무기여 잘 있거라
전쟁, 사랑, 죽음

무기여 잘 있거라
전쟁, 사랑, 죽음

ⓒ 고민곤, 2025

초판 1쇄 발행 2025년 9월 1일

지은이	고민곤
펴낸이	이기봉
편집	좋은땅 편집팀
펴낸곳	도서출판 좋은땅
주소	서울특별시 마포구 양화로12길 26 지월드빌딩 (서교동 395-7)
전화	02)374-8616~7
팩스	02)374-8614
이메일	gworldbook@naver.com
홈페이지	www.g-world.co.kr

ISBN 979-11-388-4646-2 (03840)

- 가격은 뒤표지에 있습니다.
- 이 책은 저작권법에 의하여 보호를 받는 저작물이므로 무단 전재와 복제를 금합니다.
- 파본은 구입하신 서점에서 교환해 드립니다.

무기여 잘 있거라

전쟁, 사랑, 죽음

고민곤
지음

전쟁보다 더 나쁜 것은 없다. There is nothing worse than war.
모든 사람이 이 전쟁을 증오합니다. Everybody hates this war.
패배는 전쟁 그 자체보다 더 안 좋은 것이다. defeat is worse.

전쟁에 참전한 젊은이들은 지금 이 나라를 지배하는 세력들은 어리석고 아무것도 깨닫지 못하고 깨달을 수도 없는 계급이라고 생각했다. 그리고 젊은이들에게 그 계급은, 전쟁을 겪게 만드는 존재이자 전쟁으로 돈까지 벌이들이는 사람들일 뿐이었다.

좋은땅

_____ 에게

_____ 드림

서문

    헨리의 운전병들은 "멍청하고 아무것도 깨달을 수도 없는 계급이 지금 이 나라를 지배하고 있습니다. 그런 자들 때문에 우리가 이놈의 전쟁을 하는 것입니다.", "게다가 그놈들은 전쟁으로 돈도 벌지."라고 무능한 작금의 지도자들을 비판하고 성토하는 말 속에 젊은이들의 절규와 전쟁에 대한 신랄한 비판을 하고 있다. 전쟁은 세계 역사 속에서 끊임없이 반복되는 비극이자, 인간 존재의 본질을 시험하는 가장 잔혹한 일이다. 전쟁을 통해 다른 사람들을 노예로 삼고 제국의 꿈을 위해서 젊은이들을 희생시키는 지도자들은 젊은이들과 이 세상을 부조리한 악의 구덩이로 몰아넣는다. 이 소설의 주인공 프레드릭 헨리는 자신의 고귀한 이상을 가지고 전선으로 나아갔으나, 전쟁의 현실은 그가 기대했던 고귀함과는 완전히 상반되는 모습을 드러낸다.

    또한 아무리 이렇게 죽어가면서 절규한다 해도 그들은 들어도 듣지 못하고 보아도 보지 못하고 전쟁의 현실을 이해하지 못하고 오르지, 자신의 이익에만 골몰하고 돈에만 집착하는 암담한 현실을 비판한다. 헨리는 처음에는 고통받는 인류를 돕겠다는 의도로 전쟁에 자원했지만, 전쟁의 속성과 그로 인한 비극은 그가 신성하게 믿었던 가치들을 비루하게 짓밟아 버리게 된다.

    그가 겪은 경험은 단순히 한 개인의 비극에 국한되지 않는다. 따라서 전쟁이 개인의 삶과 사회에 미치는 복합적인 영향을 깊이 탐구하자는 메시지를 내포하고 있다. 헨리는 전투 중에 사랑하는 사람들을 만나기도 하지만, 그들의 관계는 전쟁이라는 특수한 상황 속에서 고통과 슬픔으로 얼룩진다. 전쟁이 가져온 파괴와 부조리함 속에서 헨리는 어떻게 인간의 연대와 사랑이 시들어 가는지를 뼈아프게 경험하게 되고 우리는 작품을 통해서 그 고통을 이해하게 된다.

"분노는 의무와 함께 강물에 던져 버렸다."라는 그의 고백은 비참한 현실을 마주한 후, 그가 마음속에 간직하고 있던 믿음과 이상들이 어떻게 부서져 갔는지를 상징적으로 보여 준다. 전쟁을 증오하는 것은 자연스러운 반응이지만, 우리가 전쟁의 원인을 이해하고 그로 인해 발생하는 절망과 고통을 함께 나누기는 쉽지 않은 일이다. 헨리의 분노는 결국 고통받는 인류를 돕고자 하는 원대한 이상과 꿈이 어떻게 회색으로 변해 버렸는지를 잘 보여 준다.

여기서 우리는 단순히 과거의 전쟁을 비난하는 데 그치지 않고, 그 어두운 그림자를 이해하고 나아가야 한다. '전쟁보다 나쁜 것은 없다.'라는 목소리는, 전쟁이 가져오는 고통의 깊이를 인정하고, 참전한 이들이 얼마나 절망적인 상황에 부닥쳤는지를 알게 된다. 나를 포함해서 이 같은 고통의 전쟁을 경험하지 못한 세대들이 알았으면 한다. 전쟁을 일으킨 자들의 무능함과 이기심은 결국 순수한 젊은이들의 희생을 요구하며, 이로 인해 우리가 얻을 수 있는 것은 아무것도 없다는 사실을 말한다.

비극적인 상황 속에서도 피어나는 인간애와 사랑의 의미를 깊이 탐구함으로써, 우리가 직면한 현실을 돌아보게 하고, 평화의 소중함을 다시

금 일깨우고 서로 사랑하고 돕고 함께할 수 있는 공동체를 만들어야 한다. 작품 속의 헨리와 캐서린의 사랑은 비극적이지만, 그것이 결국 어떻게 우리의 영혼을 구원할 열쇠가 될 수 있는지를 탐구하는 여정이 되어야 한다. 전쟁은 우리 민족에게 힘든 단어이고 생각하기 싫은 단어이기에 다시는 우리 땅에 전쟁의 비극이 없어야 하고 그러기 위한 노력을 해야 한다. 전쟁의 참상 속에서도 빛나는 인류의 연민과 사랑이 존재하고 발견하는 것처럼 평화와 사랑이 우리 민족과 함께하길 바란다.

2025년 3월 1일

목차

서문 7

1부(Book One)

1장(Chapter I) 14
2장(Chapter II) 21
3장(Chapter III) 32
4장(Chapter IV) 43
5장(Chapter V) 53
6장(Chapter VI) 62
7장(Chapter VII) 70
8장(Chapter VIII) 80
9장(Chapter IX) 86
10장(Chapter X) 102
11장(Chapter XI) 107
12장(Chapter XII) 114

2부(Book Two)

13장(Chapter XIII) 120
14장(Chapter XIV) 129
15장(Chapter XV) 137

16장(Chapter XVI) ················ 143

17장(Chapter XVII) ················ 149

18장(Chapter XVIII) ················ 156

19장(Chapter XIX) ················ 162

20장(Chapter XX) ················ 174

21장(Chapter XXI) ················ 180

22장(Chapter XXII) ················ 191

23장(Chapter XXIII) ················ 195

24장(Chapter XXIV) ················ 203

3부(Book Three)

25장(Chapter XXV) ················ 210

26장(Chapter XXVI) ················ 218

27장(Chapter XXVII) ················ 224

28장(Chapter XXVIII) ················ 234

29장(Chapter XXIX) ················ 243

30장(Chapter XXX) ················ 249

31장(Chapter XXXI) ················ 266

32장(Chapter XXXII) ················ 273

4부(Book Four)

33장(Chapter XXXIII)	280
34장(Chapter XXXIV)	288
35장(Chapter XXXV)	299
36장(Chapter XXXVI)	310
37장(Chapter XXXVII)	320
38장(Chapter XXXVIII)	339
39장(Chapter XXXIX)	353
40장(Chapter XL)	358
41장(Chapter XLI)	364
전쟁, 사랑, 죽음	399
중심인물들(Characterization and Central Characters)	413
프레더릭 헨리(Frederic Henry)	418
캐서린 버클리(Catherine Barkley)	437
사제(Priest)	456
의사 리날디(Doctor Rinaldi)	464
헬렌 퍼거슨(Helen Ferguson)	469
미스 게이지(Miss Gage)	478
그 밖의 인물들(Minor Characters)	483
배경과 인물들(Background and Characters)	485
날씨의 상징(Weather Symbolism)	487

1부(Book One)

1장(Chapter I)

■ 1장 주요 내용

- 정체불명의 서술자 등장.
- 작품의 시대적 배경: In the summer of that year, 1915년 1차 세계대전을 의미함.
- 계절의 변화: 여름에서 겨울로 콜레라 발생.

At the start of the winter came the permanent rain and with the rain came the cholera.

- 전시 상황 묘사와 아이러니한 표현: only seven thousand

■ Summary

1장은 알려지지 않은 농촌지역에서 20세기 초반(1915년) 전쟁 기간에 『무기여 잘 있거라』(A Farwell to Arms)의 배경을 소개하는 장이다. 특히 motor cars motor truck과 같은 언급을 통해서 시간을 추측할 수가 있다. 정체불명의 서술자는 1장의 행동이 일어나는 평지 저 너머의 산에서 일어나는 싸움에 대해서 말한다. 그리고 자신의 편에서 상황이 매우 좋지 않다(thing went very badly)고 언급했다.

■ 논평

그해 늦은 여름 우리는 강과 들판 너머로 산이 보이는 어느 마을의 민가에서 지냈다.(3)

In the summer of that year we lived in a house in a village that looked across the river and plain to the mountains.(3)

In the summer of that year는 1915년 늦은 여름에서 가을로 계절 변화의 과정에 있었고 전반적인 소설 시작의 분위기가 음산하고 쓸쓸한 분위기를 보여 준다.

첫 번째 장은 매우 짧고 전쟁에 관한 상황을 잘 묘사하고 있다. 첫 장은 짧지만, 헤밍웨이가 소설 전체의 분위기를 조성하는 장이기 때문에 이것보다 더 큰 의미는 없을 것이다. 이 소설은 전쟁 이야기다. 전쟁인 것을 미화하기보다는 전쟁에 관한 냉혹한 진실(harsh truth)을 말해 준다. 전쟁은 추상적이며 그림과 같이 매력적인 것이 아니라 오히려 위험하고 따분한 것이다. 『무기여 잘 있거라』의 첫 장에서는 죽음과 죽어가는 일이 주목받는다. 1장에서 "들판에 곡식이 풍성"(The plain was rich with crops.(3) 하지만 이 소설에서 비는 죽음을 상징한다. 화자는,

"가을로 접어들어 비가 내리자, 밤나무 잎이 모두 떨어져 가지는 앙상해지고 줄기는 비에 젖어 거무스름했다. 포도밭의 나뭇가지들도 잎이 모두 져서 앙상해졌고 온 사방에 내리는 비에 갈색이 되어 생기를 잃었다."(4)고 말했다.

1부(Book One)

There was fighting for that mountains too, but it was not successful, and in the fall when the rains came the leaves all fell from the chestnut trees and the branches were bare and the trunks black with rain. The vineyards were thin and bare-branched too and all the country wet and brown and dead with autumn.

또한 화자는 비가 질병을 가져온다고 우리에게 말했다. 따라서 헤밍웨이는 비와 죽음의 명확한 관계를 설정했다.

탄약과 무기로 무장한 군인들이 행군할 때, 마치 "탄창이 든 묵직한 회색 가죽 탄약통이 튀어나와서 마치 육 개월이 된 임신부들처럼 보였다."(4)
their rifles were wet and under their capes the two leather cartridges boxes on the front of the belts, long 6.5 mm. cartridges, bulged forward under the capes so that the men, passing on the road, marched as though they were six months with child.(4)

라고 말한 것은 이 소설의 비와 죽음이 인과관계와 비극적인 결말을 암시하고 있다.

1장에서는 행군하는 부대, 노새, 무기와 보급품을 운송하는 트럭, 국왕(빅토리오 엠마누엘레 3세)(1869-1947)과 고위직 장군과 같은 장교를 운반하는 차량 등의 관찰자로서 화자는 움직이지 않으면서 전쟁이 어떻게 화자를 지나쳐 가는지를 주목해 봐야 한다. 우리는 아직 화자가 분쟁에 개입한 정황을 알지 못하지만, 그가 이 전쟁에 완전히 관여하지는 못했음을 알 수 있다. 나중에 그는 이탈리아 군대의 소위(second lieutenant)이면서 야전부대에 미국 자원병 프레더릭 헨리(Frederic Henry)라는 것을 알게 된다.

1장에서는 이 소설의 이분법이 도입된다. 즉 산과 평지(mountains and plain) 고지대와 저지대(highlands and lowlands) 사이에서 긴장을 볼 수 있다. 절제되고 순수하고 그래서 존경할 만한 행동들은 산에서 발생하고 부패하고 악한 행동들은 저지대에서 일어난다.

1장은 헤밍웨이 특유의 영향력 있는 글쓰기 스타일이 잘 드러난다. 종종 구체적인 사항이 풍부하고 짧은 선언적인 문장의 사용으로 요약된다. 작가의 전형적인 스타일처럼 그리고 심지어 더 독특한 것은 연속적으로 짧은 절을 포함하는 길고 복잡한 문장으로 ("and", "or" 그리고 "but"과 같은 짧은 연결된 단어)로 연결된 문장의 연속이다. 예를 들어,

나무줄기도 먼지를 뒤집어썼는데 그해는 나뭇잎들이 일찍 졌다. 군대가 길을 따라 행진하면 먼지가 일어나고 나뭇잎들이 미풍에 흔들리다 떨어지는 것이 보였고 그리고 나면 텅 비고 뿌연 길바닥에는 나뭇잎들만 뒹굴었다.(3)

The trunks of the trees too were dusty **and** the leaves fell early that year **and** we saw the troops marching along the road **and** the dust rising **and** leaves, stirred by the breeze, falling **and** the soldiers marching **and** afterward the road bare **and** white except for the leave.(3)

콜레라 발생에 대해 그는 "결과적으로 군대 내 희생자는 7천 명뿐이

다." 말했다. "7천 명뿐이다"(only seven thousand) 헤밍웨이 작품에 나오는 주인공들처럼『무기여 잘 있거라』의 화자는 극기심이 강하고 과장하기보다는 절제하며 자신이 바꿀 수 없는 것을 암울하게 받아들인다.

■ 1장 주요 작품 내용

In the late summer of that year we lived in a house in a village that looked across the river and the plain to the mountains. In the bed of the river there were pebbles and boulders, dry and white in the sun, and the water was clear and swiftly moving and blue in the channels. Troops went by the house and down the road and the dust they raised powered the leaves of the trees.(3)

The trunks of the trees too were dusty and the leaves fell early that year and we saw the troops marching along the road and the dust rising and leaves, stirred by the breeze, falling and the soldiers marching and afterward the road bare and white except for the leave.(3)

들판에는 곡식이 풍성하지만, 그 들판 너머 산은 헐벗고 전투로 인해 포탄에서 나오는 불빛은 들판이 가져다주는 평온함과는 거리가 먼 전시 상황을 대조적으로 잘 묘사하고 있다.

The plain was rich with crops; there were many orchards of fruit tree and beyond the plain the mountains were brown and bare. There was fighting in the mountains and at night we could see the flashes from the artillery. In the dark it was like summer lightning, but the night were cool and there was not the feeling of a storm coming.(3)

군인들의 행군과 대포를 단 포차가 달리는 소리와 포차를 초록 잎으로 위장한 상황들을 묘사함으로써 지금의 상황이 전시 상황인 것을 잘 말해 주는 대목이다.

Sometimes in the dark we heard the troops marching under the window and guns going past pulled by motor-tractors. There was much traffic at night and many mules on the roads with boxes of ammunition on each side of their pack-saddles and gray motor trucks that carried men, and other trucks with loads covered with canvas that moved slower in the traffic. There were big guns too that passed in the day drawn by tractors, the long barrels of the guns covered with green branches and green leafy branches and vines laid over the tractors.(4)

At the start of the winter came the permanent rain and with the rain came the cholera. But it was checked and in the end only seven thousand died of it in the army.(4)

2장(Chapter II)

■ 2장 주요 내용

- "우리"(We)라고 확인된 화자.
- 고지리아(Gorizia) 점령, 신부(Priest), 대위(captain), 소령(major) Free Masons 소개.

■ Summary

이듬해에 "여러 차례 승리가 있었다." 결과적으로 "우리"(We)라고 확인된 화자 측은 강을 가로질러 진격하고 점령한 적의 도시인 고리치아(Gorizia)를 점령했다.

The next year there were many victories. The mountain that was beyond the valley and hillside where the chestnut forest grew was captured and there were victories beyond the plain on the plateau to the south and we crossed the river in August and lived in a house in Gorizia that had a fountain and many thick shady trees in a walled garden and a wistaria vine purple on the side of the house.(5)

명백히 이 전쟁은 1차 세계대전이다. 그리고 2장에서 발생하는 작전(action)은 이탈리아와 현재 슬로베니아(Slovenia) 사이의 국경 주변에 있는 알프스에서 발생했다. 오스트리아 헝가리 제국(Austro-Hungarian Empire)과 독일에 대항한 러시아 프랑스 영국이 연합했다. 오스트리아 헝가리 제국과 독일에 맞서 영국, 프랑스, 러시아와 동맹을 맺은 이탈리아는 오스트리아 헝가리 군대가 독일군을 돕는 것을 막을 책임이 있었다.

장교식당에서 저녁 식사를 하는 동안, 겨울 첫눈이 내리던 날 밤, 나레이터의 동료들은 그들은 신부를 조롱하지만 중요하게도 나레이터 자신은 조롱에 참여하지 않는다.

이탈리아 장교들은 해설자가 다가오는 휴가를 다양한 저지대 이탈리아의 도시에서 보낼 것을 추천하는 반면 신부는 그에게 아브루치(Abruzzi) 여행할 것을 제한한다.

■ 논평

이 장에서 저자는 산 대 평원의 이분법과 유사한 또 다른 이분법을 소개한다. 교회와 위안소이다. 신부가 휴가 중에 나레이터를 자신의 산이 있는 고향(mountain hometown)에 방문하도록 초대할 때 두 가지 역학 관계가 교차한다. 장교들은 이 제안을 비웃습니다.

"그는 농부를 보고 싶어 하지 않습니다."이라고 한 사람이 말합니다.

"그를 문화와 문병의 중심지로 가게 하라."(8)

He doesn't want to see peasants. Let him go to centres of culture and civilization.

그런 다음 다른 장교는 나폴리에 있는 창녀 집 주소를 제공합니다. 이 사람들에게 문명과 성은 하나이고 같은 것이지만 신부님은 서술자에게 다른 더 영적인 삶의 방식을 제공하고 있습니다.

* 고리치아(Gorizia) 현재 이탈리아 북동부 도시 당시 오스트리아 땅이었다.

마을 너머 산에 있던 참나무 숲은 사라졌다. 우리가 마을에 왔던 지난여름에는 숲이 푸르렀지만 지금은 땅이 온통 파헤쳐지고 나무그루터기와 부러진 줄기만 남았는데.(6)

The forest of oak trees on the mountain beyond the town was gone. The forest had been green in the summer when we had come into the town but now there were the stumps and the broken trunks and the ground torn up….

전쟁으로 인한 황폐한 환경을 잘 보여 준다. 전쟁으로 인해서 산과 들만 파괴된 것이 아니고 전쟁에 참전한 사람들 사이의 갈등도 찾아볼 수 있다. 장교와 사제와의 대화 속에서 갈등을 찾아볼 수 있다.

"신부님, 오늘 아가씨들이랑." 대위가 신부와 나를 바라보며 말했다. 신부는 얼굴을 붉히고 미소 지으며 고개를 저었다. 대위는 신부를 자주 놀려댔다.(7)

"Priest to-day with girls," the captain said looking at the priest and me. The priest smiled and blushed and shook his head. This captain baited him often.

"교황은 이 전쟁에서 오스트리아가 이기길 바라지," 소령이 말했다. "교황은 프란츠 요제프 편이거든. 거기가 돈 나오는 데니까. 나는 무신론자야."(7)

1부(Book One)

"The Pope wants the Austrians to win the war," the major said. "He loves Franz Joseph. That's where the money comes from. I am an atheist."

유럽 역사는 가톨릭교회(Catholic Church)에 의해서 가장 잘 알려졌고 가톨릭교회는 유럽에서 2천 년 넘게 가장 강력한 존재였다. 오스트리아 프란츠 요제프(Franze Joseph) 황제는 유럽 역사에서 가장 긴 군주 통치를 하였고 가톨릭교회는 프란츠 요제프 황제의 모든 통치 활동에서 중요한 역할을 하였다. 즉 프란츠 요제프와 가톨릭교회가 밀착하여 강력한 권력을 행사했다. 이와 같은 역사적인 사실에 따라서 군인을 대표하는 장교식당에 모인 장교들은 신부를 비웃고 조롱한 것이다. 즉 종교와 정치가 결탁해서 전쟁을 일으키고 전쟁에서 한쪽을 지원하는 일을 비판하는 장면이다. 종교는 발생할지도 모르는 전쟁을 막아야 하고 중재해도 모자랄 판에 전쟁을 지원하는 비극적인 상황을 작가는 지적한다. 결국 전쟁을 통해서 젊은 군인들과 선량하고 힘없는 시민들이 희생된다. 신부도 이 같은 상황을 모르지 않을 것이다. 알고 있지만 자신에게 주어진 사명을 감당하기 위해서 나름대로 최선을 다한다. 어쩌면 신부 자신도 어쩔 수 없이 주어진 상황에서 자신의 역할을 수행할지도 모른다. 커다란 가톨릭 종교계에서 자신의 할 수 있는 역할이 극히 제한될 수 있기 때문일지도 모른다. 그래도 전쟁터에서 자신이 할 수 있는 역할을 찾아서 노력하는 모습은 인상적이다. 결국 군인들이나 신부 모두가 희생자이며 피해자라고 볼 수 있다.

장교들과 사제의 대화를 통해서 군인들을 대표로 하는 소령은 자신들이 원하지 않은 전쟁에 참여한 것에 대한 불만을 사제를 통해서 말하고 있는 것이다. 특히 교황이 전쟁에 물자를 지원한다는 말은 상당한 불만의 요인으로 작용한다. 여기서 사제는 교황으로 대표되는 전쟁을 유발한 사람들이고 소령은 원하지 않은 전쟁에 참여하게 된 젊은 전쟁 참여자가 된다. 따라서 소령이 사제를 비웃고 놀리는 것은 당연할 수 있다. 젊은이들이 원하지 않은 전쟁에서 죽어가는 것은 참으로 가슴 아픈 일이기 때문이다.

"저 친구는 농부를 보고 싶은 게 아닙니다. 문화와 문명의 중심지로 보내야죠."
"예쁜 아가씨들도 만나야지. 내가 나폴리에서 어디를 가야 할지 알려줄게. 어머니를 늘 따라다니는- 젊고 예쁜 아가씨들이 있는데. 하! 하! 하!"(8)

　　He doesn't want to see peasant. Let him go to centres of culture and civilization. "He should have fine girls. I will give you addresses of places in Napoles. Beautiful young girls-accompanies by their mothers. Ha! Ha! Ha!"

"아브루치에 다녀와요," 신부가 말했다. 다른 사람들은 소리 질러대고 있었다. "사냥하기 좋은 곳입니다. 사람들도 마음에 들 거고요. 날씨는 춥지만 맑고 건조하죠. 우리 집에 묵어도 좋습니다. 아버지는 유명한 사냥꾼이십니다."(9)
"I would like you to go to Abruzzi," the priest said. The others were shouting. : There is good hunting. You would like the people and thought it is cold it is clear and dry. You could stay with my family. My father is a famous hunter.

　　휴가에 대해서 서로 다른 장소를 추천해 주는 장면에서 서로 간의 견해차를 확인할 수 있다. 외부 세계와 단절된 생활하는 젊은 군인들의 처지에서 젊은 아가씨가 있는 곳을 추천하지만 신부는 사냥하고 마음씨도 좋은 고향에 가서 쉬기를 바란다. 전쟁은 젊은 사람들의 처지에서 보면 외부와의 철저히 단절된 세계에서 생활하는 곳이다. 신부의 처지에서는 인내하고 이해할 수도 있겠지만 젊은이들은 그렇지 못하다.

앞에 대화뿐만 아니라 휴가에 관한 대화에서도 신부와 젊은 군인들 간의 견해차를 확인하게 된다. 젊은 군인들의 처지에서는 자신들이 원하지도 않은 전쟁터 와서 고생하는 것에 대한 일종의 불만을 토로한다고 볼 수 있다.

헤밍웨이는 등장인물의 역할을 소개하기 시작한다. 첫 번째 겨울눈이 내리는 밤 장교식당의 저녁 시간에 화자의 동료 장교들은 신부를 조롱하기 시작한다. 그렇지만 중요한 것은 화자 자신은 화를 돋우는 일에 가담하지 않는다. 이탈리아 장교는 화자에게 다가오는 휴가를 저지대의 이탈리아 도시의 다양한 곳을 추천했지만 사제는 산을 여행하라고 제시한다.

이 장에서 작가는 매춘(brothel)과 교회, 평지와 산과 같은 또 다른 이분법을 도입한다. 신부가 화자에게 휴가 동안 자기 고향을 방문했을 때 산을 방문하라고 추천했을 때 둘의 역학관계가 교차한다. 장교는 이 같은 제안을 비웃었다. "그는 농부를 보고 싶은 게 아닙니다."라고 한 사람이 말했다. 또 다른 장교는 나폴리의 유곽(whorehouses)의 주소를 제공했다. 이 둘에게는 문명과 섹스는 하나이고 같은 것이다. 그러나 신부는 화자에게 다르고 보다 정신적인 삶의 방식을 제공한다.

눈이 왔을 때 싸움이 불가능하다는 것은 초기의 현대 전쟁에서는 사실이다. 그러므로 헨리와 그의 동료들에게 눈은 평화이다. 그 평화라는 것이 비록 일시적인 것일지라도 눈은 헐벗은 땅을 덮고 심지어는 대포도 덮는다. 여름철 싸움으로 갈기갈기 찢어진 오크 나무 그루터기는 하얀 담요(눈)에서 돌출된다. 따라서 눈은 단순한 연기 또는 정전(a cease fire)을 의미한다.

■ 2장 주요 작품 내용

The next year there many victories. The mountain that was beyond the valley and hillside where the chestnut forest grew was captured and there were victories beyond the plain on the plateau to the south and we crossed the river in August and lived in a house in Gorizia that had a fountain and many thick shady trees in a walled garden and a wistaria vine purple on the side of the house.(5)

The forest of oak trees on the mountain beyond the town was gone. The forest had been green in the summer when we had come into the town but now there were the stumps and the broken trunks and the ground torn up, and one day at the end of the fall when I was out where the oak forest had been I saw a cloud coming over the mountain. It came very fast and the sun went a dull yellow and then everything was gray and the sky was covered and the cloud came on down the mountain and suddenly we were in it and it was snow. The snow slanted across the wind, the bare ground was covered, the stumps of the trees projected, there was snow on the guns and there were paths on the snow going back to the latrines behind trenches.(6)

"Not true?" asked the captain. "To-day I see priest with girls."
"No," said the priest. The other officers were amused at the baiting.
"Priest not with girls," went on the captain. "Priest never with girls," he explained to me. He took my glass and filed it, looking at my eyes all the time, but not losing

sight of the priest.

"Priest every night five against one." Every one at the table laughed. "You understand? Priest every night five against one." He made a gesture and laughed loudly. The priest accepted it as a joke.

"The Pope wants the Austrians to win the war," the major said. "He loves Franz Joseph. That's where the money comes from I am an atheist."

"Did you ever read the 'Black Pig?' asked the lieutenant." "I will get you a copy. It was that which shook my faith."

"It is a filthy and vile book," said the priest. "You do not really like it."

"It is very valuable," said the lieutenant. "It tells you about those priest. You will like it," he said me. I smiled at the priest and he smiles back across the candle-light. "Don't you read it," he said.

"I will get it for you," said the lieutenant.

"All thinking men are atheists," the major said. "I do not believe in the Free Masons however."(8)

"I believe in the Free Masons," the lieutenant said. "It is a noble organization." Some one came in and as the door opened I could see the snow falling.

"There will be no more offensive now that the snow has come," I said.

"Certainly not," said the major. "You should go on leave. You should go to Rome, Naples, Sicily____"

"He should visit Amalfi," said lieutenant. "I will write you cards to my family in

Amalfi. They will love you like a son."

"He should go to Palermo."

"He should go to Capri."

"I would like you to see Abruzzi and visit my family at the Capracotta," said the priest.(8)

Listen to him talk bout the Abruzzi. There's more snow there than here. He doesn't want to see peasants. Let him go to centres of culture and civilization.

"He should have fine girl. I will give you the addresses of places in Naples. Beautiful young girls- accompanied by their mothers. Ha! Ha! Ha!"(8)

"You must go on leave at once," the major said.

"I would like to go with you and show you things," the lieutenant said.

"When you come back bring phonograph."

"Bring good opera disks."

"Bring Caruso."

"Don't bring Caruso. He bellows."

"Don't you wish you could bellow like him?"

"He bellows. I say he bellows!"

"I would like you to go to Abruzzi," the priest said. The others were shouting. "There is good hunting. You would like the people and thought it is cold it is clear and dry. You could stay with my family. My father is a famous hunter."

"Come on," said the captain. "**We** go whorehouse before it shuts."

"Good-night," I said to the priest.

"Good-night," he said. (9)

3장(Chapter III)

■ 3장 주요 내용

- 휴가 마치고 화자의 고리치아로 귀환 그리고 휴가지에서 있었던 이야기.

When I came back to the front we still lived in that town.

- 그의 룸메이트 리날디 소개

He came from Amalfi.

■ **Summary**

봄에 화자는 고리치아(Gorizia)로 돌아온다. 아말피(Amalfi) 출신이면서 동갑이고 외과 의사인 것을 자랑스러워하는 그의 친구 리날디(Rinaldi)라는 인물이 등장한다. 그는 이탈리아 군대에서 외과 의사이면서 중위인 그의 룸메이트(방을 같이 쓰는 친구)로 소개된다.

He came from Amalfi. He loved being a surgeon and we were great friends.(12)

리날디는 그의 휴가가 어떠했는지 물어본다.

"Ciaou!" he said. "What kind of time did you have?"
"Magnificent."

그리고 자신이 버클리(Barkley) "영국의 아름다운 소녀"(beautiful English girl)가 점령된 마을에 나타났다고 화자에게 말한다.

Here now we have beautiful girls. New girls never been to the front before.
"Wonderful."
"You don't believe me? We will go now this afternoon and see. And in the town we have beautiful English girls. I am now in love with Miss Barkley."(12)

저녁에 장교식당에서 화자는 신부에게 아브루치 지역을 가지 못한 것에 대해서 사과했다. 대신 휴가 동안 술 마시고 매춘부와 어울리는 데 시간을 보냈다. 그의 이탈리아 동료 장교들이 신부를 조롱하는 일이 다시 시작되었다.

■ **논평**

화자가 전선에 돌아왔을 때 앞 장에서 언급했던 "줄기차게 비가 온다"(permanent rain)라고 언급한 것이 끝이 나고 태양이 따듯하고 녹색이 완연한 봄의 시기였다. 여기에서 이 소설의 주요한 죽음의 상징이 여기에 없다는 것은 좋은 징조처럼 보였다. 그러나 매년 싸움을 멈추게 하는 유일한 것인 눈(snow)이 녹아 버렸다. 따라서 전투는 피할 수 없었다. "다음 주에 전쟁이 시작됩니다"라고 리날디 중위가 보고했다. 리날디와 신부는 매우 대조적인 인물로 묘사되지만, 헤밍웨이가 다른 작품에서 남자들의 우정에 대한 작가의 다루는 방식처럼 리날디와 화자의 관계는 따듯하고 편안한 관계이다. 이 장에서 캐서린 버클리는 거의 부수적으로 소개되고 있다.

눈과 비, 이 두 개의 기후 현상은 전쟁에서는 큰 차이점을 시사한다. 비가 오면 날이 추워지지 않아서 좋지만, 전쟁은 시작되고 날이 추워지면 눈이 오지만 대신 전쟁은 일시적으로 멈춘다. 따라서 눈과 비중에서 눈이 군인들에게는 좋은 일기일 수 있다. 나중에 소설의 뒷부분에서 나오겠지만 퇴각하는 장면에서 비가 많이 와서 길이 질퍽해서 마차를 비롯한 차량 등이 움직이지 못하는 일이 발생해서 결국 앰블런스 차를 포기하고 헨리를 비롯한 군인들이 차를 버리고 걷기 시작한 장면이 나온다. 이 장면에서도 결국 주인공인 헨리가 탈영병으로 몰리게 되는 계기가 된다. 이 소설에서 눈보다 비는 부정적인 면으로 많이 작용한다.

겉으로 보면 리날디와 신부 두 등장인물은 대조적인 면을 자주 보인다. 정신적인 가치관을 가진 신부 상대적으로 성적인 가치관을 가진 즉 인문주의자(humanist)인 리날디 중위로 볼 수 있다. 등장인물 중에서 앞장에서도 언급했지만, 군인과 젊은이들을 대표하는 장교 그리고 가톨릭 교회를 대표하는 신부 이 두 인물은 인간적으로는 화해와 용서를 할 수 있지만 신부가 속한 황제와 교황이 서로 지원하면서 전쟁을 주도한 집단이기에 장교들은 신부를 좋게 말할 수 없다. 욕을 하고 싸움하지 않은 게 신사적일 수 있다. 이 작품에서 신부를 조롱하는 장면이 많이 등장한다. 그와 같은 일은 상호 간의 불신에 의한 것이라고 볼 수 있다.

헤밍웨이의 다른 작품에서 남자들의 우정에 대한 작가의 처리처럼 리날디와 화자의 관계는 따뜻하고 편안한 관계이다. 이 작품의 여주인공인 버클리는 여담 수준(as an aside)으로 소개된다. 사람들의 커다란 축하 없이 우리 삶 속에서 가장 중요한 사람을 만났을 때처럼 작가의 정제된 가치와 현실적인 느낌과도 일치한다.

우리 인생에서 중요한 사람과의 조우는 일생일 때의 중요한 사건이고 그래서 엄청나게 큰 소란 속에서 맞이해야 해야 하는데 사실 되돌아보면 아~ 그때가 내 인생에서 중요한 사람을 만난 것이었구나 하고 생각한다. 마찬가지고 작가도 버클리와의 만남도 되돌아보면 가장 중요한 사건이지만 만남 그 당시는 무미건조한 것일 수 있다. 즉 작가는 버클리와 만남은 정제되면서도 현실성 있게 표현한다. 너무 찬란하게 만남을 표현하면 나중에 그 만남의 중요성을 강조할 공간 여력이 남지도 않고 효과도 떨어진다. 예를 들면 이 작품의 후반부에 보면 버클리의 위험한 순간 전에 코믹한 작품을 작가는 배치한다. 작가의 의도는 코믹한 장면과 위험한 순간의 배치는 등장인물의 위험한 강도를 더 강조하기 위해서 배치한 것과 같다. 신부와 화자의 이야기는 이분법적으로 산과 들판(mountain and plain)이 되풀이된다. 나는 아브루치에 가고 싶었다.

1부(Book One)

길이 꽁꽁 얼어 쇳덩이처럼 단단한 곳 날이 청명하고 춥고 건조하고 눈이 가루처럼 내리는 곳, 눈밭에 토끼 발자국이 있고 농부들이 모자를 벗어들고 나리라고 부르며 인사하는 곳, 멋진 사냥을 할 수 있는 곳은 어디도 가지 못했다.(13)

아브루치를 여행했어야만 했다는 것을 화자는 알고 있었다. 대신 그는 저지대(lowlands)의 도시에 있는 매춘부 집이나 술집을 갔다. 특별히 전쟁과 이 세상의 불화(unpleasantness)에 관한 화자의 전략은 술과 섹스를 통해서 그가 얻을 수 있는 망각으로써 언급되는 것이다. 신부가 추천한 장소에 가서 한가롭게 여행하며 사냥을 즐기면서 휴가를 보낼 수 있는 마음의 여유가 없다고 봐야 한다. 화자의 마음 상태는 일단 휴가를 얻어서 전쟁터에서 나와 있지만 여전히 마음속에 불안과 걱정 두려움으로 사로잡혀 있는 상태이다. 그 불안과 걱정 두려움을 술과 섹스를 통해서 잠시나마 잊고자 하는 상황이다. 즉 전쟁으로 인한 죽음과 죽음이 가져온 이 세상의 불안과 불화를 잊기 위해서 젊은이들이 술과 섹스에 빠져든다는 것이다. 일시적이지만 그는 정신적으로 방황한다. 그러나 이 작품의 많은 부분은 자아실현(self realization)에 대한 그의 움직임을 찾아갈 것이다.

헤밍웨이 문체를 특별하게 만드는 것은 이론적인 것보다 실질적인 것에 더 의존한다. 리날디와 함께 사용하고 있는 방에 대한 화자 묘사의 특수함에 주목해 보자. 이 방에 익숙하지만 약간 위협적인 것이라고 우리에게 말하기보다는 그는 구체적인 것에 집중한다: 창이 열려 있고 그의 침대는 담요가 말끔하게 정돈되어 있으며, 방독면이 든 양철 깡통이며 철모와 같은 것들을 언급한다. 그리고 자신의 총, 신발, 트렁크 등도 언급했다. 이와 같은 것 모두를 일반화하지 않고 작가는 군인의 스파르타식의 삶에 관해 많은 것을 우리에게 말한다. 즉 구체적인 명사들을 언급하고 일반화해서 독자들에게 말하는 것을 지양한다. 대신 명사를 통해서 군인의 삶 군인으로 사는 생활, 상황을 말해 준다. 일반적인 진술을 통해 주제나 의도를 말해 주는 대신 구체적인 진술을 통해 즉 구체적인 단어들의 배열을 통해서 독자들에게 상황에 대해 인식하도록 해 주는 기법이다. 작품의 표현기법은 화자의 겨울 휴가에 대한 환각적인 묘사에서 다시 등장한다.

그런 곳 대신 담배 연기 자욱한 카페들에 갔고, 밤마다 방안이 빙빙 돌아 그걸 멈추려면 벽을 쳐다봐야 했고, 그게 다라는 것을 알면서도 밤이면 술에 취한 채 여자와 침대로 기어들어 갔고, 잠에서 깼을 때는 상대가 누군지도 모르는 이상한 흥분을 느꼈으며, 어둠 속에서 세상은 전부 비현실적으로 느껴지고 나는 상대가 누군지도 모르고 아무것도 개의치 않으며 몹시 흥분한 상태에서 이것이 전부이고 모든 것이라고 확신하는 똑같은 일을 되풀이했다.(13)

짧은 문장이 아닌 일반적인 헤밍웨이 문체와는 대조가 된다. 이렇듯 긴 문장의 사용은 『무기여 잘 있거라』를 쓰기 전에 파리에서 알고 지낸 두 명의 작가의 영향을 보여 준다. 그 작가는 제임스 조이스(James Joyce)와 거트루드 스타인(Gertrude Stein)이다. 제임스 조이스는 마음에 흐르는 비논리적인 작동을 흉내를 내려고 시도하는 의식적 흐름(Stream of Consciousness)으로 잘 알려졌다. 스타인은 일반적인 반복뿐만 아니라 다양한 연결사의 사용에 영향을 주었다. 스타인은 "A rose is a rose is a rose and when you get there, there is no there there."(문장이 중간에 끝난 듯한 느낌을 줍니다.)

■ 3장 주요 작품 내용

When I came back to the front we still lived in that town. There were many more guns in the country around and the spring had come. The fields were green and there were small green shoots on the vines, the trees along the road had small leaves and a breeze came from the sea. I saw the town with the hill and the old castle above it in a cup in the hills with the mountains beyond, brown mountains with a little green on their slopes. In the town there were more guns, there were some new hospitals, you met British men and sometimes women, on the street, and a few more houses had been hit by shell fire. It was warm and like the spring and I walked down the alleyway of trees, warmed from the sun on the wall, and found we still lived in the same house and that it all looked the same as when I had left it. The door was open, there was a soldier sitting on a bench outside in the sun, an ambulance was waiting by the side door and inside the door, as I went in, there was smell of marble floors and hospital. It was all as I had left it except that now it was spring. I looked in the door of the big room and saw the major sitting at his desk, the window open and the sunlight coming into the room. He did not see me and I did not know whether to go in and report or go upstairs first and clean up. I decided to go on upstairs.(10)

The room I shared with the lieutenant Rinalidi looked out on the courtyard. The window was open, my bed was made up with blankets and my things hung on the wall, the gas mask in an oblong tin can, the steel helmet on the same peg.

At the foot of bed was my flat trunk, and my winter boots, the leather shiny with oil, were on the trunk. My Austrian sniper's rifle with its blued octagon barrel and the lovely dark walnut, cheek-fitted, schutzen stock, hung over the two beds. The telescope that fitted it was, I remembered, locked in the trunk. The lieutenant, Rinalidi, lay asleep on the other bed. He woke when he heard me in the room and sat up.

"Ciaou!" he said. "What kind of time did you have?"

"Magnificent."

We shook hands and he put his arm around my neck and kissed me.

"Oughf," I said.

"You're dirty," he said. "You ought to wash. Where did you go and what did you do? Tell me everything at once."

"I went everywhere. Milan, Florence, Room, Napoles, Villa San Giovanni, Messina, Taormina------"

"You talk like a time-table. Did you have any beautiful adventures?"

"Yes."

"Where?"

"Milan, Florence, Room, Napoli------"

"That's enough. Tell me really what was the best."

"In Milano."

"That was because it was first. Where did you meet her? In the Cova? Where did you go? How did you feel? Tell me everything at once. Did you stay all night?"(11)

That night at the mess I sat next to the priest and he was disappointed and suddenly hurt that I had not gone to the Abruzzi. He had written to his father that I was coming and they had made preparations. I myself felt as badly as he did and could not understand why I had not gone. It was what I had wanted to and I tried to explain how one thing had led to another and finally he saw it and understood that I had really wanted to go and it was almost all right. I had drunk much wine and afterward coffee and Strega and I explained, winefully, how we did not do the thing we wanted to do; we never did such things.

We two were talking while the others argued. I had wanted to go to Abruzzi. I had gone to no place where the roads were frozen and hard as iron, where it was clear cold and dry and the snow was dry and powdery and hard-tracks in the snow and the peasants took off their hats and called you Lord and there was good hunting. I had gone to no such place but to the smoke of cafes and nights when the room whirled and you needed to look at the wall to make it stop, nights in bed, drunk, when you knew that that was all there was, and the strange excitement of waking and not knowing who it was with you, and the world all unreal in the dark and so exciting that you must resume again unknowing and not caring in the night, sure that this was all and all and all and not caring. Suddenly to care very much and to sleep to wake with it sometimes morning and all that had been there gone and everything sharp and hard and clear and sometimes a dispute about the cost. Sometimes still pleasant and fond and warm and breakfast and lunch. Sometimes all niceness gone and glad to get out on the street but always another day starting and then another night. I tried to tell about the night and the difference between the night and the day and how the night was better unless the day was very clean and cold and I could not tell it; as I cannot tell it now. But if you have had it you know. He had not had it but he understood that I had really wanted to go to the Abruzzi but had not gone and we were still friends, with many tastes alike, but with the difference between us. He had always known what I did not know and what, when I learned it, I was always able to forget. But I did not know that then, although I learned it later. In the meantime we were all at the mess, the meal was finished, and the argument went on. We two stopped talking and the captain shouted, "The priest not happy. Priest not happy without girls."

"I am happy," said the priest.

"Priest not happy. Priest wants Austrians to win the war," the captain said. The others listened. The priest shook his head.

"No," he said.

"Priest wants us never to attack. Don't you want us never to attack?"

"No. If there is a war I suppose we must attack."

"Must attack. Shall attack!"

The priest nodded.

"Leave him alone," the major said. "He's all right."

"He can't do anything about it anyway," the captain said. We all got up and left the table.(14)

4장 (Chapter IV)

- **4장 주요 내용**

- 화자의 정체를 알게 됨.
- 캐서린 버클리와 첫 만남.
- 헬렌 퍼거슨(Helen Ferguson) 등장.

- **Summary**

드디어 전쟁에서 화자의 개입(involvement) 정체를 알게 되었다.

The battery in the next garden woke me in the morning and **I saw** the sun coming through the window and got out of the bed **I went** to the window and looked out. …. I could not see the guns but they were evidently firing directly over us.(15)

그는 구급차 기사들을 관리한다. 4장이 시작하면서 기사들과 차의 상태에 대해서 간단하게 이야기한다.

The mechanics were working on one out in the yard. Three others were up in the mountains at dressing stations.(15)

"Fine," I said. "What's the matter with this machine?"

It's no good. One thing after another.

"What's the matter now?"

"New rings."

리날디는 버클리를 만나러 갈 때 함께 갈 것이라고 확신한다. 해가 질 무렵 영국 병원으로 개조된 독일 주택에서 화자와 두 간호사가 만났다. 버클리는 왜 입대했고 왜 이탈리아 군대에 있는지 궁금해했다.

The British hospital was a big villa built by Germans before the war.(18)

"How do you do?" Miss Barkley said. "You're not an Italian are you?"

"Oh, no."

Rinaldi was talking with the other nurse. They were laughing.

"What an odd thing-to be in the Italian army."

"It's not really the army. It's only the ambulance. Why did you do it?"

"It's very odd though," I said. "There isn't always an explanation for everything."

"I don't know," I said.(18)

버클리(Barkley)와 그녀의 친구 헬렌 퍼거슨(Helen Ferguson) 버클리와 화자는 전쟁과 그 이전의 전투에서 죽은 그녀의 약혼자(fiance)에 대해서 말했다.

I thought she was very beautiful. She was carrying a thin ratten stick like a toy riding-crop, bound in leather.

"It belonged to a boy who was killed last year."

"I'm awfully sorry."

"He was a very nice boy. He was going to marry me and he was killed in the Somme."(18)

■ 논평

4장은 극적으로나 주제적으로나 주요한 장이다. 소설 사건의 관점에서 이 작품의 주동 인물이 소설의 여주인공 버클리와의 만남이 이루어지는 장이다. 그들이 얼마나 빨리 친밀해졌는지를 주목해 보자.

버클리는 그녀가 약혼한 남자의 죽음에 관해서 이야기했다. 그리고 화자는 그가 누구도 사랑하지 않았다고 인정했다. 작가는 비상한 상황(극적인 상황, extraordinary stress)에서도 인간이 얼마나 빨리 가까워지는지를 이해했다.

주제적으로 이 소설의 극단적인 행동인 이탈리아 부대에서 그의 탈영을 화자는 이미 합리화를 준비하고 있었다. 그는 부대의 성공적인 작전에 그의 휴가가 영향을 받지 않는다고 우리와 자신에게 말함으로써 그곳에서 탈영은 안 했지만, 복선으로 언급된다.

"내가 점검을 하나 하지 않나 별다른 차이가 없는 것 같다."
"내가 떠나 있는 동안 모든 일이 전보다 더 잘 돌아가고 있던 것 같았다."(117)

1부(Book One)

It evidently made no difference whether I was there to look after things or not.
Evidently it did not matter whether I was there or not.(16)
The whole thing seemed to run better while I was away(17)

달리 말하면 화자가 언젠가 발생할 원인에 대한 자신의 책무를 포기하는 것을 선택한다면 이것은 전쟁에 대해 알아볼 수 없는 부정적인 영향을 주지 않는다. 이런 관점에서,

"이상하네요- 이탈리아 군에 있다니."
"사실 군대라고 할 수 없습니다. 구급 수송대죠."
"그래도 이상해요. 왜 입대했어요."
"저도 모르겠습니다." 나는 말했다. "만사에 다 이유가 있는 건 아니니까요."(18)
"What an old thing- to be in the Italian army."
"It's not really the army. It's only the ambulance."
"It's very odd though. Why did you do it?"
"I don't know," I said. "There isn't always an explanation for everything."

라는 버클리의 관찰은 매우 중요하다. 화자에게 탈영을 허락하는 최초의 언급이라 볼 수 있다. 자원해서 입대했지만, 자신이 싸우는 전쟁이 자신의 조국을 위해 싸우는 것이 아니기 때문에 위안이 되는 부분이다. 버클리와 퍼거슨을 만나러 가기 전에 리날디와 화자는 두 잔을 마셨다. 『무기여 잘 있거라』를 포함해서 헤밍웨이 작품에 흐르는 주제 중의 하나는 이성 간의 만남이 전쟁터에서의 전투만큼이나 끔찍하고 위험하다.

결국에는 그들의 사랑은 두 명의 죽음을 가져오게 되는 끔찍한 사랑이었다. 따라서 그들의 만남을 위해서 자신들을 강화할 필요가 있다.

등장인물에 대해 물리적인 묘사를 하지 않는 것은 헤밍웨이의 전형적인 스타일이다. 예를 들면,

"미스 버클리는 꽤 키가 컸다. 간호사 제복을 인 듯 옷을 입었고 금발에 연갈색 피부, 회색 눈이었다. 나는 그녀가 무척 아름답다고 생각했다."(18)

작가의 이 같은 구체성의 결여는 두 가지를 얻게 해 준다는 것을 알게 된다.
첫째는 독자들에게 상상에 의한 독자를 자신만의 구체성으로 작가가 남겨 놓은 빈 공간을 채우게 한다.
둘째는 등장인물에 대한 보편성의 감성을 준다. 어떤 의미에서 모든 사람이 『무기여 잘 있거라』에서 남주인공과 여주인공이 될 수 있다.

■ 4장 주요 작품 내용

The battery in the next garden woke me in the morning and I saw the sun coming through the window and got out of bed. I went to the window and looked out. The gravel paths were moist and the grass was wet with dew. The battery fired twice and the air came each time like a blow and shook the window and made the front of my pajamas flap. I could not see the guns but they were evidently firing directly over us. It was a nuisance to have them there but it was a comfort that they were no bigger. As I looked out at the garden I heard a motor truck starting on the road. I dressed, went downstairs, had some coffee in the kitchen and went out to the garage.(15)

Ten cars were lined up side by side under the long shed. They were top-heavy, blunt-nosed ambulances, painted gray and built like moving vans. The mechanics were working on one out in the yard. Three others were up in the mountains at dressing station.

"Do they ever shell that battery?" I asked one of the mechanics.

"No, Signor Tenente. It is protected by the little hill."

"How's everything?"

"Not so bad. This machine is no good but the others march."

He stopped working and smiled. "Were you on permission?"

"Yes."

He wiped his hands on his jumper ad grinned. "You have a good time?" The others all grinned too.

"Fine," I said. "What's the matter with this machine?"

"It's no good. One thing after another."

"What's the matter now?"

"New rings."

I left them working, the car looking disgraced and empty with the engine open and parts spread on the work bench, and went in under the shed and looked at each of the cars. They were moderately clean, a few freshly washed, the others dusty. I looked at the tires carefully, looking for cuts or stone bruises. Everything seemed in good condition. It evidently made no difference whether I was there to look after things or not. I had imagined that the condition of the cars, whether or not things were obtainable, the smooth functioning of the business of removing wounded and sick from the dressing stations, hauling them back from the mountains to the clearing station and then distributing them to the hospitals named on their papers depended to considerable extent on myself. Evidently it did not matter whether I was there or not.(16)

"All right," I said. We drank the second grappa, Rinaldi put away the bottle and we went down the stairs. It was hot walking through the town but the sun starting to go down and it was very pleasant. The British hospital was a big villa built by Germans before the war. Miss Barkley was in the garden. Another nurse was with her. We saw their white uniforms through the trees and walked toward them. Rinaldi saluted. I saluted too but more moderately.

"How do you do?" Miss Barkley said. "You're not an Italian, are you?"

"Oh, no."

Rinaldi was talking with the other nurse. They were laughing.

"What an odd thing- to be in the Italian army."

"It's not really the army. It's only the ambulance."

"It's very odd though. Why did you do it?"

"I don't know," I said. "There isn't always an explanation for everything."

"Oh, isn't there? I was brought to think there was."

"That's awfully nice."

"Do we have to go on and talk this way?"

"No," I said.

"That's a relief. Isn't it?"

"what is the stick?" I asked. Miss Barkley was quite tall. She wore what seemed to me to be a nurse's uniform, was blonde and had a tawny skin and gray eyes. I thought she was very beautiful. She was carrying a thin rattan stick like a toy riding-crop, bound in leather.

"It belonged to a boy who was killed last year."

"I'm awfully sorry."

"He was a very nice boy. He was going to marry me and he was killed in the Somme."

"It was a ghastly show."

"Were you there?"

"No."

"I've heard about it," she said. "There's not really any war of that sort down here. They sent me the little stick. His mother sent it to me. They returned it with his things."

"Had you been engaged long?"

"Eight years. We grew up together?"

"And why didn't you marry?"

"I don't know," she said. "I was a fool not to. I could have given him that anyway. But I thought it would be bad for him."

"I see."

"Have you ever loved any one?"

"No," I said.

We sat down on a bench and I looked at her.

"You have beautiful hair," I said.

"Do you like it?"

"Very much."

"I was going to cut it all off when he died."

"No."

"I wanted to do something for him. You see I didn't care about the other thing and he could have had it all. He could have had anything he wanted if I would have known. I would have married him or anything. I know all about it now. But then He wanted to go to war and I didn't know."

I did not say anything.

"I didn't know about anything then. I thought it would be worse for him. I thought perhaps he couldn't stand it and then of course he was killed and that was the end of it."

"I don't know."

"Oh, yes," she said. "That's the end of it."

We looked at Rinaldi talking with the other nurse.

"What is her name?"

"Fergurson. Helen Fergurson. Your friend is a doctor, isn't he?"

"Yes. He's very good."

"That's splendid. You rarely find any one any good this close to the front. This is close to the front, isn't it?"(19)

5장 (Chapter V)

■ 5장 주요 내용

- 화자와 버클리와의 만남. 그리고 키스함.

I kissed her hard and held her tight and tried to opened he lips; they were closed tight.

- 오스트리아 군과 이탈리아 군의 대치 플라바(Plava) 지역 등장.

I had been up the river to the bridgehead at Plava. It was there that the offensive was to begin.

- 이탈리아 군대에 입대한 이유를 묻는다.

"Tell me. Why did you join up with the Italian?"

■ Summary

화자는 버클리를 찾아갔다. 그때 병원 수간호사(head nurse)는 그녀는 근무 중이라고 말했다.

안에서 만난 수간호사는 미스 버클리는 근무 중이라고 알려 줬다. "아시다시피 전쟁 중이니까요."(22)

Inside I saw the head nurse, who said Miss Barkley was on duty- "there's a war on, you know."

공격이 개시될 지점인 강 상류 쪽 플라바(Plava)의 교두보(bridge-head)를 다녀왔다. 오스트리아 군과 이탈리아 군이 대치한 지점이기도 하다. 서로 간에 교두보를 확보하고 상황만 주시하고 있다. 그는 오스트리아를 공격하기 위해서 이탈리아 공격의 준비상태를 점검했다. 그가 그 지역을 정찰하는 동안 세 번의 포탄이 폭발했다.

나는 강 상류 쪽 플라바의 교두보에 다녀왔다. 공격이 개시될 지점이었다.(23)
내 생각에는 오스트리아 군도 강 하류 쪽에 교두보를 확보했기 때문에 서로 묵인하는 것 같았다.

I had been up the river to the bridgehead at Plava. It was there that the offensive was to begin.(23)

I suppose it was mutual tolerance because the Austrians still kept a bridgehead further down the river.(23)

저녁 식사 후 화자는 버클리를 찾아간다. 그리고 그녀와 키스했다. 버클리는 미스 퍼거슨과 달리 간호사가 아니고 일은 죽어라 하고 누구도 인정해 주지 않는 VAD이다. 자신이 하는 일에 대한 원망을 토로한다.

"아, 아니에요. 저는 VAD예요. 죽어라 일해도 아무것도 인정해 주지 않죠."

"Oh, no. I'm something called a *V.A.D. We work very hard but no one trusts us."(25)

저녁 식사 후 화자는 버클리를 다시 찾아갔다. 그리고 그녀와 키스했다.

* VAD: 1차 세계대전 때 영국 적십자사가 조직한 구급 간호봉사대.

■ 논평

화자의 저돌적인 돌진에 그녀의 저항 이후에 버클리와 화자의 사랑은 시작된다. 분명 그들은 서로 다른 의제를 갖고 있다. 화자는 그들의 관계를 체스 게임(Chess game)으로 보았다. 이와 대조적으로 버클리는 화자에 대해서 자신의 죽은 약혼자에 대한 사랑을 나타내주는 것처럼 보였다. 그들이 처음 키스했을 때 그녀는 울었다. 그리고 그녀는 화자에게 잘해 달라고 간청했다. 그리고 그녀는 불가사의하게도 "우리는 이상한 삶을 살게 될 테니까요."(27)

I held her close against me and could feel her heart beating and lips opened and her head went back against my hand and then she was crying on my shoulder. "Oh, darling," she said. "You will be good to me, won't you?"

"Because we're going to have a strange life."(27)

화자 탈영의 전조는 그가 이탈리아 군대에 입대한 것을 이상하다고 생각한 수간호사의 대화에서 지속된다. 자신도 이탈리아인들에게 경례하는 것이 불편했다. 버클리와 이야기할 때 화자는 다음과 같이 제시했다.

"전쟁 이야기는 그만하시죠." "안 하기 힘들어요. 온통 그 얘기뿐이니까."(26)
"Let's drop the war." "It's very hard. There's no place to drop it."

그녀가 키스하려고 하는 화자를 때린 후에 그는 "전쟁 이야기도 잊어버렸고요."(26)라고 농담했다. "We have gotten away from the war." 그녀는 웃었다. 이야기의 핵심은 버클리는 전쟁을 잊을 수 없다는 것을 알고 있다는 사실이다. 사랑하는 사람을 잃은 비극적인 손실이 그녀에게 많은 것을 가르쳐 준 것처럼 전쟁은 매우 중요하다. 그러나 화자는 아직은 이 같은 사실을 인식하지 못한다. 젊은 두 남녀 간의 사랑에서 한 사람은 전쟁의 비극을 잘 알고 있지만 한 사람은 전쟁이 어떤 결과를 가져오는지에 대해 알지 못하는 기막힌 상황이 전개된다.

"이탈리아 군에 있다는 그 미국인인가요?" 그녀가 물었다.
"네, 부인."
"어쩌다 그랬어요? 왜 우리 군에 들어오지 않은 거죠?"
"모르겠습니다." 나는 말했다. "지금이라도 들어갈 수 있을까요?"
"지금은 어려울 것 같은데요. 말해 줘요. 왜 이탈리아 군에 들어갔어요?"(22)
"이탈리아에 있었고," 나는 말했다. "이탈리아어를 했거든요."
"You're the American in the Italian army?" she asked.

"Yes, ma'am."

"How did you happen to do that? Why didn't you join up with us?"

"I don't know," I said. "Could I join now?"

"I'm afraid not now. Tell me. Why did you join up with the Italians?"

"I was in Italy," I said, and "I spoke Italian."(22)

■ 5장 주요 작품 내용

The next afternoon I went to call on Miss Barkely again. She was not in the garden and I went to the side door of the villa where the ambulances drove up. Inside I saw the head nurse, who said Miss Barkley was on duty- "there's a war on, you know."

I said I knew.

"You're the American in the Italian army?" she asked.

"Yes, ma'am."

"How did you happen to do that? Why didn't you join up with us?"

"I don't know," I said. "Could I join now?"

"I'm afraid not now. Tell me. Why did you join up with the Italians?"

"I was in Italy," I said, "and I spoke Italian."

"Oh," she said. "I'm learning it. It's beautiful language."

"Somebody said you should be able to learn it in two weeks."

"Oh, I'll not learn it in two weeks. I've studied it for months now. You may come and see her after seven o'clock if you wish. She'll be off then. But don't bring a lot of Italians."(22)

At dinner I ate very quickly and left for the villa where the British had their hospital. It was really very large and beautiful and there were fine trees in the grounds. Miss Barkley was sitting on a bench in the garden. Miss Ferguson was with her. They seemed glad to see me and in a little while Miss Ferguson excused herself and went away.

"I'll leave you two," she said. "You get along very well without me."

"Don't go, Helen," Miss Barkley said.

"I'd really rather. I must write some letters."

"Good-night," I said.

"Good-night, Mr. Henry."

"Don't write anything that will bother the censor."

"Don't worry. I only write about what a beautiful place we live in and how brave the Italians are."

"That way you'll be decorated."

"That will be nice. Good-night, Catherine."

"I'll see you in a little while," Miss Barkley said. Miss Ferguson walked away in the dark.

"She's nice," I said.

"Oh, yes, she's very nice. She is a nurse."

"Aren't you a nurse?"

"Oh, no. I'm something called a V.A.O. We work very hard but no one trusts us."

"Why not?"

"They don't trust us when there's nothing going on. When there is really work they trust us."

"What is the difference?"

"A nurse is like a doctor. It takes a long time to be. A V.A.D is a short cut."

"I see."

"The Italians didn't want women so near the front. So we're all on very special behavior. We don't go out."

"I can come here though."(25)

"Oh, yes. We're not cloistered."

"Let's drop the war."

"It's very hard. There's no place to drop it."

"Let's drop it anyway."

"All right."

We looked at each other in the dark. I thought she was very beautiful and I took her hand. She let me take it and I held it and put my arm around under her arm.

"No," she said. I kept my arm where it was.

"Why not?"

"No."

"Yes," I said. "Please." I leaned forward in the dark to kiss her and there was a sharp stinging flash. She had slapped my face hard. Her hand had hit my nose and eyes, and tears came in my eyes from the reflex.

"I'm so sorry," she said. I felt I had a certain advantage.

"You were quite right."

"I'm dreadfully sorry," she said. "I just couldn't stand the nurse's evening- off aspect of it. I didn't mean to hurt you. I did hurt you, didn't I?"

She was looking at me in the dark. I was angry and yet certain, seeing it all ahead like the moves in a chess game.

"You did exactly right," I said. "I don't mind at all."

"Poor man."

"You see I've been leading a sort of a funny life. And I never even talk English. And then you are so very beautiful." I looked at her.

"You don't need to say a lot of nonsense. I said I was sorry. We do get along."

"Yes," I said. "And we have gotten away from the war."

She laughed. It was the first time I had ever heard her laugh. I watched her face.

"You are sweet," she said.

"No, I'm not."

"Yes. You are a dear. I'd be glad to kiss you if you don't mind."

I looked in her eyes and put my arm around her as I had before and kissed her. I kissed her hard and held her tight and tried to open her lips; they were closed tight. I was still angry and as I held her suddenly she shivered. I held her close against me and could feel her heart beating and her lips opened and her head went back against my hand and then she was crying on my shoulder.

"Oh, darling," she said. "You will be good to me, won't you?"

What the hell, I thought. I stroked her hair and patted her shoulder. She was crying.

"You will, won't you?" She looked up at me. "Because we're going to have a strange life."(27)

6장(Chapter VI)

■ 6장 주요 내용

- 화자가 헨리(Frederick Henry)로 바뀜.
- "Good morning, Mr Henry." she said.
- 버클리 캐서린(Catherine Barkley)으로 정식으로 바뀜.

■ Summary

처음으로 6장에서 화자가 헨리로 바뀐다. 독자들은 그동안 화자 즉 주동 인물이 누구인지 궁금함으로 느껴 왔는데 이제 그 실마리가 드러난 셈이다. 화자가 Mr, Henry로 바뀐다. "안녕하세요, 미스터 헨리." 그녀가 말했다. (29) "Good morning, Mr Henry." she said. 삼 일 후 화자가 버클리를 방문했다. 이때 작가는 캐서린(Catherine)이라는 이름을 처음으로 드러냈다. 즉 버클리가 캐서린으로 정식으로 바뀐 것이다. 그들은 영국 병원 근처 정원에 앉았다. 그리고 말했다. 그녀는 그에게 자신을 안심시키는 말을 요청했고 그는 그렇게 했다. 캐서린은 그에 대한 자신의 사랑에 대해서 말했다. 나중에 그녀는 슬프게도 게임이라 언급했고 키스를 한 후에 헤어졌다.

■ 논평

구성의 관점에서 이 소설의 후반부에 중요하다고 증명되는 문체가 6장에서 소개된다. 화자가 가지고 다니는 권총(pistol)이다.

우리는 자동 권총을 소지하게 돼 있어야 하는데, 군의관과 위생장교도 예외는 아니었다.(29)
"Also, we were required to wear an automatic pistol, even doctors and sanitary officers."

전쟁과 관련된 단어들을 통해서 상대적으로 평화로운 장에서도 우리는 끊임없이 전쟁이 우리 가까이 있음을 알게 된다. 반면 화자가 거짓말이라고 말한다고 할지라도 캐서린은 화자로부터 사랑의 맹세를 원한다. 게임이나 브리지에 비교하면서 화자는 자세히 말한다.

"나는 캐서린 버클리를 사랑하지 않았고 그럴 생각도 없었다."(30)
이건 게임이었다. 카드가 아니라, 말로 하는 브리지 같은 게임. 브리지처럼 돈을 따기 위해 게임을 하거나 내기를 걸고 하는 척하면 그만이었다.(31)
I knew I did not love Catherine Barkley nor had any idea of loving her. This was a game, like bridge, in which you said things instead of playing cards. Like bridge you had to pretend you were playing for money or playing for some stakes.

그러나 상황은 반전된다. 캐서린은 화자의 팔을 자기 어깨에 놓지 못하게 하고 키스도 거부한다. 그리고 그녀는 그가 게임하고 있다는 것을 드러낸다. 그녀도 역시 게임을 하고 있다.

"나를 사랑하는 척할 필요 없어요…. 정신이 나간 게 아니에요."(31)
"You don't have to pretend you love me…. You see I'm not mad."(31)

캐서린은 처음에 보였던 그때보다도 더 현명해졌다. 어떤 면에서는 화자 자신보다도 더 현명해졌다. 헤밍웨이만의 전형적인 기법으로 6장을 끝낸다.

작가는 등장인물의 느낌을 등장인물의 마음을 읽어서 말하는 방식과 등장인물의 행동을 묘사하고 대사를 인용하는 방식을 취하지 않고 등장인물들이 다른 사람에게 불어넣은 반응을 독자에게 제공함으로써 작가는 등장인물들이 어떻게 느끼는지를 우리에게 알려 준다. 명료하게 말하지 않지만, 캐서린 버클리 간호사를 만난 후 우리는 그의 행동에 대한 룸메이트의 반응 때문에 화자가 기분이 좋지 않다는 사실을 안다.

"아하!" 그가 말했다. "일이 잘 안 되나 보군요. 우리 베이비가 당황스러워 보이는데."(32)

"Ah, ha!" he said. "It does not go so well. Baby is puzzle."

■ 6장 주요 작품 내용

There were many marble busts on painted wooden pillars along the walls of the room they used for an office. The hall too, that the office opened on, was lined with them. They had the complete marble quality of all looking alike. Sculpture had always seemed a dull business-still, bronzes looked like something. But marble busts all looked like a cemetery. There was one fine cemetery though-the one at Pisa. Genoa was the place to see the bad marbles.(28)

I sat on a chair and held my cap. We were supposed to wear steel helmets even in Gorizia but they were uncomfortable and too bloody theatrical in a town where the civilian inhabitants had not been evacuated. I wore one when we went up to the posts and carried English gas mask. We were just beginning to get some of them. They were a real mask. Also we were required to wear an automatic pistol; even doctors and sanitary officers. I felt it against the back of the chair. You were liable to arrest if you did not have one worn in plain sight. Rinaldi carried a holster stuffed with toilet paper. I wore real one and felt like a gunman until I practised firing it. It was an Astra 7.65 caliber with a short barrel and it jumped so sharply when you let it off that there was no question of hitting anything.(29)

I saw Catherine Barkley coming down the hall, and stood up. She did not seem tall walking forward me but she looked very lovely.

"Good-evening, Mr. Henry." she said.

"How do you do?" I said. The orderly was listening behind the desk.

"Shall we sit here or go out in the garden?"

"Let's go out. It's much cooler."

I walked behind her out into the garden, the orderly looking after us. When we were out on the gravel drive she said, "Where have you been?"

"I've been out on post."(29)

"You couldn't have sent me a note?"

"No," I said. "Not very well. I thought I was coming back."

"You ought to have let me know, darling."

We were off the driveway, walking under the trees. I took her hands, then stopped and kissed her.

"Isn't there anywhere we can go?"

"No," she said. "We have to just walk here. You've been away a long time."

"This is the third day. But I'm back now."

She looked at me, "And you do love me?"

"Yes."

"You did, say you loved me, didn't you?"

"Yes," I lied. "I love you." I had not said it before.

"And you call me Catherine?"

"Catherine." We walked on a way and were stopped under a tree.

"Say," I've come back to Catherine in the night.

"I've come back to Catherine in the night."

"Oh, darling, you have come back, haven't you?"

"Yes."

"I love you so. and it's been awful. You won't go away?"

"No. I'll always come back."

"Oh, I love you so. Please put your hand there again."

"It's not been away." I turned her so I could see her face when I kissed her and I saw that her eyes were shut. I kissed both her shut eyes. I thought she was probably a little crazy. It was all right if she was. I did not care what I was getting into. This was better than going every evening to the house for officers where the girls climbed all over you and put your cap on backward as a sign of affection between their trips upstairs with brother officers. I knew I did not love Catherine Barkley nor had any idea of loving her. This was a game, like bridge, in which you said things instead of playing cards.(30)

Like bridge you had to pretend you were playing for money or playing for some stakes. Nobody had mentioned what the stakes were. It was all right with me.

"I wish there was some place we could go," I said. I was experiencing the masculine difficulty of making love very long standing up.

"There isn't any place," she said. She came back from wherever she had been.

"We might sit here just for a little while."

We sat on the flat stone bench and I held Catherine Barkley's hand. She would let me put my arm around her.

"Are you very tired?" she asked.

"No."

She looked down at the grass.

"This is a rotten game we play, isn't it?"

"What game?"

"Don't be dull."

"I'm not, on purpose."

"You're a nice boy," she said. "And you play it as well as you know how. But it's a rotten game."

"Do you always know what people think?"

"Not always. But I do with you. You don't have to pretend you love me. That's over for the evening. Is there anything you'd like to talk about?"

"But I do love you."

"Please let's not lie when you don't have to. I had a very fine little show and I'm all right now. You see I'm not mad and I'm not gone off. It's only a little sometimes."

I pressed her hand, "Dear Catherine."

"It sound very funny now- Catherine. You don't pronounce it very much alike. But you're very nice. You're very good boy."

"That's what the priest said."

"Yes, you're very good. And you will come and see me?"

"Of course."(31)

"And you don't have to say you love me. That's all over for a while."She stood up and put out her hand. "Good-night."

I wanted to kiss her.

"No," she said. "I'm awfully tired."

"Kiss me, though," I said.

"I'm awfully tired, darling."

"Kiss me."

"Do you want to very much?"

"Yes."

We kissed and broke away suddenly. "No. Good-night, please, darling." We walked to the door and I saw her go in and down the hall. I liked to watch her move. She went on down the hall. I went on home. It was a hot night and there was a good deal going on up in the mountains. I watched the flashes on San Gabriele.(32)

I stopped in front of the Villa Rossa. The shutters were up but it was still going on inside. Somebody was singing. I went on home. Rinaldi came in while I was undressing.

"Ah, ha!" he said. "it does not go so well. Baby is puzzled."

"Where have you been?"

"At the Villa Rossa. It was very edifying, baby. We all sang. Where have you been?"

"Calling on the British."

"Thank God I did not become involved with the British."(32)

7장 (Chapter VII)

■ 7장 주요내용

- 낙오자(stragger) 출현으로 전쟁터의 부조리한 점을 지적.

A soldier came along after the last of the stragglers.

- 캐서린에 대해 쉽게 생각하고.

I had treated seeing Catherine very lightly

- 헨리가 캐서린에 대해 더 그리워하기 시작.

when I could not see her there I was feeling lonely and hollow.

■ Summary

화자가 엠블런스를 타고 운전하는 동안 미국인 동료를 만났다. 그는 탈장(Hernia 헤르니아)로 인해서 매우 고통을 받고 있었고 이탈리아어를 사용하면서 전투에서 면제받기를 원하는 미국인 보병(infantryman)과 마주했다. 그 보병은 의도적으로 자기 머리에 상처를 낸다.

"무슨 문제지?"

"전쟁이 문제죠."

"다리는 왜 그러죠?"

"다리가 아닙니다. 탈장입니다."

"왜 수송차를 타지 않았지?" 내가 물었다.

"왜 병원에 가지 않았어?"

"보내 주지 않았습니다. 우리 중위님은 제가 일부러 탈장띠를 풀었다고 하십니다."(34)

"What's the trouble?"

"----- the war."

"What's wrong with your leg?"

"It's not my leg. I got a rupture."

"Why don't you ride with the transport?" I asked. "Why don't you go to the hospital?"

"They won't let me. The lieutenant said I slipped the truss on purpose."

"이 빌어먹을 전쟁을 어떻게 생각하십니까?"

"최악이지."

"정말 그렇습니다. 젠장, 정말 최악입니다."

"미국에 살았나?"

"네, 피츠버그에 있었습니다. 저는 중위님이 미국인이란 걸 알아봤습니다."(35)

"How you like this goddam war?"

"Rotten."

1부(Book One)

"I say it's rotten. Jesus Christ, I say it's rotten."

"Were you in the States?"

"Sure, In Pittsburgh. I knew you was an American."(35)

"들어 봐." 내가 말했다. "차에서 내린 다음 자네는 아무 데서나 넘어져 머리에 혹을 만들어 봐. 그럼 내가 돌아오는 길에 자네를 태워 병원에 데려갈 테니까. 여기서 잠깐 멈춰, 알도." 우리는 길가에 차를 세웠다. 나는 그가 내리도록 부축했다.(35)

"Listen," I said. "You get out and fall down by the road and get a bump on your head and I'll pick you up on our way back and take you to a hospital. We'll stop by the road here, Aldo." We stopped at the side of the road. I helped him down.(35)

이윽고 말이 끄는 구급차 한 대가 길가에 서 있는 것이 보였다. 두 사람이 탈장된 병사를 들어오려 차에 태우고 있었다. 그들이 병사를 데리러 돌아온 것이었다. 병사는 나를 향해 고개를 저었다. 철모는 벗겨지고 이마에서는 아래로 피가 흐르고 있었다. 콧등이 까지고 피가 흐르는 부분과 머리카락은 먼지투성이였다.(36)

Then we saw a horse ambulance stopped by the road. Two men were lifting the hernia man to put him in. They had come back for him. He shook his head at me. His helmet was off and his forehead was bleeding below the hair line. His nose was skinned and there was dust on the bloody patch and dust in his hair.(36)

이 장면은 부조리한 전쟁터를 말해 준다. 부상이 아니면 수송차에 탈 수 없다는 규정은 전쟁터에 있는 군인들을 힘들게 하는 면이다. 중위는 일부러 그랬다고 주장하는 현실에서 병사의 고통은 더 힘들어진다.

나중에 숙소에서 집으로 편지를 쓸 때 화자는 그의 상황에 대해 대안을 생각하고 밀라노(Milan)의 호텔 방에서 버클리와 사랑에 대해 상상했다. 장교식당에서 캐서린을 만나기 위해서 가는 도중에 화자는 취해 있었다. 반면 장교들은 신부를 다시 학대했다. 우리는 그의 이름이 프레더릭 헨리(Frederic Henry)라는 것을 알게 되는 서술기법에서 매우 중요하다. 결국 헨리는 늦게 나타나서 캐서린을 못 만난다. 그는 집으로 오면서 외로움과 허전함을 느낀다.

캐서린과 만나는 것을 아주 가볍게 생각했고 술을 마시느라 약속을 잊을 뻔하기도 했지만, 막상 그녀를 만나지 못하자 외롭고 허전했다.(41)
I had gotten somewhat drunk and had nearly forgotten to come but when I could not see her there I was feeling lonely and hollow.(41)

■ 논평

보병이 전투에서 탈출을 선택할 수 있다는 의미를 나타내 주는 썩은 전쟁(rotten war)에 참여한 피츠버그(pittsburgh) 출신의 군인과 생각을 같이해서 헨리 중위의 탈영을 다시 한번 조짐을 보여 준다. 이것은 전쟁에 대한 환멸이 헨리 자신에게 한정된 것이 아니라는 것을 보여 주기 때문에 이야기는 중요하다.

화자의 이름은 중위의 의지만큼이나 부조리한 전쟁의 상처를 나타내 주는 『전사의 용기』(The Red Badge of Courage)라는 미국의 반전 소설의 주동 인물(protagonist)을 내비친다. 헤밍웨이는 이 작품의 작가인 스테판 크레인(Stephen Crane)을 칭송했다. 지금까지 헨리라는 이름을 드러내는 것을 거부한 작가의 의도는 주동 인물이 누구나 될 수 있다는 또 다른 전략이다. 이것은 전쟁 기간 군인들에게서 서로 볼 수 있는 본성인 정체 불성(faceless)을 강조한다. 특히 전쟁의 책임자들에게 그렇다. 헤밍웨이는 한 명의 구급차 운전병은 어느 다른 운전병과 같다. 즉 모든 사람은 다 똑같이 중요하다고 말하려는 것이다. 잘못된 몇 명에 의해서 이루어진 전쟁터에서 이루어진 부조리한 행동들을 누가 책임을 추궁할 수 있으며 이 부조리한 전쟁터를 탈영한들 누가 그 책임을 물을 수 있는지 반문한다. 한 명 한 명 모두 소중하고 중요하다. 그리고 이 전쟁에서 발생하는 모든 일들은 누구에게도 일어날 수 있는 일이다. 즉 우리의 문제이다.

헨리와 캐서린 버클리와의 대화로 드러난 전쟁에 관한 단순한 생각이 매우 명확히 드러난다.

나는 죽지 않을 것이다. 이 전쟁에서는 아니다. 이 전쟁은 나와 아무런 상관이 없다. 나에게 이 전쟁은 영화 속 전쟁만큼이나 위험하지 않은 느낌을 주었다.(37)
Well, I knew I would not be killed. Not in this war. It did not have anything to do with me. It seemed no more dangerous to me myself than war in the movies.

캐서린은 전쟁에서 약혼자를 잃은 결과를 간직하고 있어서 전쟁은 잔혹한 현실인 것을 알고 있다. 그러나 헨리는 그와 같은 경험을 하고 있지 않다. 그러나 캐서린은 헨리가 곧 전쟁이란 것이 어떤 것인지를 알게 될 것이란 것을 알고 있다. 그의 무심함과 두려움의 부재가 전쟁의 위험과 전쟁의 현실이 존재하지 않고 그가 위험과 현실 영향을 받지 않는다는 것을 의미하지 않는다.

헨리는 신부를 괴롭히는 일에 가담하지 않는다. 냉소적이고 허무적인 장교들이 신부를 놀리는 것과는 달리 그는 사제가 무언가를 상정한다는 것도 알고 있다. 사제를 화나게 하는 일에 동참하는 것을 거부한 것은 그가 사제를 존경한다는 것이고 이런 점에서 그가(신부) 잠재력을 가졌다는 것을 우리에게 보여 준다.

문체적으로 작가는 짧은 문장과 평서문을 결합해서 사용했다. 이 방식은 캐서린과 밀라노 호텔 방에서 함께 한다는 헨리의 몽상 속에서 조이스적인 의식의 흐름(Joycean Stream of Consciousness)으로 잘 알려져 있다. 강조하는 점이 성적인 것처럼 보일지라도 헨리는 "우리 밤새도록 서로 사랑한다."라고 말한 점을 주목하자. 즉 그녀에 대한 그의 깊은 감정의 무의식적인 시인이라고 볼 수 있다. 그가 장교들과 술을 마셨기 때문에 그는 저녁 그녀와의 약속에 열성적이지 않았다. 결국 그날 저녁 그녀를 만나지 못했다. 반면 그 후에 그렇게 한 것에 대해서 후회했다. 그리고 헨리는 점점 더 캐서린에게 가까이 다가가고 있었다.

1부(Book One)

■ 7장 주요 작품 내용

There were stragglers going by long after the regiment had passed-men who could not keep up with their platoons. They were sweety, dusty and tired. Some looked pretty bad. A soldier came along after the last of the stragglers. He was walking with a limp. He stopped and sat down beside the road. I got down and went over.

"What's the matter?"

He looked at me, then stood up.

"I'm going on."

"What's the trouble?"

"----- the war."

"What's wrong with your leg?"

"It's not my leg. I got a rupture."

"Why don't you ride with the transport?" I asked. "Why don't you go to the hospital?"

"They won't let me. The lieutenant said I slipped the truss on purpose."

"Let me feel it."

"It's way out."

"Which side is it on?"

"Here."

"I felt it."

"Cough," I said.

"I'm afraid it will make it bigger. It's twice as big as it was this morning."

"Sit down," I said. "As soon as I got the papers on these wounded I'll take you along the road and drop you with your medical officers."

"He'll say I did it on purpose."

"They can't do anything." I said. "It's not a wound. You've had it before, haven't you?"

"But I lost the truss."

"They'll send you to a hospital."

"Can't I stay here, Tenente?"

"No, I haven't any papers for you."

The driver came out of the door with the papers for the wounded in the car.

"Four for 105. Two for 132," he said. They were hospitals beyond the driver.

"You drive," I said. I helped the soldier with the rupture up on the seat with us.(35)

"Listen," I said. "You get out and fall down by the road and get a bump on your head and I'll pick you up on our way back and take you to a hospital. We'll stop by the road here, Aldo." We stopped at the side of the road. I helped him down.

"I'll be right here, Lieutenant." he said.

"So long," I said. We went on and passed the regiment about a mile ahead. then crossed the river, cloudy with snow-water and running fast through the spiles of the bridge, to ride along the road across the plain and deliver the wounded at the town hospitals. I drove coming back and went fast with the empty car to find

1부(Book One)

the man from Pittsburgh. First we passed the regiment, hotter and slower than ever: then the stragglers. Then we saw a horse ambulance stopped by the road. Two men were lifting the hernia man to put him in. They had come back for him. He shook his head at me. His helmet was off and his forehead was bleeding below the hair line. His nose was skinned and there was dust on the bloody patch and dust in his hair.(36)

Still I would probably have been killed. Not in the ambulance business. Yes, even in the ambulance business. British ambulance drivers were killed sometime. **Well, I knew I would not be killed. Not in this war. It did not have anything to do with me. It seemed no more dangerous to me myself than war in the movies.** I wish to God it was over though. Maybe it would finish this summer. Maybe the Austrians would crack. They had always cracked in other wars. What was the matter with this war? Everybody said the French were through. Rinaldi said that the French had mutinied and troops marched on Paris. I asked him what happened and he said, "Oh, they stopped them." I wanted to go to Austria without war. I wanted to go to the Black Forest. I wanted to go the Hartz Mountains. Where were the Hartz mountains anyway? There were fighting in the Carpathians. I did not want to go there anyway. It might be good though. I could go to Spain if there was no war. The sun was going down and the day was cooling off.(37)

After supper I would go and see Catherine Barkley. I wish she were here now. I wish I were in Milan and her. I would like to eat at the Cova and then walked down the Via Manzoni in the hot evening and cross over and turn off along the canal and go to the hotel with Catherine Barkley. Maybe she would. Maybe she would pretend that I was her boy that was killed and we would go in the front door and the porter would take off his cap and I would stop at the concierge's desk and ask for the key and she would stand by the elevator and then we would get in the elevator and it would go up very slowly clicking at all the floors and then our floor and the boy would open the door and stand there and she would step out and I would step out and we would walk down the hall and I would put the key in the door and open it and go in and then take down the telephone and ask them to send a bottle of capri bianca in a silver bucket full of ice and she would hear the ice against the pail coming down the corridor and the boy would knock and I would say leave it outside the door please. Because we would not wear any clothes because it was so hot and the window open and the swallows flying over the roofs of the houses and when it was dark afterward and you went to the window very small bats hunting over the houses and close down over the trees and we would drink the capri and the door locked and it hot and only a sheet and the whole night and we would both love each other all night in the hot night in Milan. That was how it ought to be. I would eat quickly and go and see Catherine Buckley.(37-38)

I went out the door and suddenly I felt lonely and empty. I had treated seeing Catherine very lightly. I had gotten somewhat drunk and had nearly forgotten to come but when I could not see her there I was feeling lonely and hollow.(41)

8장 (Chapter VIII)

■ 8장 주요 내용

- 공격 준비를 위한 출격.

The next afternoon we heard there was to be an attack up the river that night and that we were to take four cars there.

- 캐서린과의 이별.

I looked back and saw her standing on the steps. She waved and I kissed my hand and hold it out.

■ Summary

야간 공격 준비를 위해서 헨리 중위는 강 쪽으로 구급차를 이동하라는 지시받은 후에 헨리는 영국 병원에 잠시 멈춘다. 그곳에서 캐서린과 작별 인사를 하고 그녀는 그에게 성 안토니오 메달(Saint Anthony Medal)을 준다.

■ 논평

사실 헤밍웨이는 헨리 중위가 성 베드로 대성전에 대해 말한 것처럼 그러한 행동을 분명히 예견하고 있다. 안토니오 메달을 내가 다친 이후로 찾지 못했다. 일반적으로 작가는 드라마를 과소평가하고 멜로드라마를 피한다: 캐서린과 헨리는 서로 작별 인사를 하면서도 키스하지 않는다. 아마도 병원의 예절이나 그녀의 영국인들의 유보하는 태도 때문일 것이다. 그리고 앞장에서처럼 우리는 서술자 자신이 아니라 다른 인물의 반응을 통해 헨리의 감정을 배운다.

캐서린은,

"안 돼요. 여기서 키스하면 안 돼."라고, 말했다.(43)
"No, you can't kiss me here. You can't."

소설의 상징성 측면에서 헨리가 영웅적인 행위로 그의 첫 번째 만남을 위해서 저지대에서 언덕으로 올라간다는 것은 매우 중요하다. 그리고 그가 먼 곳에 있는 하얀 산에 대해서 말하고,

그것들은 모두 오스트리아의 산이었고 우리 쪽에는 그런 산이 없었다.(45)
These were all the Austrians' mountains and we had nothing like them.

라고 말하는 것은 흥미롭다 그는 오스트리아군과 달리 이탈리아인들은 규율이 없으므로 아마도 그들은 싸울 가치가 없을 것이라고 제한한

다. 헨리는 이탈리아 군대에서 그에게 곧 있을 유기(탈영) 없다고 시사(암시)에 대한 이유(근거)와 알리바이(albeit)를 만드는 것처럼 보였다. 이장은 제9장에서 극적인 사건을 위해 여러 가지 무대를 만든 장으로 본다. 사실 작가는 그 같은 행동을 명시적으로 나타냈다.

She was unclasping something from her neck. She put it in my hand. "It's a Saint Anthony," she said. "And come to-morrow night."(43)

"그 뒤로 곧 그것을 잃어버렸다. 부상당한 뒤로 끝내 찾지 못했다."(44)
"Then I forgot about him. After I was wounded I never found him. Some one probably got it at one of the dressing stations."(44)

라고 헨리 중위가 말했다. 평상시처럼 작가는 극을 덜 심각하게 보이게 했다. 멜로드라마를 피했다. 캐서린과 헨리는 서로 작별하는 동안 키스하지 않았다. 병원의 예의 때문이었을 수도 있다. 앞장에서 보았듯이 우리는 화자 자신으로부터 헨리의 감정(느낌)을 알 수 있는 게 아니고 다른 등장인물의 반응을 통해서 알 수 있다.

그녀는 목에서 뭔가를 풀어 내 손에 쥐어 주었다.
"성 안토니오예요." 그녀가 말했다. "내일 밤에 와요."(43)
She was unclasping something from her neck. She put it in my hand. "It's a Saint Anthony," she said. "And come to-morrow night."(43)

■ 8장 주요 작품 내용

　　The next afternoon we heard there was to be an attack up the river that night and that we were to take four cars there. Nobody knew anything about it although they all spoke with great positiveness and strategical knowledge. I was riding in the first car and as we passed the entry to the British hospital I told the driver to stop. The other cars pulled up. I got out and told the driver to go on and that if we had not caught up to them at the junction of the road to Cormons to wait there. I hurried up the driveway and inside the reception hall I asked for Miss Barkley.

"She's on duty."

"Could I see her just for a moment?"

They sent an orderly to see and she came back with him.

"I stopped to ask if you were better. They told me you were on duty, so I asked to see you."

"I'm quite well," she said. "I think the heat knocked me over yesterday."

"I have to go."

"I'll just step out the door a minute."

"And you're all right?" I asked outside.

"Yes, darling. Are you coming to-night?"

"No. I'm leaving now for a show up above Plava."

"A show?"

"I don't think it's anything."

"And you'll be back?"

"To-morrow."

She was unclasping something from her neck. She put it in my hand. "It's a Saint Anthony." she said. "And come to-morrow night."

"You're not a Catholic, are you?"

"No. But they say a Saint Anthony's very useful."

"I'll take care of him for you. Good-by."

"No," she said, "not good-by."

"All right."

"Be a good boy and be careful. No, you can't kiss me here. You can't."

"All right."

I looked back and saw her standing on the steps. She waved and I kissed my hand and held it out. She waved again and then I was out of the driveway and climbing up into the seat of the ambulance and we started. The Saint Anthony was in a little white metal capsule. I opened the capsule and spilled him out into my hand.

"Saint Anthony?" asked the driver.

"Yes."

"I have one." His right hand left the wheel and opened a button on his tunic and pulled it out from under his shirt.

"See?"

I put my Saint Anthony back in the capsule, spilled the thin gold chain together and put it all in my breast pocket.

"You don't wear him?"

"No."

"It's better to wear him. That's what it's for."

"All right," I said. I undid the clasp of the gold chain and put it around my neck and clasped it. The saint hung down on the outside of my uniform and I undid the throat of my tunic, unbuttoned the shirt collar and dropped him in under the shirt. I felt him in his metal box against my chest while we drove. Then I forgot about him. After I was wounded I never found him. Some one probably got it at one of the dressing stations.(44)

9장 (Chapter IX)

■ 9장 주요 내용

- 참호 안에서 운전병들과 부조리한 전쟁에 관한 대화.

■ Summary

전쟁보다 더 나쁜 것은 없다.
There is nothing worse than war.(50)

"모든 사람이 이 전쟁을 증오합니다."
"Everybody hates this war."(51)

"이 나라를 지배하는 세력들은 어리석고 아무것도 깨닫지 못하고 깨달을 수도 없는 계급이 지배하고 있어서 이 같은 전쟁을 우리가 겪어야 한다고 맹비난한다." "게다가 전쟁으로 돈까지 벌어들이는 사람이라고 비난한다."

"There is a class that controls a country that is stupid and does not realize anything never can. That is why we have this war." "Also they make money out of it."(50-51)

패배는 전쟁 그 자체보다 더 안 좋은 것이다.

defeat is worse.(50)

- 전반부 소설에서 가장 주요한 장

    파시니(Passini), 마네라(Manera), 고르디니(Gordini), 가부치(Gavuzzi) 등장

- 파시니 죽음

나는 각반을 풀기 시작했지만 그사이에 그가 이미 죽어 애써 지혈대를 만들 필요가 없다는 것을 깨달았다.

I unwound the puttee and while I was doing it I saw there was no need to try and make a tourniquet because he was dead already. I made sure he was dead.(55)

- 헨리의 부상

"나보다 부상이 훨씬 심한 사람들이 많아. 나는 괜찮아."(58)
"There are much worse wounded than me. I'm all right."

■ 논평

이장(9장)은 이 소설의 두 번째 중요한 전환점(turning point)을 극적으로 제시한다. 헨리 중위가 전쟁에서 입은 부상으로 인해서 전쟁에서 더 이상 싸울 수 없고 그래서 이송되게 되고 캐서린 버클리와 사랑에 빠

지는 일이 발생하게 된다.

주제적인 측면에서 작가는 전쟁 또는 1차 세계대전(world war I)에 대한 자신의 믿음(신념)을 표현하기 위해서 참호 속에서 운전병들과 토론을 활용해서 표현했다. 작가는 공화주의(republican)의 열렬한 지지자이고 파시즘과 나치즘에 강력한 반대를 했다. 이 소설의 9장에서 헨리는 경험이 없고 순진했기 때문에 파시니는 다음과 같이 자기 생각을 표현했다.

전쟁보다 더 나쁜 것은 없다. 그게 얼마나 나쁜 건지 구급차를 운전하는 우리야 아무것도 모르겠죠. 그걸 깨닫는다고 하더라도 모두가 이미 미쳐 버려 멈추게 할 수도 없을 거고요. 절대 깨닫지 못하는 사람들도 있습니다. 그냥 장교들을 두려워하는 사람들도 있고요. 그런 사람들 때문에 전쟁이 계속되는 겁니다.

"There is nothing worse than war. We in the auto-ambulance cannot even realize at all how had it is. When people realize how bad it is they cannot do anything to stop it because they go crazy. There are some people who never realize. There are people who are afraid of their officers. It is with them the war is made."(50) 전쟁은 사람들을 미치게 만든다. 자신들의 상관을 두려워하는 사람들이 전쟁에 책임이 있다.

"모든 사람이 이 전쟁을 증오합니다." Everybody hates this war.(51) 라고 파시니가 말했다.

"한쪽이 그만두어야 합니다. 왜 우리는 그만두지 못하는 겁니까? 만약 적들이 이 탈리아로 쳐들어온다 해도 결국은 지쳐 물러갈 겁니다."(50)

"One side must stop fighting. Why don't we stop fighting? If they come down into Italy they will get tired and go away."

라고 파시니가 말했을 때 파시니는 헨리의 머릿속에 단독강화(separate peace)의 생각을 심어 주었다. 또한 지금에 이 나라를 지배하는 세력들은 어리석고 아무것도 깨닫지 못하고 깨달을 수도 없는 계급이 지배하고 있어서 이 같은 전쟁을 우리가 겪어야 한다고 맹비난한다. 게다가 전쟁으로 돈까지 벌어들이는 사람이라고 비난한다.

"There is a class that controls a country that is stupid and does not realize anything never can. That is why we have this war." "Also they make money out of it."(50-51)

대조적으로 헨리는 포격이 두려웠다고 인정하면서도 용기에 대해서 여전히 말한다. 그는 포기(give up)에 대해서 반론을 폈다.

"우리가 멈추면 상황은 오히려 나빠질 거야."(49)
패배는 전쟁 그 자체보다 더 안 좋은 것이다. defeat is worse.(50)

라고 말했다. 탈영(desertion)이란 주제가 명시적으로 다뤄졌다. 우리 부대가 공격하지 않을 때 운전병 중의 한 명이 헌병들이 열에 한 명씩 총살했다고 헨리에게 말했다.

"척탄병(granatieri)이 공격에 나서지 않아 열에 한 명씩 총살을 당했을 때 중위님도 거기 계셨습니까?"

"아니."

"정말입니다. 일렬로 죽 세워 놓고 열 번째 병사마다 죽였어요. 헌병이 총으로 쐈죠."(49)

"Were you there, Tenente, when they wouldn't attack and they shot every tenth man?"

"No."

"It is true. They lined them up afterward and took every tenth man. Carabinieri shot them."(49)

헨리는 이탈리아 부대에서 그에게 곧 있을 위기(탈영)에 대한 이유(근거)와 알리바이(albeit)를 만드는 것처럼 보였다. 오스트리아인과 달리 이탈리아인들은 훈련이 잘 안 되었고 싸울 가치가 없다는 듯 암시했다.

파시니에 따르면 탈영 가족들도 처벌받는다. 작가는 헌병들의 잔혹함에 관한 정보를 어떻게 주입하는지를 잘 생각해 봐야 한다. 나중에 작가의 이런 계획된 생각들이 독자와 작가에게 모두 성과를 올리게 된다. 이 소설의 1장과도 일치하게 9장에서도 전쟁은 매력적이지 못하고 좋지 않은 그것이라는 작가의 신념을 아주 강하게 보여 준다.

주목해야 할 점은 용감하게 영웅적인 위업(업적)을 수행하는 중이 아니고 차가운 스파게티를 먹는 동안에 파시니는 죽고 헨리는 부상을 당한다는 것이다.

헨리 자신이 부상으로 인해서 고통을 당하고 있음에도 파시니의 목숨을 구하려는 헨리의 시도는 확실히 영웅적인 행위였다. 그러나 이장은 위대하기보다는 더 부조리(불합리)하다.

이장에서 헨리는 전투 현장의 현실에 노출되었다. 죽어 가는 동료의 피가 자신에게 떨어지는 것은 말할 것도 없고 동료의 죽음을 목격한 자신의 정신적인 충격(trauma)과 극심한 고통의 결과로써 헨리는 이 전쟁에 자신의 참전 그리고 자신에게 영향을 주는 전쟁의 잠재력(영향력)을 더 이상 부정할 수 없다.

앞장에서 보여 준 순진함은 사라지고 헨리는 삶에 대한 이해에 다가가기 시작한다. 마지막으로 헤밍웨이가 헨리에게 상처를 입힌 폭발에 대한 허세 가득한 묘사뿐만 아니라 작은 방식으로 어떻게 구체적이고 구체적인 것에 계속 집중하는지 주목해 보자. 헨리와 고르디니가 음식을 가지고 참호 안으로 돌아오는 동안 헨리는 우리에게 "나는 치즈를 들고 그들 쫓고 있었고 그 표면은 벽돌 먼지로 덮여 있었다."고 말한다. 치즈에 붙은 벽돌 먼지의 세부 사항은 현장의 생동감을 있게 한다.

I was after him, holding the cheese, its smooth surface covered with brick dust.(53)

■ 9장의 주요 작품 내용

I went back to the major's dugout and he said the field kitchen would be along and the drivers could come and get their stew. He would loan them mess tins if they did not have them. I said I thought they had them. I went back and told the drivers I would get them as soon as the food came. Manera said he hopes it would come before the bombardment started. They were silent until I went out. They were all mechanics and hates the war.(48)

I went out to look at the cars and see what was going on and then came back and sat down in the dugout with the four drivers. We sat on the ground with our backs against the wall and smoked. Outside it was nearly dark. The earth of the dugout was warm and dry and I let my shoulders back against the wall, sitting on the small my back, and relaxed.

"Who goes to the attack?" asked Gavuzzi.

"Bersaglieri?"

"All Bersaglieri?"

"I think so."

"There aren't enough troops here for a real attack."

"It is probably to draw attention from where the real attack will be."

"Do the men know that who attack?"

"I don't think so."

"Of course they don't," Manera said. "They wouldn't attack if they did."

"Yes, they would," Passini said. "Bersaglieri are fools."

"They are brave and have good discipline," I said.

"They are big through the chest by measurement, and healthy. But they are still fools."

"The granatieri are tall," Manera said. This was a joke. They all laughed.

"Were you there, Tenente, where they wouldn't attack and they shot every tenth man?" "No."(48)

"It is true. They lined them up afterward and took every tenth man. Carabinieri shot them." **indicate foreshadow**

"Carabinieri," said Passini and spat on the floor. "But those grenadiers; all over six feet. They wouldn't attack."

"If everybody would not attack the war would be over," Manera said.(49)

"I believe we should get the war over." I said. **"It would not finish it if one side stopped fighting. It would only be worse if we stopped fighting."**

"It could not be worse." Passini respectfully. **"There is nothing worse than war."**(49)

"Defeat is worse."

"I don't believe it," Passini said still respectfully. "What is defeat? You go home."

"They come after you. They take your home. They take your sisters."

"I don't believe it," Passini said. "They can't do that to everybody. Let everybody defend his home. Let them keep their sisters in the house."

"They hang you. They come and make you be a soldier again. Not in the auto-ambulance, in the infantry."

"They can't hang every one."

"An outside nation can't make you be a soldier," Manera said.

"At the first battle you all run." "Like the Tchecos."

"I think you do know anything about being conquered and so you think it is not bad."

"Tenente," Passini said. "We understand you let us talk. Listen. There is nothing as bad as war. We in the auto-ambulance cannot even realize at all how bad it is. When people realize how bad it is they can not do anything to stop it because they go crazy. There are some people who never realize. There are people who are afraid of their officers. It is with them the war is made."(50)

"I know it is bad but we must finish it."

"It doesn't finish. There is no finish to a war."

"Yes there is."

Passini shook his head. "**War is not won by victory.** What if we take San Gabriele? What if we take the Carso Monfalcone and Trieste? Where are we then? Did you see all the far mountains to-day? Do you think we could take all them too? **Only if the Austrians stop fighting. One side must stop fighting. Why don't we stop fighting?** If they come down into Italy they will get tired and go away. They have their own country. But no, instead there is a war."

"You're an orator."

"We think. We read. We are not peasants. We are mechanics. But even the peasants know better than to believe in a war. **Everybody hates this war.**"

"There is a class that controls a country that is stupid and does not realize anything never can. That is why we have this war." "Also they make money out of it."(50-51)

The major was at the telephone sitting on a box. One of the medical captains said the attack had been put forward an hour. He offered me a glass of cognac. I looked at the board tables, the instruments shining in the light, the basins and the stoppered bottles, Gordini stood behind me. The major got up from the telephone.

"It starts now," he said. "It has been put back again."

I looked outside, it was dark and the Austrian search-lights were moving on the mountains behind us. It was quiet for a moment still, then from all the guns behind us the bombardment started.

"Savoia," said the major.

"About the soup, major." I said. He did not hear me. I repeated it.

"It hasn't come up."

A big shell came in and burst outside in the brickyard. Another burst and in the noise you could hear the smaller noise of the brick and dirt raining down.

"What is there to eat?"

"We have a little pasta asciutta," the major said.

"I'll take what you can give me."

The major spoke to an orderly who went out of sight in the back and came back with a medal basin of cold cooked macaroni. I handed it to Gordini.

"Have you any cheese?"

The major spoke grudgingly to the orderly who ducked back into the hole again and came out with a quarter of a white cheese.

"Thank you very much," I said.

"You'd better not go out."(52)

Gordini got up and ran for the dugout. I was after him, holding the cheese, its smooth surface covered with brick dust. Inside the dugout were the three drivers sitting against the wall, smoking.

"Here, you patriots." I said.

"How are the cars?" Manera asked.

"All right."

"Did they scare you, Tenente?"

"You're dammed right," I said.

I took out my knife, opened it, wiped off the blade and pared off the dirty outside surface of the cheese. Gavuzzi handed me the basin of macaroni.

"Start in to eat, Tenente."

"No," I said. "Put it on the floor. We'll all eat."

"There are no forks."

"What the hell," I said in English.

I cut the cheese into pieces and laid them on the macaroni.

"Sit down to it," I said. They sat down and waited. I put thumb and fingers into the macaroni and lifted. A mass loosened.

"Lift it high, Tenente."(53)

I lifted it to arm's length and the strands cleared. I lowered it into mouth, sucked and snapped in the ends, and chewed, then took a bite of cheese, chewed, and then a drink of wine. It tasted of rusty metal. I handed the canteen back to Passini.

"It's rotten," he said. "It's been in there too long. I had it in the car."

They were all eating, holding their chins close over the basin, tipping their heads back, sucking in the ends. I took another mouthful and some cheese and a rinse of wine. Something landed outside that shook the earth.

"Four hundred twenty or minnenwerfer," Gavuzzi said.

"There aren't any four hundred twenties in the mountains," I said.

"They have big Skoda guns. I've seen the holes."

"Three hundred fives."

We went on eating. There was a cough, a noise like a railway engine starting and then an explosion that shook the earth again.(54)

I ate the end of my piece of cheese and took a swallow of wine. Through the other noise I heard a cough, then came the chuh-chuh-chuh-chuh then there was a flash, and when a blast-furnace door is swung open, and a roar that started white and went red and on and on in a rushing wind. I tried to breath but my breath would not come and I felt myself rush bodily out of myself and out and out and out and out and all the time bodily in the wind. I went out swiftly, all of myself, and I knew I was dead and that it had all been a mistake to think you just died. Then I floated, and instead of going on I felt myself slide back. I breathed and I was back. The ground was torn up and in front of my head there was s splintered beam of wood. In the jolt of my head, I heard somebody crying. I thought somebody was screaming. I tried to move but I could not move. I heard the machine-guns and rifles firing across the river and all along the river. There was a great splashing and I saw the star-shells go up and burst and float whitely and rockets going up and heard the bombs, **all this in a moment, and then I heard close to me some one saying "Mama Mia! Oh, mama Mia!"** I pulled and twisted and got my legs loose finally and turned around and touched him. It was Passini and when I touched him he screamed. **His legs were toward me and I saw in the dark and the light that they were both smashed above the knee. One leg was gone and the other was held by tendons and part of the trouser and the stump twitched and jerked as thought it were not connected. He bit his arm and moaned, "Oh mama mia, mama Mia," then, "Dio te slave, Maria, Oh Jesus shoot me Christ shoot me mama mia mama Mia oh purest lovely Mary shoot me. Stop it. Stop it. Stop it. Oh Jesus lovely Mary stop it. Oh oh oh oh," then choking, "Mama mama mia." Then he was quiet, bitting his arm, the stump of his leg twitching.** (55)

"Porta feriti!" I shouted holding my hands cupped. "Porta feriti!" I tried to get closer to Passini to try to put a tourniquet on the legs but I could not move. I tried again and my legs moved a little. I could pull backward along with my arms and elbows. Passini was quiet now. I sat beside him, undid my tunic and tried to rip the tail of my shirt. It would not rip and I bit the edge of the cloth to start it. Then I thought of his puttees. I had no wool stockings but Passini wore puttees. All the drivers wore puttees but Passini had only one leg. I unwound the puttee and while I was doing it I saw there was no need to try and make a tourniquet because he was dead already. I made sure he was dead. There were three others to locate. I sat up straight and as I did so something inside my head moved like the weights on a doll's eyes and it hit me inside in back of my eyeballs. My legs felt warm and wet and my shoes were wet and warm inside. I knew that I was hit and leaned over and put my hand on my knee. My knee wasn't there. My hand went in and knee was down on my shin. I wiped my hand on my shirt and another floating light came very slowly down and I looked at my leg and was very afraid. Oh, God, I said, get me out of here. I knew, however, that there had been three others. There were four driver. Passini was dead. That left three. Some one took hold of me under the arms and somebody else lifted my legs.

"There are three others," I said. "One is dead."

"It's Manera. We went for a stretcher but there wasn't any. How are you, Tenente?"

"Where is Gordini and Gavuzzi?"

"Gordini's at the post getting bandaged. Gavuzzi has your legs. Hold on to my neck, Tenente. Are you badly hit?"

"In the leg. How is Gordini?"

"He is all right. It was a big trench mortar shell."

"Passinin's dead."

"Yes, He's dead."

A shell fell close and they both dropped to the ground and dropped me. "I'm sorry, Tenente," said Manera. "Hang onto my deck."

"If you drop me again."

"It was because we were scared."

"Are you unwounded?"

"We are both wounded a little."

"Can Gordini drive?"

"I don't think so."

They dropped me once more before we reached the post. "You sons of bitches," I said. "I am sorry, Tenente," Manera. "We won't drop you again." Outside the post a great many of us lay on the ground in the dark.(56)

"Here is the American Tenente," he said in Italian.

"I'd rather wait," I said. "There are much worse wounded than me. I'm all right."

"Come, come, he said." Don't be a bloody hero. "Then in Italian: Lift him very carefully about the legs. His legs are very painful. He is the legitimate son of President of Wilson."(58)

"He is American," one of the other captains said.

"I thought you said he was a Frenchman. He talks French," the captain said. "I've known him before. I always thought he was French."(60)

As the ambulance climbed along the road, it was slow in the traffic, sometimes it stopped, sometimes it backed on a turn, then finally it climbed quite fast. I felt something dripping. At first it dropped slowly and regularly, then it pattered into a stream. I shouted to the driver. He stopped the car and looked in through the hole behind his seat.

"What is it?"

"The man on the stretcher over me has a hemorrhage."

"We're not far from the top. I woundn't be able to get the stretcher out alone." He started the car. The stream kept on. In the dark I could not see where it came from the canvas overhead. I tried to move sideways so that it did not fall on me. Where it had run down under my shirt it was warm and sticky. I was cold and my leg hurt so that it made me sick. After a while the stream from the stretcher above lessened and started to drip again and I heard and felt the canvas above move as the man on the stretcher settled more comfortably.

"How is he?" the Englishman called back. "We're almost up."

"He's dead I think," I said.

The drops fell very slowly, as they fall from an icicle after the sun has gone. It was cold in the car in the night as the road climbed. At the post on the top they took the stretcher out and put another in and we went on.(61)

10장 (Chapter X)

■ 10장 주요 내용

- 헨리 야전 병원에 입원. 리날디와 신부 병문안.

In the ward at the field hospital they told me a visitor was coming to see me in the afternoon.

■ Summary

리날디는 헨리 중위가 입원한 야전 병원을 방문해서 이탈리아 군에 의해서 전투에서 승리했다고 말했다. 그리고 리날디는 캐서린이 병원에 방문하도록 하겠다고 말했다.

In the ward at the field hospital they told me a visitor was coming to see me in the afternoon.(63)

■ 논평

이 장은 리날디와의 따뜻한 우정을 강조할 뿐만 아니라 헨리 중위의 신체적 불편함과 부상을 극화했다. 전반적으로 작가는 주인공을 겸손할 뿐만 아니라 인내심이 강한 인물로 묘사했다.

　무슨 일이 있었는지 정확히 말해 봐. 영웅적인 행동을 했을 거야. "잘 떠올려 봐."
"아니", 내가 말했다. "우린 치즈를 먹다가 포탄을 맞았을 뿐이야." "진지하게 생각해 봐. 그전이나 그 후에 분명 뭔가 영웅적인 행동을 했을 거야. 잘 떠올려 봐."(63)
　"Tell me exactly what happened. Did you do any heroic act?"
　"No," I said. "I was blown up while we were eating cheese."
　"Be serious. You must have done something heroic either before or after. Remember carefully."

　라고 리날디로부터 재촉을 받았음에도 불구하고 헨리는 파시니를 구하기 위해 자신의 칭찬받을 노력에 관해서 아무 말도 하지 않았다. 오히려 자신이 대원들을 위해 어떤 일을 하지 않았다고 단호하게 말한다.

　이 장은 거의 대화로 구성되었다. 그리고 대화라는 꼬리표를 붙이지 않는다. 주로 "그는 말했다."(he said)로 처리한다. 이 기법은 1927년 『여자 없는 남자』(Men Without Women)단편 모음집에 수록된 「하얀 코끼리 같은 언덕」(Hills Like White Elephants)처럼 초기 단편소설에서 헤밍웨이가 발전시킨 기법이다. 주목해야 할 것은 헤밍웨이가 대화할 때도 가능한 한 "말했다."(said), "물어봤다"(asked)처럼 가능한 한 단순하게 처리했다.

■ 10장의 주요 작품 내용

"How are you, baby? How do you feel? I bring you this-----" It was a bottle of cognac. The orderly brought a chair and he sat down, "and good news. You will be decorated. They want to get you the medaglia d'argento but perhaps they can get only the bronze."

"What for?"

"Because you are gravely wounded. They say if you can prove you did any heroic act you can get the silver. Otherwise it will be the bronze."

"Tell me exactly what happened. Did you do any heroic act?"

"No," I said. "I was blown up while we were eating cheese."

"Be serious. You must have done something heroic either before or after. Remember carefully."

"I did not."

"Didn't you carry anybody on your back? Gordini says you carried several people on your back but the medical major at the first post declares it is impossible. He had to sign the proposition for the citation."

"I didn't carry anybody. I couldn't move."

"That doesn't matter," said Rinaldi.

He took off his gloves.

"I think we can get you the silver. Didn't you refuse to be medically aided before the others?"

"Not very firmly."

"That doesn't matter. Look how you are wounded. Look at your valorous conduct in asking to go always to the first line. Besides, the operation was successful."(63)

"Open the bottle. Bring a glass. Drink that, baby. How is your poor head? I looked at your papers. You haven't any fracture. That major at the first post was a hog-butcher. I would take you and never hurt you. I never hurt anybody. I learn how to do it. Every day I learn to do thing smoother and better. You must forgive me for talking so much, baby. I am very moved to see you badly wounded. There, drink that. It's good. It cost fifteen lire. It ought to be good. Five stars. After I leave here I'll go see that English and he'll get you an English medal."

"They don't give them like that."

"You are so modest. I will send the liaison officer. He can handle the English."

"Have you seen Miss Barkley?"

"I will bring her here. I will go now and bring her here."

"Don't go," I said. "Tell me about Gorizia. How are the girls?"

"There are no girls. For two weeks now they haven't changed them."(64-65)

"I don't go there any more. It is disgraceful. They aren't girls; they are old war comrades."

"You don't go at all?"

"I just go to see if there is anything new. I stop by. They all ask for you. It is a disgrace that they should stay so long that they become friends."

"Maybe girls don't want to go to the front any more."

"Of course they do. They have plenty of girls. It is just bad administration. They are keeping them for the pleasure of dugout hiders in the rear."

"Poor Rinaldi," I said. "All alone at the war with no new girls."

Rinaldi poured himself another glass of the cognac.

I don't think it will hurt you, baby. You take it.

I drank the cognac and felt it warm all the way down. Rinaldi poured another glass. He was quieter now. He held up the glass. "To your valorous wounds. To the silver medal. Tell me, baby, when you lie here all the time in the hot weather don't you get excited?"

"Sometimes."

"I can't imagine lying like that. I would go crazy."

"I wish you were back. No one to come in at night from adventures. No one to make fun of. No one to lend me money. No blood brother and roomate. Why do you get yourself wounded?"(65)

"I will send her. Your lovely cool goodness. English goodness. My God what would a man do with a woman like that except worship her? What else is an Englishwoman good for?"(66)

11장 (Chapter XI)

- **11장 주요 내용**

- 신부의 헨리 병문안.

It was dusk when the priest came.

- 전쟁은 특정한 사람에 의해서 만들어지고 다른 사람들에 의해서 실행된다.

the war is made by certain people and executed by others.

- **Summary**

신부는 헨리가 있는 야전 병원을 방문했다. 그들은 군대에서 신부의 소외와 전쟁에 대한 혐오에 관해서 이야기했다. 또한, 헨리의 전통적인 믿음의 부족에 관해 이야기했다.

- **논평**

"해가 져서 어둠이 내리고 그 어둠이 이어지자 아주 어린 시절로 돌아간 기분이

들었다. 일찌감치 저녁 먹고 나서 침대에 눕혀진 것 같았다."(68)

It made me feel very young to have the dark come after the dusk and then remain. It was like being put to bed after early supper.(68)

라고 헨리 중위는 우리에게 말했다. 주목할 것은 우리는 그의 유년 시절과 청소년 시절에 대해서 모르고 어떻게 왜 그가 전쟁에 참전하게 되었는지도 알지 못한다.

일반적으로 작가는 가능한 이 같은 종류의 배경을 아주 적게 제공하면서 효과적으로 이야기하려고 노력한다. 헨리의 입장에서 이타주의의 징후가 캐서린을 만나기 전 자신이 부족한 윤리적인 규범(ethical code)을 암시하기 때문에 작가는 주동 인물의 문제에 관한 이야기를 복잡하게 만드는 것을 피하고 싶어 한다.

다시 말하면 작가는 헨리 중위를 다음과 같이 묘사했다. 캐서린을 만나기 전 헨리는 이기적이고 본능적인 인물에게 가까운 사람이었다. 작가의 처지에서 주동 인물이 이기적인 인물로 계속 묘사되는 것은 좋지 않은 것이고 그래서 헨리 중위의 내면적인 마음의 변화를 주는 데 그 시점이 캐서린을 만나기 전과 후의 헨리의 변화를 일으킨다. 작가는 이 같은 변화의 동기에 대해서 복잡하게 이야기하는 것을 피하고 독자들에게 단순하게 이 같은 결과를 말하고자 했다.

헤밍웨이가 작품에서 주장하는 것처럼 전쟁이 우리의 삶과 같다면서 우리가 전쟁에 참전하는 문제는 선택의 여지가 없다. 그래서 작가는 그

일의 원인과 이유에 집착하지 않고 헨리의 이야기에 집중하기를 원한다. 신부는 헨리에게 전쟁을 싫어한다고 말한다. 그리고 전쟁이란 특정한 사람에 의해서 만들어지고 다른 사람에 의해서 실행된다는 파시니가 도입했던 주제를 반복한다.

신부는 당신이 사랑하게 될 거라고 그에게 안심시켰다. 확실한 것은 신부는 헨리가 자신이 알고 있는 것보다 헨리는 자신을 충분히 알고 있다는 것을 알고 있다. 신부가 떠난 후에 헨리는 신부의 고향인 아브루치(Abruzzi)에서 순순한 삶에 대해서 생각하면서 다시 두 부분으로 나눠서 싸우는 산 아래쪽을 다시 생각했다.

"전혀 사랑하지 않습니까?" 그가 물었다.
"때로 밤중에 그분이 두렵다는 생각이 들긴 합니다."
"그분을 사랑해야 합니다."
"저는 누구든 별로 사랑하지 않습니다."
"아닙니다." 신부가 말했다. "중위님도 사랑할 겁니다."(72)
"You do not love Him at all?" he asked.
"I am afraid of Him in the night sometimes."
"You should love Him."
"I don't love much."
"Yes," he said. "You do."

리날디와 신부 둘 사이에 대조적인 본질을 주목할 필요가 있다. 신부는 평화를 사랑하지만 리날디는 따뜻하고 호감이 가는 반면 전시와 관련된 성(Sex) 와 폭력(violence)에 매료가 되는 성격이다. 마치 교차로에서 어느 한쪽으로 가야 하는 처지일 때 『무기여 잘 있거라』라는 작품은 이 시점에서 헨리는 이 둘 중에 어느 곳에 있는가. 헨리가 최근에 충격적이고 고통스러운 경험을 했음에도 불구하고 그는 어느 길을 따라갈지 분명하지 않다.

■ 11장 주요 작품 내용

"How do you do?" he asked. He put some packages down by the bed, on the floor.

"All right, father."

He sat down in the chair that had been brought for Rinaldi and looked out of the window embarrassedly. I noticed his face looked very tired.

"I can only stay a minute," he said. "It is late."

"It's not late. How is the mess?"

He smiled. "I am still a great joke," he sounded tired too.

"Thank God they are all well."

"I am so glad you are all right," he said. "I hope you don't suffer." He seemed very tired and I was not used to seeing him tired. (69)

"What's the matter, father? You seem very tired."

"I am tired but I have no right to be."

"It's the heat."

"No. This is only the spring. I feel very low."

"You have the war disgust."

"No. But I hate the war."

"I don't enjoy it," I said. He shook his head and looked out of the window.

"You do not mind it. You do not see it. You must forgive me. I know you are wounded."

"That is an accident."

"Still even wounded you do not see it. I can tell. I do not see it myself but I feel it a little."

"When I was wounded we were talking about it. Passini was talking."

The priest put down the glass. He was thinking about something else.

"I know them because I am like they are," he said.

"You are different though."

"But really I am like they are."

"The officers don't see anything."

"Some of them do. Some are very delicate and feel worse than any of us."

"They are mostly different."

"It is not education or money. It is something else. Even if they had education or money men like Passini would not wish to be officers. I would not be an officer."

"You rank as an officer. I am an officer."

"I am not really. You are not even an Italian. You are a foreigner. But you are nearer the officers than you are to the men."(70)

"What is the difference?"

"I cannot say it easily. There are people who would make war. In this country there are many like that. There are other people who would not make war."

"But the first ones make them do it."

"Yes."

"And I help them."

"You are a foreigner. You are a patriot."

"And the ones who would not make war? Can they stop it?"

"I do not know."

He look out of the window again. I watched his face. "Have they ever been able to stop it?"

"They are not organized to stop things and when they get organized their leaders sell them out."

"Then it's hopeless." It is never hopeless. But sometimes I cannot hope. I try always to hope but sometimes I cannot.

"Maybe the war will be over."

"I hope so."(71)

"How about loving woman? If I really loved some woman would it be like that?"

"I don't know about that. I never loved any woman."

"What about your mother?"

"Yes, I must have loved my mother."

"Did you always love God?"

"Ever since I was a little boy."

"Well," I said. I did not know what to say. "You are a fine boy," I said.

"I am a boy," he said. "But you call me father."

"That's politeness."

He smiled.(72)

12장 (Chapter XII)

- **12장 주요 내용**

- 밀라노 병원으로 이송되기 전에 리날디와 소령의 방문.
- 캐서린 버클리가 그 병원에 오게 된다는 소식 전함.

- **Summary**

헨리는 특별한 치료를 받기 위해 밀라노(Milan)에 있는 미국인이 운영하는 병원으로 이송되기 전날 밤에 리날디와 소령이 야전 병원에 있는 헨리 중위를 방문했다. 그들은 함께 술을 마시고 캐서린 버클리가 그 병원에 있을 것이라는 소식도 전해 주었다. 헨리는 기차로 밀라노로 출발했다.

- **논평**

이 장에서 이야기의 또 다른 전환점이 발생한다. 헨리와 캐서린 버클리가 같은 병원으로 보내진다는 점이다. 헨리가 밖의 정원에 묻히게 될 환자들과 병실에서 죽어 가는 환자들에 대해서 말할 때 처음으로 헤밍웨이는 우리에게 일반적인 상황의 심각성을 상기시켰다.

사람들이 나를 침대에서 들어올려 치료실로 데려갈 때 창밖으로 마당에 새로 만든 무덤이 보였다.(75)

When they lifted you up out of bed to carry you into the dressing room you could look out of window and see the new graves in the garden.(75)

문체상으로는 작가는 리날디와 소령이 방문해서 술 마시고 취하는 것을 묘사한 긴 단락에서 의식적인 흐름과 직간접적인 담론을 결합했다. 즉 작가는 상황을 요약하기보다는 그들의 대화를 통해서 직접 인용했다. 그러나 인용부와 단락을 통해서 개인적인 말 앞에 배경의 대화를 배치했다. 이러한 관습은 술에 취한 사람의 경험 모방 속에서 함께 이어져 간다.

■ 12장 주요 작품 내용

The room was long with windows on the right-hand side and a door at the far end that went into the dressing room. The row of beds that mine was in faced the windows and another row, under the windows, faced the wall. If you lay on your left side you could see the dressing-room door. There was another door at the far end that people sometimes came in by. If any one were going to die, they put a screen around the bed so you could not see them die, but only the shoes and puttees of doctors and men nurses showed under the bottom of the screen and sometimes at the end there would be whispering. Then the priest would come out from behind the screen and afterward the men nurses would go back behind screen to come out again carrying the one who was dead with a blanket over him down the corridor between the beds and some one folded the screen and took it away.(74)

When they lifted you up out of bed to carry you into the dressing room you could look out of the window and see the new graves in the garden. A soldier sat outside the door that opened onto the garden making crosses and painting on them the names, rank, and regiment of the men who were buried in the garden. He also ran errands for the ward and in his spare time made me a cigarette lighter out of an empty Austrian rifle cartridge. The doctors were very nice and seemed very capable. They were anxious to ship me to Milan where there were better X-ray facilities and where, after the operation, I could take mechanotherapy. I wanted to go to Milan too. They wanted to get us all out and back as far as possible because all the beds were needed for the offensive, when it should start.(75)

The next day in the morning we left for Milan and arrived forty-eight hours later. It was a bad trip. We were sidetracked for a long time this side of Mestre and children came and peeked in. I got a little boy to go for a bottle of cognac but he came back and said he could only get grappa. I told him to get it and when it came I gave him the change and the man beside me and I got drunk and slept until past Vicenza where I woke up and was very sick on the floor. It did not matter because the man on that side had been very sick on the floor several times before. Afterward I thought I could not stand the thirst and in the yards outside of Veronta I called to a soldier who was walking up and down beside the train and he got me a drink of water. I woke Georgetti, the other boy who was drunk, and offered him some water. He said to pour on his shoulder and went back to sleep. The soldier would not take the penny I offered him and brought me a pulpy orange. I sucked on that and spit out the pith and watched the soldier pass up and down past a freight-car outside and after a while the train gave a jerk and started.(77-78)

2부(Book Two)

13장 (Chapter XIII)

■ 13장 주요 내용

- 밀리노 병원에 도착함.

We got into Milan.

- 워커 부인(Mrs Walker), 밴 켐펀(Miss Van Campen), 미스 게이지 (Miss Gage) 등장.

■ Summary

헨리 중위가 밀라노에 도착했을 때 두 명의 간호사를 제외하고는 텅 빈 미국병원에 구급차로 실려 왔다. 물론 그 병원에 캐서린 버클리는 없었다.

■ 논평

이 장에서 작가는 헨리 중위의 전쟁에서의 소외 이탈(alienation)이라는 주제를 간단히 반복한다. 그리고 작가는 전쟁 참전으로부터 그의 궁극적인 탈출을 위한 그와 우리가 준비하도록 했다. 그가 도착한 병원은 의사도 없어서 기능을 전혀 하지 못하는 미국병원에 유일하면서 최초의 환자였다. 작가는 주로 이곳을 헨리와 캐서린의 사랑을 위한 무대로 설치했다. 밀라노에 있는 미국병원은 헨리가 2부 마지막에 전방(front)으로 복귀하기 전까지 그들의 사랑을 위한 일종의 도피처(refuge)를 제공했다.

주목할 점은 이장의 마지막에 헨리가 밤에 잠을 잘 자지 못한다는 것이다. 병원에 있는 동안 내내 그는 주로 낮에 잠을 잔다. 헤밍웨이 영웅들은 종종 어두움을 두려워한다.

■ 13장 주요 작품 내용

We got into Milan early in the morning and they unloaded us in the freight yard. An ambulance took me to the American hospital. Riding in the ambulance on a stretcher I could not tell what part of town we were passing through but when they unloaded the stretcher I saw a market-place and an open wine shop with a girl sweeping out. They were watering the street and it smelled of the early morning. They put the stretcher down and went in. The porter came out with them. He had gray mustaches, wore a doorman's cap and was in his shirt sleeves. The stretcher would not go into the elevator and they discussed whether it was better to lift me off the stretcher and go up in the elevator or carry the stretcher up the stairs. I listened to them discussing it. They decided on the elevator. They lifted me from the stretcher. "Go easy," I said. "Take it softly."

In the elevator we were crowded and as my legs bent the pain was very bad. "Straighten out the legs," I said.

"We can't, Signor Tenente. There isn't room." The man who said this had his arm around me and my arm was around his neck.(81)

His breath came in my face metallic with garlic and red wine.

"Be gentle," the other man said.

"Son of a bitch who isn't gentle!"

"Be gentle I say," the man with my feet repeated.

I saw the doors of the elevator closed, and the grill shut and the fourth-floor button pushed by the porter. The porter looked worried. The elevator rose slowly.(82)

"Where are they ?" the stretcher-bearers asked.

"I don't know," said the porter. "They sleep down stairs."

"Get somebody."

The porter rang the bell, then knocked on the door, then he opened the door and went in. When he came back there was an elderly woman wearing glasses with him. Her hair was loose and half-falling and she wore a nurse's dress.

"I can't understand," she said. "I can't understand Italian."

"I can speak English," I said. "They want to put me somewhere."

"None of the rooms are ready. There isn't any patient expected."

She tucked at her hair and looked at me near-sightedly.

"Show them any room where they can put me."

"I don't know," she said. "There's no patient expected. I couldn't put you in just any room."

"Any room will do," I said. Then to the porter in Italian, "Find an empty room."

"There are all empty," said the porter. "You are the first patient."

He held his cap in his hand and looked at the elderly nurse.

"For Christ's sweet sake take me to some room. The pain had gone on and on with the legs bent and I could feel it going in and out of the bone. The porter went in the door, followed by the gray-haired woman, then came hurrying back. "Follow me," he said. They carried me down a long hallway and into a room with drawn blinds. It smelled of new furniture There a bed and a big wardrobe with a mirror. They laid me down on the bed. "I can't put on sheets," the woman said. "The sheets are locked up."(82-83)

"Is Miss Barkley here?"

"No. There's no one by that name here."

"Who was the woman who cried when I came in?"

The nurse laughed. "That's Mrs. Walker. She was on night duty and she'd been asleep. She wasn't expecting any one."

While we were talking she was undressing me, and when I was undressed, except for the bandages, she washed me, very gently and smoothly. The washing felt very good. There was a bandage on my head but she washed all around the edge.

"Where were you wounded?"

"On the Isonze north of Plava."

"Where is that?"

I could see that none of the places meant anything to her.(84)

"Do you have a lot of pain?"

"No. Not much now."

She put a thermometer in my mouth.

"The Italians put it under the arm," I said.

"Don't talk."

When she took the thermometer out she read it and then shook it.

"What's the temperature?"

"You're not supposed to know that."

"Tell me what it is ."

"It's almost normal."

"I never have any fever. My legs are full of iron too."

"What do you mean?"

"They're full of trench-mortar fragments, old screws and bed-springs and things."

She took her head and smiled.

"If you had any foreign-bodies in your legs they would set up an inflammation and you'd have fever."

"All right," I said. "We'll see what come out."

She went out of the room and came back with the old nurse of the early morning. Together they made the bed with me in it. That was new to me and an admirable proceeding.

"Who is in charge here?"

"Miss Van Campen."

"How many nurses are there?"

"Just us two."

"Won't there be more?"

"Some more are coming."

"When will they get here?"

"I don't know. You ask a great many questions for a sick boy."

"I'm not sick," I said. "I'm wounded."

They had finished making the bed and I lay with a clean smooth sheet under me and another sheet over me.(85)

Mrs. Walker went out and came back with a pajama jacket. They put that on me and I felt very clean and dressed.

"You're awfully nice to me," I said. The nurse called Miss Gage giggled. "Could I have a drink of water?" I asked.

"Certainly. Then you can have breakfast."

"I don't want breakfast. Can I have the shutters opened please?"

The light had been dim in the room and when the shutters were opened it was bright sunlight and I looked out on a balcony and beyond were the tile of roofs of the houses and chimneys. I looked out over the tiled roofs and saw white clouds and the sky very blue.

"Don't you know when the other nurses are coming?"

"Why? Don't we take good care of you?"

"You're very nice."

"Would you like to use the bedpan?"

"I might try."

They helped me and held me up but it was not any use. Afterward I lay and looked out the open doors onto the balcony.

"When does the doctor come?"

"When he gets back. We've tried to telephone to Lake Como for him."

"Aren't there there any other doctors?"

"He's the doctor for the hospital."

Miss Gage brought a pitcher of water and a glass. I drank three glasses and then they left me and I looked out the window a while and went back to sleep. I ate some lunch and in the afternoon Miss Van Campen, the superintendent, came up to see me. She did not like me and I did not like her. She was small and neatly suspicious and too good for her position. She asked many questions and seemed to think it was somewhat disgraceful that I was with the Italians.

"Can I have wine with the meals?" I asked her.

"Only if the doctor prescribes it."(86)

"I can't have it until he comes?"

"Absolutely not."

"You plan on having him come eventually?"

"We've telephoned him at Lake Como."

She went out and Miss Gage came back.

"Why were you rude to Miss Van Campen?" She asked after she had done something for me very skillfully.

"I didn't mean to be. But she was snooty."

"She said you were domineering and rude."

"I wasn't. But what's the idea of a hospital without a doctor?"

"He's coming. They've telephoned for him to Lake Como."

"What does he do there? Swim?"

"No. He has a clinic there."

"Why don't they get another doctor?"

"Hush. Hush. Be a god boy and he'll come."(87)

14장 (Chapter XIV)

■ 14장 주요 내용

- 이탈리아 부대에 근무하면서 이탈리아인들에 의해서 동맹국으로 인정을 받지 못함.

"I am an Italian. I will not communicate the enemy."(90)

- 캐서린과 재회 헨리와 캐서린은 사랑에 빠진다.

When I saw her I was in love with her. Everything turned over inside me.(91)

■ Summary

적대적인 이발사(Barber)가 헨리 중위를 면도해 주었다. 나중에 이발사는 헨리가 미국인이 아니라 오스트리아인이라고 생각했다는 것을 알게 되었다. 캐서린 버클리가 도착했다. 그녀와 헨리는 그들의 사랑을 서로서로 확인했다.

■ 논평

이발사의 장면은 희극적인 기분 전환(comic relief)을 제공한다. 그러나 이것은 소외감에 대한 주제를 다시 반복한다. 헨리 중위는 그가 근무하는 군대에서 이탈리아인들에 의해서 동맹국으로 인정받지 못한다. 헨리가 캐서린을 다시 만났을 때 그녀를 유혹하는 수단으로써 그의 사랑을 그녀에게 고백했다. 그러나 그는 우리에게 다음과 같이 말했다.

"나는 그녀를 본 순간에 사랑에 빠졌다. 내 안에 모든 것이 요동쳤다."(91)
When I saw her I was in love with her. Everything turned over inside of me.(91)

그리고 14장 끝부분에서도 다음과 같이 말했다.

하늘에 맹세하지만 나는 그녀와 사랑에 빠지고 싶지 않았다. 누구와도 사랑에 빠지고 싶지 않았다. 그런데 하늘에 맹세하지만 나는 사랑에 빠지고 말았고 밀라노 어느 병실 침대에 누워 있는 나의 머릿속에는 온갖 상념이 오갔지만 그래도 행복했다.(93)

God knows I had not wanted of all in love with her. I had not wanted to fall in love with any one. But God knows I had and lay on the bed in the room of the hospital in Milan and all sorts of things went through my head but I felt wonderful.(93)

헨리를 위해서 캐서린과의 그의 정사(affair)는 더는 게임이 아니었다.

그리고 이 같은 변화는 전쟁에서 그의 부상을 가져온 것이 매우 중요했다. 이 같은 경험은 헨리를 성숙하게 했고 그를 캐서린의 지혜 수준까지 올려 주었다.

■ 14장 주요 작품 내용

It was bright sunlight in the room when I woke. I thought I was back at the front and stretched out in bed. My legs hurt me and I looked down at them still in the dirty bandages, and seeing them knew where I was. I reached up for the bell-cord and pushed the button. I heard it buzz down the hall and then some one coming on rubber soles along the hall. It was Miss Gage and she looked a little older in the bright sunlight and not so pretty.

"Good morning," she said. "Did you have a good night?"

"Yes. Thanks very much," I said. "Can I have a barber?"

"I came in to see you and you were asleep with this in the bed with you."

She opened the armoire door and held up the vermouth bottle. It was nearly empty. "I put the other bottle from under the bed in there too," she said. "Why didn't you ask me for a glass?"

"I thought maybe you wouldn't let me have it."

"I'd have had some with you."

"You're a fine girl."(89)

"It isn't good for you to drink alone." she said. "You mustn't do it."

"All right."

"Your friend Miss Barkley's come," she said.

"Really?"

"Yes. I don't like her."

"You will like her. She's awfully nice."

She shook her head. "I'm sure she's fine. Can you move just a little to this side? That's fine. I'll clean you up for breakfast." She washed me with a cloth and soap and warm water. "Hold your shoulder up," she said. "That's fine."

"Can I have the barber before breakfast?"

"I'll send the porter for him." She went out and came back.

"He's gone for him," she said and dipped the cloth she held in the basin of water.

The barber came with the porter. He was a man of about fifty with an upturned mustache. Miss Gage was finished with me and went out and the barber lathered my face and shaved. He was very solemn and refrained from talking.

"What's the matter? Don't you know any news?" I asked.

"What news?"

"Any news. What's happened in the town?"

"It is time of war," he said. "The enemy's ears are everywhere."

I looked up at him. "Please hold your face still," he said and went on shaving.

"I will tell nothing."

"What's the matter with you?" I asked.

"I am an Italian. I will not communicate with the enemy."

I let it go at that. If he was crazy, the sooner I could get out from under the razor the better. Once I tried to get a good look at him. "Beware," he said. "The razor is sharp."

I paid him when it was over and tipped him half a lira. He returned the coins.

"I will not. I am not at the front. But I am an Italian."(90)

"Get the hell out of here."

"With your permission," he said and wrapped his razors in newspaper. He went out leaving the five copper coins on the table beside the bed. I rang the bell. Miss Gage came in. "Would you ask the porter to come please?"

"All right."

The porter came in. He was trying to keep from laughing.

"Is that barber crazy?"

"No, signorino. He made a mistake. He doesn't understand very well and he thought I said you were an Austrian officer."(91)

He went out and I heard him laughing in the hall. I heard some one coming down the hallway. I looked toward the door. It was Catherine Barkley.

She came in the room and over to the bed.

"Hello, darling," she said. She looked fresh and young very beautiful. I thought I had never seen any one so beautiful.

"Hello," I said. When I saw her I was in love with her. Everything turned over inside of me. She looked toward the door, saw there was no one, then she sat on the side of the bed and leaned over and kissed me. I pulled her down and kissed her and felt her heart beating.

"You sweet," I said. "Weren't you wonderful to come here?"(91)

"It wasn't very hard. It may be hard to stay."

"You've got to stay," I said. "Oh, you're wonderful." I was crazy about her. I could not believe she was really there and held her tight to me.

"You mustn't," she said. "You're not well enough."

"Yes, I am. Come on."

"No. You're not strong enough."

"Yes. I am. Yes. Please."

"You do love me?"

"I really love you. I'm crazy about you. Come on please."

"Feel our hearts beating."

"I don't care about our hearts. I want you. I'm just mad about you."

"You really love me?"

"Don't keep on saying that. Come on. Please, please Catherine."

"All right but only for a minute."

"All right," I said. "Shut the door."

"You can't. You shouldn't."

"Come on. Don't talk. Please come on."

Catherine sat in a chair by the bed. The door was open into the hall. The wildness was gone and I felt finer than I had ever felt.

She asked "Now do you believe I love you?"

"Oh, you're lovely," I said. "You've got to stay. They can't send you away. I'm crazy in love with you."

"We'll have to be awfully careful. That was just madness. We can't do that."

"We can at night."

"We'll have to be awfully careful. That was just madness. We can't do that."

"We can at night."

"We'll have to be awfully careful. You'll have to be careful in front of other people."

"I will."(92)

"You'll have to be. You're sweet. You do love me, don't you?"

"Don't say that again. You don't know what that does to me."

"I'll be careful then. I don't want to do anything more to you. I have to go now, darling, really."

"Come back right away."

"I'll come when I can."

"Good-by."

"Good-by, sweet."

She went out. God knows I had not wanted to fall in love with her. I had not wanted to fall in love any one. But God knows I had and I lay on the bed in the room of the hospital in Milan and finally Miss Gage came in.

"The doctor's coming," she said. "He telephoned from Lake Como."

"When does he get here?"

"He'll be here this afternoon."(93)

15장 (Chapter XV)

■ 15장 주요 내용

- 세 명의 의사가 제안한 수술을 거부하고 발렌티니의 다음 날 수술을 받아들임.

"육 개월 동안 뭘 한다고요?" 내가 물었다.

"피낭이 이물질을 둘러쌀 때까지 육 개월은 기다려야 무릎을 안전하게 열 수 있단 말입니다."(96)

"Six months for what?" I asked.

"Six months for the projectile to encyst before the knee can be opened safely."

"다른 외과 의사를 불러주실 수 있습니까?"

"Could another surgeon see it?"

"수술은 언제 할 수 있습니까?"

"내일 아침."

"When do you think it can be operated on?"

"To-morrow morning."

■ Summary

캐서린과 재회: 헨리와 캐서린은 사랑에 빠짐.

세 명의 의사가 헨리 중위의 부상과 엑스레이(X-ray)를 함께 검토한 후에 그의 다리를 수술하기 전에 6개월을 기다려야 한다고 권고했다. 그러나 헨리는 다른 사람의 의견을 듣고 싶어 했다. 닥터 발렌티니(Dr Valentini)라고 불리는 이탈리아 의사에게 봐 달라고 했다.

소령은 다음날 수술하자고 제안했다.

■ 논평

마치 전쟁을 일으킨 사람들과 전쟁에 나가서 싸우는 사람들과 비슷하게 이 장에서 관료들과 (the bureaucratic)과 현역 장교(the active) 사이의 대조적인 면을 극화시켰다. 간호사 반 캠펜(Van Campen)과 간호사 게이지(Miss Gage)도 이러한 대조를 극화한다. 헨리 중위를 처음으로 검사한 세 명의 의사는 능력도 없고 우유부단한 사람들이었다. 헨리는 우리에게 다음과 같이 말한다.

"진찰 경험이 부족한 의사들은 상의하고 도우려는 경향이 있다는 것을 나는 알고 있다."(95)

I have noticed that doctors who fail in the practice of medicine have a tendency to seek one another's company and aid in consultation.(95)

이와 반대로 발렌티니는 삶의 기쁨(joie de vivre)이 가득 찼고 헨리는 그는 항상 웃는다고 말했다. 그리고 헨리와 함께 술 마시는 것도 동의할 정도로 활기찬 사람이다.

이탈리아인이라기보다는 미국인 것처럼 보였고 헨리와 관심사가 같은 것처럼 보였다. 발렌티니는 캐서린의 아름다움을 인정하면서도 다음과 같이 말했다.

"건배하자. 간호사 당신에게도 건배."(99)
"Cheer up. Cherry Oh to you."

15장은 전조(foreshadowing)가 많이 보인다. 단락에서 헨리는 우리에게 다음과 같이 말했다. "스노(snow)인지 뭔지 하는 국소마취제를 사용했는데"(95)

He used anesthetic called something or other "snow" which froze the tissue and avoided pain until the probe, the scalpel or the forceps got below the frozen portion.

눈이라는 것은 전쟁에서 전투를 방지해 주는 것일 것을 상기시켜 주고 마음속에 눈의 상징을 품는다. 그리고 이 작품에서 마지막 3분의 1 동안 눈의 상징을 염두에 둬야 한다. 또한 발렌티니 박사의 제안을 기억해야 한다.
"당신은 모든 출산 업무를 무료로 해 드리겠습니다. 그녀는 당신을 훌륭한 소년으로 만들어 줄 것입니다."라고 캐서린에 대해 말한다. I will do all your maternity work free. Does she understand that? She will make you a fine boy.

■ 15장 주요 작품 내용

Nothing happened until afternoon. The doctor was a thin quiet little man who seemed disturbed by the war. He took out a number of small steel splinters from my thighs with delicate and refined distaste. He used a local anesthetic called something or other "snow" which froze the tissue and avoided pain until the probe, the scalpel or the forceps got below the frozen portion. The anesthetized area was clearly defined by the patient and after a time the doctor's fragile delicacy was exhausted and he said it would be better to have an X-ray. Probing was unsatisfactory, he said.(94)

Before he came back three doctors came into the room. I have noticed that doctors who fail in the practice of medicine have a tendency to seek one another's company and aid in consultation. A doctor who cannot take out your appendix properly will recommend to you a doctor who will be unable to remove your tonsils with success. These were three such doctors.

"This is young man," said the house doctor with the delicate hands.
"How do you do?" said the tall gaunt doctor with the beard. The third doctor, who carry the X-ray plates in their red envelopes, said nothing.(95)

"Only one thing I can say," the first captain with the beard said. "It is a question of time. Three month, six months probably."(96)

"Yes. I can't wait six months to be operated on. My God, doctor, did you ever stay in bed six months?" "You won't be in bed all the time. You must first have the wounds exposed to the sun. Then afterward you can be on crutches."(97)

"Could another surgeon see it?"(98)

Two hours later Dr.Valentini came into the room. He was in a great hurry and the points of his mustache stood straight up. He was a major, his face was tanned and he laughed all the time.

"How did you do it, this rotten thing?" he asked. "Let me see the plates. Yes. Yes. That's it. You looks healthy as a goat. Who's the pretty girl? Is she your girl? I thought so. Isn't this a bloody war? How does that feel? You are a fine boy. I'll make you better than new. Does that hurt? You bet it hurts. How they love to hurt you, these doctors. What have they done for you so far? Can't that girl talk Italian? She should learn. What a lovely girl. I could teach her. I will be a patient here myself. No, but I will do all your maternity work free. Does she understand that? She will make you a fine boy. A fine blonde like she is. That's fine. That's all right. What a lovely girl. Ask her if she eat supper with me. No I won't take her away from you. Thank you. Thanks you very much, Miss. That's all."

"That's all I want to know." He patted me on the shoulder. "Leave the dressing off."

"Will you have a drink, Dr. Valentini?"

"A drink? Certainly. I will have ten drinks. Where are they?"

"In the armoire. Miss Barkley will get the bottle."

"Cheery oh. Cheery oh to you. Miss. What a lovely girl. I will bring you better cognac than that." He wiped his mustache.

"When do you think it can be operated on?"

"To-morrow morning. Not before. Your stomach must be emptied. You must be washed out".(99)

16장(Chapter XVI)

■ 16장 주요 내용

- 수술 전 병원의 일상.

■ Summary

헨리 중위와 캐서린 버클리는 수술 전날 밤 병실에서 함께 보냈다.

■ 논평

작가는 이번 장에서 평화로운 장을 만들어서 둘만의 여유로운 시간을 보낼 수 있도록 설정했으면서도 대공포(air-craft)와 탐조등(search-lights)과 같은 것들을 통해서 전시 상황인 것을 우리에게 상기시킨다. 작가는 조심스럽게 선정한 세부 사항들을 가지고 배경설정을 한다. 예를 들면 밖에서 오는 이슬 냄새 병원 근처 지붕 위에 있는 군인들이 마시는 커피 냄새 등을 통해서 세심하고 구체적인 상황들을 묘사한다. 그러한 친밀한 감각의 세부 사항들은 독자를 장면 그 자체에 넣습니다. 전쟁 중이지만 인간들이 살아가면서 보고 듣고 마시고 하는 일상들을 잘 묘사했다. 목숨이 왔다 갔다 하는 위중한 상황에서 인간들은 오롯이 자신의 목숨을 지키기 위한 노력만을 할 것 같지만 평온한 일상에서 우리가 하는 일들을 한다는 것을 보여 준다. 전시 중에서도 사랑도 하고 밥도 먹고 일상에서 하던 일들을 한다는 것을 말하고 있다. 매우 자연스러운 일상이다. 전쟁이란 것이 매우 특별한 상황이지 전쟁 중에서 인간들은 평상시에서 하는 행동들과 매우 같은 행동을 한다. 이 같은 우리 일상과 친밀한 세부 사항들을 묘사함으로 인해서 독자들이 그 장면에 머물 수 있도록 한다.

헨리 중위의 소박하면서도 역동적인 면과 캐서린 버클리의 경험과 성숙함은 계속 반복되어 나타난다. 헨리는 수술 후에, 밖에서 데이트하자고 말하지만 캐서린은 수술 후에 나를 전혀 보려고 하지 않을 것이라고 말했다. 이 소설의 말미(ending)를 두 사람 간의 장난스러운 대화를 통해서 조짐을 보여준다. 어린아이의 체온과 헨리가 수술에서 회복하면 함께 어딘가를 가자고 하는 캐서린의 주장에 관한 두 사람의 장난스러운 대화에서 조짐을 보여준다. "아마 전쟁이 끝날 것이고 계속 진행되지 못할 것이라고"("maybe the war will be over. It can't always go on."(103) 캐서린은 희망적으로 말했다. 매춘에 대한 헨리 경험의 토론은 진정한 사랑과 섹스의 차이를 보여 준다. 헨리는 캐서린에게 당신을 만나기 전에 누구도 사랑하지 않았다고 말했다. 그러나 그가 파트너에게 사랑을 고백하지 않았다고 말했을 때 그는 그녀에게 거짓말을 했다는 것을 독자들에게 인정한 것이다.

이 장면 동안에 아침 태양은 밀라노 성당의 첨탑을 비춰 준다. 그리고 우리에게 신부를 상기시켜 준다. 헨리는 이렇게 말했다.

"나는 몸 안팎을 깨끗이 하고 의사를 기다렸다."(105)

I was clean inside and outside and waiting for the doctor.

이 말의 의미는 적어도 당분간이라도 리날디와 다른 장교들보다는 사제와 자기 자신을 연결하게 했다. 이 시점에서 자신은 다른 장교들의 행동보다는 사제(priest)의 행동에 맞춰서 생활하고 앞으로 캐서린을 사랑하겠다는 의미를 알 수 있다. 또한 몸 안팎으로 깨끗하다는 말속에서 단순히 수술받기 위해서라기보다는 새롭게 태어났고 앞으로 깨끗하게 살겠다는 캐서린에 대한 다짐이다.

16장은 거의 전적으로 인용 대화 없는 대화로 구성되었다. 인용의 내용뿐만 아니라 단어 및 문장의 구조 선택이 일반적인 속성을 불필요하게 만들었다는 것에 주목해야 한다. 캐서린은 종종 헨리를 "자기야"(darling)이라고 부르며 그녀의 연설은 그의 연설보다 더 노골적이고 감정적인 경향이 있다.

■ 16장 주요 작품 내용

That night a bat flew into the room through the open door that led onto the balcony and through which we watched the night over the roofs of the town. It was dark in our room except for the small light of the night over the town and the bat was not frightened but hunted in the room as though he had been outside. We lay and watched him and I do not think he saw us because we lay so still. After he went out we saw a searchlight come on and watched the beam move across the sky and then go off and it was dark again. A breeze came in the night and we heard the men of anti-aircraft gun on the next roof talking. It was cool and they were putting on their capes.(101)

"Come back to bed, Catherine. Please," I said.

"I can't. Didn't we have a lovely night?"

"And can you be night duty to-night?"

"I probably will. But you won't want me."

"Yes, I will."

"No, you won't. You've never been operated on. You don't know how you'll be."

"I'll be all right."

"You'll be sick and I won't be anything to you."

"Come back then now."

"No," she said. "I have to do the chart, darling, and fix you up."

"You don't really love me or you'd come back again."

"You're such a silly boy." She kissed me. "That's all right for the chart. Your temperature always normal. You've such a lovely temperature."(102)

"Maybe the war will be over. It can't always go on."

"I'll get well," I said. "Valentini will fix me."

"He should with those mustaches. And, darling, when you're going under the ether just think about something else- not us. Because people get very blabby under an aesthetic."

"What should I think about?"

"Anything. Anything but us. Think about your people. Or even any other girl."

"No."

"Say your prayers then. That ought to create a splendid impression."

"Maybe I won't talk."

"That's true. Often people don't talk."

"I won't talk."

"Don't drag, darling. Please don't drag. You're so sweet and you don't have to brag."

"I won't talk a word."

"Now you're bragging, darling. You know you don't need to brag. Just start your prayers or poetry or something when they tell you to breathe deeply. You'll be lovely that way and I'll be so proud of you. I'm very proud of you anyway. You have such a lovely temperature and you sleep like a little boy with your arm around the pillow and think it's me. Or is it some other girl? Some fine Italian girl?"

"It's you."

"Of course it's me. Oh I do love you and Valentini will make you a fine leg. I'm glad I don't have to watch it."

"And you'll be on night duty to-night."

"Yes. But you won't care."

"You wait and see."

"There, darling. Now you're all clean inside and out. Tell me. How many people have you ever loved?"

"Nobody."

"Not me even?"

"Yes, you."

"How many others really?"

"None."

"How many have you- how do you say it?-stayed with?"

"None."

"You're lying to me."

"Yes."(104)

Outside the sun was up over the roofs and I could see the points of the cathedral with the sunlight on them. I was clean inside and outside and waiting for the doctor.(105)

17장(Chapter XVII)

■ 17장 주요 내용

- 캐서린이 등장하지 않는 장.

- 헬렌 퍼거슨의 조언.

- 퍼거슨은 당신들은 결혼을 절대 못 한다고 주장했다.

"You will never get married."(108)

- 대신 그녀는 결혼하기 전에 싸울 것이라고, 말하자 우리는 안 싸운다고 말하자 아니면 죽겠죠라고 주장한다.

"You will fight before you will marry."(108) "We never fight."(108) "You will die then. Fight or die. That's what people do. They don't marry."(108)

- 같은 병원에 입원한 미국인: 포탄을 전쟁 기념품으로 준비하던 중 부상.

■ Summary

17장은 수술 후에 헨리와 캐서린이 사랑에 빠진 일상(routine)을 요약했다. 그녀는 자발적으로 밤에 헨리와 함께 있기 위해서 밤 근무를 신청했다. 그리고 헨리는 낮에 잠을 잤다. 캐서린의 친구 헬렌 퍼거슨(Helen Ferguson)은 사랑에 관해서 냉소적으로 말했고 캐서린이 쉬게 하려고 헨리가 캐서린에게 야간근무 못 하도록 하라고 당부했다.

■ 논평

"캐서린에게 야간근무는 그만하라고 해요 많이 피곤해해요."(109)
"You ought to her not to do night duty for a while. She's getting very tired."

캐서린 버클리가 주로 빠진 17장은 헨리와 헬렌 퍼거슨과의 토론에서 불길한 조짐(전조)들로 가득한 장이다.

헨리가 헬렌 퍼거슨 간호사에게 캐서린과의 결혼식을 올 수 있는지 물어봤다. ("Will you come to our wedding, Fergy?") 그러자 퍼거슨은 당신들은 결혼을 절대 못 한다고 주장했다. ("You will never get married."(108)) 대신 그녀는 결혼하기 전에 싸울 것이라고, 말하자 우리는 안 싸운다고 말하자 아니면 죽겠죠라고 주장한다. ("You will fight before you will marry."(108) "We never fight."(108) "You will die then. Fight or die. That's what people do. They don't marry."(108))

울면서 그녀는 계속해서 다음과 같이 말했다. "하지만 캐서린을 힘들게 하지 말아요. 그랬다간 내가 가만히 안 놔둘 거예요."(But watch out you don't get her in trouble. You get her in trouble and I will kill you. (108))

헨리는 약속하지 않았다. 그러자 헬렌은 "캐서린이 전쟁고아를 갖는 꼴은 보고 싶지 않으니까." "I don't want her with any these war babies."(109)라고, 반응했다.

대신 작가는 전쟁에서 전투원들 사이에 진행되는 전투에서부터 섹스와 결혼, 커플들 사이의 전투(종종 성전투라고 불린다), 출산, 그리고 다시 돌아오는 전투까지 이어지는 연속체를 그린다. 사랑과 전쟁은 정반대인 것처럼 보이지만 작가는 그들이 실제로 연결되어 있다고 미묘하게 암시하고 있다.

또한, 작가는 같은 병원에 입원하게 된 다른 세 명의 미국 군인들의 언급을 통해서 이탈리아 군대로부터 헨리의 소외라는 주제를 반복하고 있다. 그중 한 명은 집에 기념품으로 가져가기 위해서 오스트리아군이 사용한 혼합 탄의 뇌관 뚜껑을 분해하려다가 상처를 입은 젊은이다. 이것이 함축하는 것은 이 전선에 참여한 미국인들은 호사가들(dilettantes)이다. 그들은 전쟁의 원인에 대해 생각하지도 않고 전쟁의 결과에 대해서도 생각하지 않는다. 아니 인식하지도 못하고 있다. 자신의 부상을 받아들이기 전에 헨리 자신에게도 이 같은 일들이 진실이다.

헨리 눈에 비친 미국 젊은 군인들의 모습은 자신의 마음속에 있는 전쟁, 전쟁의 참전 그리고 그로 인해 심각한 결과에 대해서 생각하지 못하는 자신과 같다는 의미이다. 사실 전쟁이란 전쟁에 참여한 젊은이들이 원한 것도 그들이 일으킨 것도 아니다. 그러나 전쟁터에 나온 것은 젊은 이들이고 실상 전쟁을 일으킨 사람들은 전쟁터에 나오지도 않는 역설적인 일이 발생한다. 따라서 아무것도 모르고 전쟁터에 나온 젊은이들은 아무것도 모르는 천진난만한 어린이들처럼 포탄을 전쟁에 나온 기념품으로 집에 가져가야겠다는 생각을 하게 된다. 웃기지도 않는 비참한 현장이다. 그렇다고 어린아이들처럼 행동하는 것을 조롱하거나 비웃는 일은 적절치 못하다. 한 가지 행동이나 일순간의 행동을 통해서 젊은이들의 전체적인 진실을 부정하거나 평가하는 일은 적절치 못하다.

■ 17장 주요 작품 내용

There were three other patients in the hospital now, a thin boy in the Red Cross from Georgia with malaria, a nice boy, also thin, from New York, with malaria and jaundice, and a fine boy who had tried to unscrew the fuse-cap from a combination shrapnel and high explosive shell for a souvenir. This was a shrapnel shell used by the Austrians in the mountains with a nose-cap which went on after the burst and exploded on contact.(108-109)

Catherine Barkley was greatly liked by the nurses because she would do night duty indefinitely. She had quite a little work with the malaria people, the boy who had unscrewed the nose-cap was a friend of ours and never rang at night, unless it was necessary but between the times of working we were together. I loved her very much and she loved me. I slept in the daytime and we write notes during the day when we were awake and sent them by Ferguson. Ferguson was a fine girl. I never learned anything about her except that she had a brother in the Fifty-Second Division and a brother in Mesopotamia and she was very good to Catherine Barkley.

"Will you come to our wedding, Fergy?" I said to her once.

"You'll never get married."

"We will."

"No you won't."

"Why not?"

"You'll fight before you'll marry."

"We never fight."

"You've time yet."

"We don't fight."

"You'll die then. Fight or die. That's what people do. They don't marry."

I reached for her hand. "Don't take hold of me," she said. "I'm not crying. Maybe you'll be all right you two. But watch out you don't get her in trouble. You get her in trouble and I'll kill you."

"I won't get her I trouble."

"Well watch out then. I hope you'll be all right. You have a good time."(108)

"We have a fine time."

"Don't fight then and don't get her into trouble."

"I won't."

"Mind you watch out. I don't watch her with any of these war babies."

"You are fine girls, Fergy."

"I'm not. Don't try to flatter me. How does your leg feel?"

"Fine."

"How is your head?" She touched the top of it with her fingers. It was sesitive like a foot that had gone to sleep. "It's never bothered me."

"A bump like that could make you crazy. It never bothers you?"

"No."

"You're a lucky young man. Have you the letter done? I'm going down."

"It's here," I said.

"You ought to ask her not to do night duty for a while. She's getting very tired."(109)

18장 (Chapter XVIII)

■ 18장 주요 내용

- 수술 후 캐서린과 즐겁게 지냄.

We had a lovely time that summer.

■ Summary

헨리가 회복하는 동안 헨리와 캐서린은 함께 여름을 보냈다. 그리고 저녁에 밀라노에 있는 식당도 같이 가서 밤에도 함께 보내고 결혼에 관해서도 이야기했다.

■ 논평

헨리가 더욱더 잘 움직이면서 즉 침대에만 있다가 목발로 움직이면서 캐서린과의 사랑은 여름이고 전쟁 중에도 불구하고 그들의 사랑은 만개한 꽃과 같았다. 그들이 함께하는 어느 날 저녁 그들은 결혼에 대해서 말했다. 그 결혼에 대해서 헨리는 원했지만, 캐서린은 실질적인 이유 들어 거절했다.

"나는 아이가 생길지도 모른다는 우려에 결혼하고 싶었지만 이미 결혼한 부부처럼 지냈기 때문에 크게 걱정하지 않았고 사실 결혼하지 않고 지내는 것을 더 즐겼던 것도 같다."(115)

이것은 그들의 분리를 필요하게 만들었다. 사랑은 하지만 결혼은 할 수 없는 현실에 대한 인식 때문이다. 그리고 그녀는 그에게 죽은 군인에 대한 관련된 경험을 상기시켰다.

이 앞장에서 퍼거슨 간호사처럼 캐서린은 사랑과 죽음은 논리적인 연관성이 없다는 것을 직감했다. 캐서린이 헨리에게 나는 종교를 갖고 있지 않다고 말했을 때 우리는 신부와 장교들을 통해서 소설의 시작 시점인 역동적인 장면으로 돌아갔다. 그러나 그녀는 자기 말을 바로 수정한다. 그리고 그녀는 허무주의자(nihilist)는 아니다. 그녀는 명확한 가치 시스템에 의해서 생활한다. 그리고 그녀가 중요하게 생각하는 것은 사랑이다. 헨리는 어느 정도 전통적인 종교를 거부할 수 없어서 헨리는 사적인 비밀스러운 결혼을 제안했다. 로미오와 줄리엣(Romeo and Juliet)처럼 작가는 비극의 예감을 암시했다. 18장의 마지막 부분에서 캐서린은 불길하게 다음과 같이 말했다.

"우리는 온갖 무서운 일을 겪게 될 수도 있어요. 하지만 그것만큼은 걱정 안 해도 돼요."(116)

"I suppose all sorts of dreadful things will happen to us. But you don't have to worry about that."(116)

작가는 다가올 재앙에 대한 징후를 반복해서 암시하면서 우리에게도 그런 예감을 하도록 해 준다.

■ 18장 주요 작품 내용

At the door of the hospital the porter came out to help with the crutches. I paid the driver, and then we rode upstairs in the elevator. Catherine got off at the lower floor where the nurses lived and I went on up and went down the hall on crutches to my room; sometimes I undressed and got into bed and sometimes I sat out on the balcony with my leg up on another chair and watched the swallows over the roofs and waited for Catherine. When she come upstairs it was as though she had been away on a long trip and I went along the hall with her on the crutches and carried the basins and waited outside the doors, or went in with her; it depending on whether they were friends of ours or not, and when she had done all there was to be done we sat out on the balcony outside my room. Afterward I went to bed and when they were all asleep and she was sure they would not call she came in. I loved to to take her hair down and she sat on the bed and kept very still, except suddenly she would dip down to kiss me while I was doing it, and I would take out the pins and lay them on the sheet and it would be loose and I would watch her while she kept very still and then take out the last two pins and it would all come down and she would drop her head and we would both be inside of it and it was the feeling of inside a tent or behinds a falls.(114)

I wanted to be really married but Catherine said that if we were they would send her away and if we merely started on the formalities they would watch her and would break us up. We would have to be married under Italian law and the formalities were terrific. I wanted us to be married really because I worried about having a child if I thought about it, but we pretended to ourselves we were married and did not worry much and I suppose I enjoyed out being married, really. I know one night we talked about it and Catherine said, "But, darling, They'd send me away."

"Maybe they wouldn't."

"They would. They'd send me home and then we would be apart until after the war."

"I'd come on leave."

"You coudn't get to Scotland and back on a leave. Besides, I won't leave you. What good would it do to marry now? We're really married. I couldn't be any more married."

"I only wanted to for you."

"There isn't any me. I'm you. Don't make up a separate me."(115)

"Only being sent away from you. You're my religion. You're all I've got."

"All right. But I'll marry you the day you say."

"Don't talk as though you had to make an honest woman of me, darling. I'm a very honest woman. You can't be ashamed of something if you're only happy and proud of it. Aren't you happy?"

"But you won't ever leave me for some one else." No, darling. I won't ever leave you for some one else. I suppose all sorts of dreadful things will happen to us. But you don't have to worry about that."(116)

"Yes and if he hadn't I wouldn't have meet you. I'm not unfaithful, darling. I've plenty of faults but I'm very faithful. You'll be sick of me I'll be so faithful."

"I'll have to go back to the front pretty soon."

"We won't think about that until you go. You see I'm happy, darling. and we have a lovely time. I haven't been happy for a long time and when I met you Perhaps I was nearly crazy. perhaps I was crazy. But now we're happy and we love each other. Do let's please just be happy. You are happy, aren't you? Is there anything I do you don't like? Can I do anything to please you? Would you like me to take down my hair? Do you want to play?"

"Yes and come to bed."

"All right. I'll go and see the patients first."(116)

19장(Chapter XIX)

■ 19장 주요 내용

- 계절이 여름을 지나감. (The summer went that away)

- 에레토(Ettore)를 통해서 자신이 원하는 인물상을 제시함. 자만하지 않는 사람을 좋아하고 마이어스 부부를 좋아하지 않음.

"We have heroes too," she said. "But usually, they're much quieter."(124)
"No, darling. I only want you to have enough rank so that we're admitted to the better restaurants." "That's just the rank I have."(125)

- 에토레(Ettore) 모레티(Moretti), 부영사(vice-consul) 마이어스 부부 (Mr. and Mrs. Meyers), 시먼스(Simmons) 등장.

- 캐서린의 비에 대해 좋지 않은 예감을 제시함.

"All right. I'm afraid of the rain because I see me dead in it."

■ Summary

오스트리아 전선에서 "신문에 승리 소식이 자주 실렸다."(117)

The summer went that way. I do not remember much about the days, except that they were not hot and that there were many victories in the paper.(117)

이런 기사가 실릴 때인 여름에 헨리 중위는 회복하고 있었다. 그는 밀라노 주변에서 전문 도박사인 미국인 부부인 마이어스(Mr. Mayer)를 만난다. 그리고 샌프란시스코에서 온 이탈리아인으로 이탈리아 군에 입대한 에토레 모레티(Ettore Moretti)도 만났다. 그는 이탈리아 부대에서 대위이고 그들은 오페라를 공부하는 학생이다.

■ 논평

헤밍웨이는 이번에도 밀라노에 있는 다른 미국인들과 헨리 중위를 비교함으로써 헨리 중위가 이탈리아인으로부터 소외되었다는 주제로 다시 들어간다. 소문에 따르면 마이어스는 감옥에서 풀려나 죽을 때까지 이탈리아에 살고 있고 비록 그들은 이탈리아어를 제대로 발음하지 못하지만, 두 오페라 학생은 그들의 미국 이름을 이탈리아 이름으로 바꿨다.

헨리에 따르면 샌프란시스코에서 온 이탈리아인으로 이탈리아 군에 입대한 에토레 모레티는 "진정한 영웅이지만 만나는 모든 사람을 지루하게 했다."(124)

He was a legitimate hero who bored every one he met.(124)

  이 같은 사람 중에서 왜 헨리 자신은 이탈리아 군대에 있는가 에 대해서 질문하는 사람이 아무도 없었다. 다시 한번 작가는 작품 후반부에 헨리가 탈영하게 되는 이유를 제공한다.

  성격묘사에 있어서 헨리는 에토레 모레티를 이해하는 반면 캐서린은 매우 싫어한다. 이 소설 현시점에서 캐서린은 헨리보다 더 성숙할 뿐만 아니라 그녀는 작가가 만들어 낸 주인공으로 더 발전된 인물이다.

  "여기도 영웅이 많아요." 그녀는 말했다. "하지만 그 사람들은 대체로 훨씬 조용하죠." Catherine could not stand him. "We have heroes too," she said. "But usually, darling, they're much quieter."(124)

  캐서린은 금욕의 미덕(virtues of stoicism)과 겸손을 더 존중한다. 이 미덕은 캐서린뿐만 아니라 헨리에게도 구현되고 더 나아가서 헤밍웨이 문체에도 잘 나타난다.

  인물이란 작가의 산물이고 작가의 문체를 통해서 인물의 특징을 잘 볼 수 있다. 헤밍웨이는 처음부터 끝까지 모든 것들을 진술하고 설명하지 않고 핵심적인 것들만 표현해서 나타내는 문체의 특징을 가지고 있다. 따라서 금욕의 미덕이란 캐서린이 말한 그것처럼 영웅은 많지만, 자신을 드러내지 않는 것이 진정한 영웅이란 의미를 말하고 있다.

  즉 이 작품의 두 주인공 헨리와 캐서린의 말과 행동을 통해서 작가가 말하고자 하는 영웅의 의미를 잘 말해 주고 있다. 비의 깊은 의미가 명확하게 드러난 것은 19장에서이다. 캐서린은 헨리에게 다음과 같이 말했다.

"내가 비를 무서워하는 건 가끔 빗속에서 죽은 나를 보기 때문이에요."

"말도 안 돼."

"빗속에서 죽은 당신을 볼 때도 있어요."(126)

"All right. I'm afraid of the rain because I see me dead in it."

"No."

"And sometimes I see you dead in it."(126)

"비가 쏟아져도 변함없이?"

"그럼."

좋아요. 나는 비가 무섭거든요.

"And the rain won't make any difference?"

"No."

"That's good. Because I'm afraid of the rain."(125)

따라서 헤밍웨이는 상징성과 예지력을 하나의 이미지로 결합했고 우리가 작품을 계속해서 읽어 나감에 따라서 비가 올 때마다 등장인물의 운세에 특히 관심을 기울이게 된다. 물론 헨리는 이 작품의 이야기하는 인물이기 때문에 (character telling the story) 죽지 않겠지만 어느 정도 이 시점부터 작품을 읽으면서 캐서린이 죽는지 죽지 않는지 헨리가 죽는지 죽지 않는지를 생각하면서 작품을 읽게 된다.

■ 19장 주요 작품 내용

Sometime I stopped in at Anglo-American Club and sat in a deep leather-cushioned chair in front of the window and read the magazines. They would not let us go out together when I was off crutches because it was unseemly for a nurse to be seen unchaperoned with a patient why did not look as though he needed attendance, so we were not together much in the afternoons. Although sometimes we could go out to dinner if Ferguson went along. Miss Van Campen had accepted the status that we were great friends because she got a great amount of work out of Catherine. She thought Catherine came from very good people and that prejudiced her in her favor finally. Miss Van Campen admired family very much and came from an excellent family herself. The hospital was quite busy, too, and that kept her occupied. It was a hot summer and I knew many people in Milan but always was anxious to get back home to to the hospital as soon as the afternoon was over. At the front they were advancing on the Carso, they had taken Kuk across from Plava and were taking the Bainsizza plateau. The west front did not sound so good. It looked as though the war were going on for a long time. We were in the war now but I thought it would take a year to get any great amount of troops over and train them for combat. Next year would be a bad year, or a good year maybe. The Italians were using up an awful amount of men. I did not see how it could go on. Even if they took all the Bainsizza and Monte San Gabriele there were plenty of mountains beyond for the Austrains. I had seen them. All the highest mountains were beyond. On the Carso they were going forward but there were marshes and swamps down by the sea. Napoleon would have whipped the Austrians on the plains. He never would have fought them in the mountains. He would have let them come down and whipped them around Verona. Still nobody was whipping any one on the Western front. Perhaps wars weren't won any more. Maybe they went on forever. Maybe it was another Hundred Years' War. I put the paper back on the rack and left the club. I went down the steps carefully and walked up the Via Manzoni. Outside the Gran Hotel I met old Meyers and his wife getting out of a carriage. They were coming back from the races.(117-118)

"How do you do? How do you do?" She shook hands. "Hello," said Meyers.

"How were the races?"

"Fine. They were just lovely. I had three winners."

"How did you do?" I asked Meyers.

"All right. I had a winner."

"I never know how he does," Mrs. Meyers said. "He never tells me."

"I do all right," Meyers said. He was being cordial. "You ought to come out." While he talked you had the impression that he was not looking at you or that he mistook you for some one else.

"I will," I said.

"I'm coming up to the hospital to see you," Mrs Meyers said. "I have somethings for my boys. You're all my boys. You certainly are my dear boys."

"They'll be glad to see you."

"Those dear boys. You too. You're one of my boys."

"I have to get back," I said.

"You give my love to all those dear boys. I 've got lots of things to bring. I've some fine marsala and cakes."

"Good-by," I said. "They'll be awfully glad to see you."

"Good-by," said Meyers. "You come around to the galleria. You know where my table is. We're all there every afternoon." I went on up the street. I wanted to buy something at the Cova to take to Catherine. Inside, at the Cova, I bought a box of chocolate and while the girl wrapped it up I walked over to the bar. There were a couple British and some aviators. I had a martini alone, paid for it, picked up the box of chocolate at the outside counter and walked on home toward the hospital. Outside the little bar up the street from the Scala there were some people I knew, a vice-councul, two fellows who studied singing, and Ettore Moretti, an Italian from San Francisco who was in the Italian army. I had a drink with them. One of singers was named Ralph Simmons, and he was singing under the name of Enrico DelCredo. I never knew how well he could sing but he was always on the point of something very big happening. He was fat and looked shopworn around the nose and mouth as though he had hayfever. He had come back from singing in Piacenza. He had sung Tosca and it had been wonderful.(119-120)

"Where were you wounded, Ettore?" asked the vice consul.

Ettore pulled up his sleeve. "Here," he showed the deep smooth red scar. "Here on my leg. I can't show you that because I got puttees on; and in the foot. There's dead bone in my foot that stinks right now. Every morning I take new little pieces out and it stinks all the time."

"What hit you?" asked Simmons.

"A hand-grenade. One of those potato mashers. It just blew the whole side of my foot off. You know those potato mashers? He turned to me."

"Sure."

"I saw the son of a bitch throw it," Ettore said. "It knocked me down and I thought I was dead all right but those damn potato mushers haven't got anything in them. I shot the son of a bitch with my rifle. I always carry a rifle so they can't tell I'm an officer."

"How did he look?" asked Simmons.

"That was the only one he had," Ettore said. "I don't know why he threw it. I guess he always wanted to throw one. He never saw any real fighting probably. I shot the son of a bitch all right."

"How did he look when you shot him?" Simmons asked.

"Hell, how should I know?" said Ettore. "I shot him in the belly. I was afraid I'd miss him if I shot him in the head."(121-122)

"So long," I said. "I'm glad you're going to be promoted captain."

"I don't have to wait to be promoted. I'm going to be a captain for merit of war. You know. There stars with the crossed swords and crown above. That's me."

"Good luck."

"Good luck. When you going to be back the front?"

"Pretty soon."

"Well, I'll see you around."

"So long."

"So long. Don't take any bad nickels."

I walked on down a back street that led to a cross-cut to the hospital. Ettore was twenty-three. He had been brought up by an uncle in San Francisco and was visiting his father and mother in Torino when war was declared. He had a sister, who had been sent to America with him at the same time to live with the uncle, who would graduate from normal school this year. He was a legitimate hero who bored every one he met. Catherine could not stand him.

"We have heroes too," she said. "But usually, darling, they're much quieter."

"I don't mind him."

"I wouldn't mind him if he wasn't so conceited and didn't bore me, and bore me and bore me."

"He bores me."

"You're sweet to say so, darling. But you don't need to. You can picture him at the front and you know he's useful but he's so much the type of boy I don't care for."

"I know."

"You're awfully sweet to know, and I try and like him but he's a dreadful, dreadful boy really."

"He said this afternoon he was going to be a captain."

"I'm glad," said Catherine. "That should please him."

"Wouldn't you like me to have some more exalted rank?"(124)

"No, darling. I only want you to have enough rank so that we're admitted to the better restaurants."

"That's just the rank I have."

"You have a splendid rank. I don't want you to have any more rank. It might go to your head. Oh, darling, I'm awfully glad you're not conceited. I'd have married you even if you were conceited but it's very restful to have a husband who's not conceited."

We were talking softly out on the balcony. The moon was supposed to rise but there was a mist over the town and it did not come up and in a little while it started to drizzle and we came in. Outside the mist turned to rain and in a little while it was raining hard and we heard it drumming on the roof. I got up and stood at the door to see if it was raining in but it wasn't, so I left the door open.(125)

"You are all her dear boys," Catherine said. "She prefers the dear boys. Listen to it rain."

"It's raining hard."

"And you'll always love me, won't you?"

"Yes."

"And the rain won't make any difference?"

"No."

"That's good. Because I'm afraid of the rain."

"Why?" I was sleepy. Outside the rain was falling steadily.

"I don't know, darling. I've always been afraid of the rain."

"I like it."

"I like to walk in it."

"But it's very hard on loving."

"I'll love you always."

"I'll love you in the rain and in the snow and in the hail and--- what else is there?"

"I don't know. I guess I'm sleepy."

"Go to sleep, darling, and I'll love you no matter how it is."

"You're not really afraid of the rain are you?"

"Not when I'm with you."

"Why are you afraid of it?"

"I don't know."

"Tell me."

"Don't make me."

"Tell me."

"No."

"All right. I'm afraid of the rain because sometimes I see me dead in it."

"No."

"And sometimes I see you dead in it."

"That's more likely."

"No, it's not, darling, because I can keep you safe. I know I can. But nobody can help themselves."

"Please stop it. I don't want you to get Scotch and crazy tonight. We won't be together much longer."

"No, but I am Scotch and crazy. But I'll stop it. It's all nonsense."

"Yes it's all nonsense."

"It's all nonsense. It's only nonsense. I'm not afraid of the rain. I'm not afraid of the rain. Oh, oh, God, I wish I wasn't." She was crying. I comforted her and she stopped crying. But outside it kept on raining.(125-126)

20장 (Chapter XX)

■ 20장 주요 내용

- 헬렌 퍼거슨, 크로얼 로저스, 마이어스 부부와 함께 경마장에 감.

- 사기 경마를 싫어하는 캐서린.

"don't like this crooked racing!"(129)

- 부패한 그것들을 참아내는 헨리와 순수함을 요구하는 캐서린.

■ Summary

헨리와 캐서린은 헬렌 퍼거슨과 크로얼 로저스(Crowell Rodgers) 그리고 마이어스 부부와 함께 경마장에 갔다. 크로얼 로저스는 기념품을 챙기려다 다친 미국 군인이다.

■ 논평

작가는 캐서린의 영웅적인 지위(heroic status)를 반복하고 있다. 그녀는 마이어가 연관된 조작 경주 내기에 매우 괴로워했다.

"이런 사기 경마 마음에 안 들어!" "I don't like crooked racing!"(129)라고 캐서린은 선포했다. 비록 다섯 필이 뛰는 경주에서 4위를 했다 할지라도 캐서린은 헨리에게 한 번도 들어 보지 못한 말에게 돈을 걸자고 제안했다. 그렇지만 캐서린은 "기분이 상쾌해요."(131)라고 말했다.

여기서 주목할 점은 부정적인 내기(crooked betting)에서 헨리와 캐서린이 멀리하고 있는 동안 경주 말이 지나갈 때 그들은 멀리 있는 산을 볼 수 있다는 점이다.

이 장면은 부패한 평지와 순순한 산으로 구분한 작가의 지리적 이분법적인 묘사를 나타낸다. 또한, 헨리는 많은 부패한 것들을 참아내지만 캐서린은 순수함을 계속 요구한다.

이 장은 뒷부분에서 헨리와 캐서린이 선언하는 단독강화(separate peace)의 조짐이 나타난다.

그들이 다른 사람들과 분리되어 있고 승리를 거두지 못할 것 같은 말에 돈을 건 이후에 그녀는 헨리에게

"우리 둘만 있는 게 더 좋지 않아요."
"Don't you like it better when we're all alone?"(132)

"다른 사람과 같이 있을 때 항상 외로웠어요."
"I felt very lonely when they were all there."(132)

■ 20장 주요 작품 내용

Crowell's head was bandaged and he did not care much about these races but read the racing paper constantly and kept track of all the horses for something to do. He said the horses were a terrible lot but they were all the horses we had. Old Meyers liked him to tips. Meyers won on nearly every race but disliked to give tips because it brought down the prices. The racing was very crooked. Men who had been ruled off the turf everywhere else were racing in Italy. Meyers' information was good but I hated to ask him because sometimes he did not answer, and always you could see it hurt him to tell you, but he felt obligated to tell us for some reason and he hated less to tell Crowell. Crowell's eyes had been hurt, one was hurt badly, and Meyers had trouble with his eyes and so he liked Crowell. Meyers never told his wife what horses he was playing and she won or lost, mostly lot, and talked all the time.(128)

We went up in the grand-stand to watch the race. They had no elastic barrier at San Siro then and the starter lined up all the track, and then sent them off with a crack of his long whip. They came past us with the black horse well in front and on the turn he was running away form the others. I watched them on the far side with the glasses and saw the jockey fighting to hold him in but he could not hold him and when they came around the turn and into the stretch the black horse was fifteen lengths ahead of the others. He went way on up and around the turn after the finish.

"Isn't it wonderful," Catherine said. "We'll have over three thousand lire. He must be a splendid horse."

"I hope his color doesn't run," Crowell said, "before they paid off."

"He was really a lovely horse," Catherine said. "I wonder if Mr. Meyers backed him."

"Did you have the winner?" I called to Meyers. He nodded.

"I didn't," Mrs. Meyers said. "Who did you children bet on?"

"Japalac."

"Really? he's thirty-five to one!"

"We liked his color."

"I didn't. I thought he looked seedy. They told me not to back him."

"He won't pay much." Meyers said.

"He's marked thirty-five to one in the quotes," I said.

"He won't pay much. At the last minute," Meyers said. "they put a lot of money on him."

"Who?"

"Kempton and boys. You'll see. He won't pay two to one."

"Then we won't get three thousand lire," Catherine said. "I don't like this crooked racing!"(129)

"We'll get two hundred lire."

"That's nothing. That doesn't do us any good. I thought we were going to get three thousand."

"It's crooked and disgusting," Ferguson said.

"Of course," said Catherine, "if it hadn't been crooked we'd never have backed him at all. But I would have liked the three thousand lire."(130)

We backed a horse named Light For Me that finished fourth in a field of five. We leaned on the fence and watched the horses go by, their hoofs thudding as they went past, and saw the mountains off in the distance and Milan beyond the trees and the fields. I feel so much cleaner, Catherine said. The horses were coming back, through the gate, wet and sweating, the jockeys quieting them and riding up to dismount under the trees.

"Wouldn't you like a drink? We could have one out here and see the horses."

"I'll get them," I said.(131)

"The boy will bring them," Catherine said. She put her hand up and the boy came out from the Pagoda bar beside the stables. We sat down at a round iron table.

"Don't you like it better when we're alone?"

"Yes," I said.

"I felt very lonely when they were all there."

"It's grand here," I said.

"Yes. It's really a pretty course."

"It's nice."

"Don't let me spoil your fun, darling. I'll go back whenever you want."

"No." I said. "We'll stay here and have our drink. Then we'll go down and stand at the water jump for the steeplechase."

"You're awfully good to me," she said.

After we had been alone awhile we were glad to see the others again. We had a good time.(132)

21장 (Chapter XXI)

- **21장 주요 내용**

- 소설이 정점을 향해 달리는 장이다.
- 여름이 가고 가을이 시작. (in September the first cool nights came)
- 에토레(Ettore) 전선 복귀. 산가브리엘(San Gabriele) 점령 못 함.
- 크로엘(Crowell) 로마를 걸쳐서 미국으로 송환.
- 토리노(Turin)에 반전시위 발생.
- 이탈리아 15만 명 손실. (one hundred and fifty thousand men)
- 이탈리아가 과도한 욕심을 부림. (Italians had better off more than they could chew)
- 플랑드르(Flanders) 전선의 공격도 패색.
- 카르소(Cars)에서 4만 명 잃음.
- cooked라는 단어를 계속 사용함. 134페이지.
- 헨리 중위는 3주간 요양 휴가 후 복귀하라는 공문(official letter) 받음.
- 캐서린이 아이를 가짐. (임신 3개월)

I'm going to have a baby, darling. It is almost three months.

■ **Summary**

헨리는 3주 동안 요양 휴가 후에 전선으로 복귀하라는 명을 받았다. 그가 떠나기 전에 캐서린은 임신 3개월이라는 사실을 그에게 말했다. 계절적으로는 여름이 끝날 무렵인 21장은 두 개의 중심적인 전환점을 보여 주기 때문에 매우 극단적이면서도 중요한 장이다.

■ **논평**

헨리는 전선으로 다시 오라는 통보를 받았고 캐서린은 임신 3개월이라는 사실을 헨리에게 말한다. 이 장은 구체적으로 매우 중요한 장중의 하나이다.

헨리 중위에게 전달된 공문(official letter)은 헨리와 우리에게 이 이야기의 중심 부분이 곧 결론에 이르게 된다는 것을 말해준다. 21장의 시작과 관련된 정보를 생각하면 이것은 나쁜 소식이다. 즉 독일과 싸우는 연합군이 러시아와 서부 전선뿐만 아니라 그 지역에서도 밀리고 있다. 더욱이 헨리가 이야기한 영국 소령은 독일이 이탈리아를 침공할 것으로 예측했다. 헨리가 부대에 다시 돌아가는 각본(시나리오)에는 캐서린과 여름에 싹틔운 사랑에 부정적인 영향을 준다. 캐서린의 임신은 엄청나게 중요한 구성 전개(plot development)를 구성한다. 그들 간의 사랑의 결과이면서 책임이 따르는 것이다. 캐서린은 자신의 믿음을 분명히 했다. 그리고 다음과 같이 말했다.

2부(Book Two)

"우리 두 사람 이외에 나머지 세상 사람들은 모두가 남이니까. 우리 사이에 무슨 일이 생기면 우리는 끝나는 거고 사람들에게 휘둘릴 거예요."(139)

"Because there's only us two and in the world there's all the rest of them. If anything comes between us we're gone and then they have us."

그러나 다른 삶이 등장함으로 인해 이것은 명백히 진실이 아니다. 성격묘사의 관점에서 캐서린의 특별히 용감한 생각은 이 장에서 명백히 드러난다. 특히 겸손함으로 그녀는 용감하게 극복하겠다고 암시했다. 그리고 헨리는 보통밖에 안 되는 야구선수의 재능과 자신의 용맹을 비교함으로써 놀라운 자기 인식을 보여준다. 그러나 헨리는 살아가는 방법을 배우고 있다.

"용감한 사람에게는 아무 일도 벌어지지 않아." "Nothing ever happens to the brave."(139)라고 헨리가 순진하게 말했을 때 경험이 많은 캐서린은 "그런 사람도 죽기는 하죠." "They died of course."(139)라고 말하고 불길한 예견을 한다. 이 소설은 계속 기계가 끊임없이 움직이게 하려면 연료를 제공하는 것처럼 작가는 21장을 기점으로 더욱 힘차게 움직이도록 하기 위한 연료를 제공하고 있다.

21장을 기점으로 헨리와 캐서린은 작별해야 한다. 사랑하지만 전쟁으로 인한 작별이고 앞장에서 퍼거슨이 말한 것처럼 전쟁 아이를 낳을 수 있는 상황이라서 좀처럼 두 사람은 마음 상태를 가늠하기 어려운 상황으로 몰고 간다. 이 소설의 정점을 향해서 달리는 기차와 같다. 목적지도 모르고 어떤 일이 벌어질지도 상상할 수 없는 그런 상황으로 몰고 간다. 두 연인뿐만 아니라 이 소설을 읽는 독자들도 매우 심각한 지점에 이

르렀다는 것을 느낄 수 있는 장이다. 헤밍웨이는 소설은 계속해서 달리기 위해서 연료를 공급해야 하는 효율적인 기계와 같다고 말한다. (The novel is like an efficient machine that Hemingway refuel constantly.)

■ 21장 주요 작품 내용

In September the first cool nights came. then the days were cool and the leaves on the trees in the park began to turn color and we knew the summer was gone. The fighting at the front went very badly and they could not take San Gabriele. The fighting on the Bainsizza plateau was over and by the middle of the month the fighting for San Gabriele was about over too. They could not take it. Ettore was gone back to the front. The horses were gone to Rome and there was no more racing. Crowell had gone to Rome too, to be sent back to America. There were riots twice in the town against the war and bad rioting in Turin. A British major at the club told me the Italians had lost one hundred and fifty thousand men on the Bainsizza plateau and on San Gabriele. He said they had lost forty thousand on the Carso besides. He had a drink and he talked. He said the fighting was over for the year down here and that the Italians had bitten off more than they could chew. He said the offensive in Flanders was going to the bad. If they killed men as they did this fall the Allies would be **cooked** in another year. He said we were all **cooked** but we were all right as long as we did not know it. We were all **cooked**. The thing was not to recognize it. The last country to realize they were **cooked** would win the war. We had another drink. Was I on somebody's staff? No. He was. It was all balls. We were alone in the club sitting back in one of the big leather sofas. His boots were smoothly polished dull leather. They were beautiful boots. He said it was all balls. They thought only in divisions and man-power. They all squabbled about divisions and only killed them when they got them. They were all **cooked**. The Germans won the victories. By God they were soldiers. The old Hun was a soldier. But they were **cooked** too. We were all **cooked**. I asked about Russia. He said they were **cooked** already. I'd soon see they were **cooked**. Then the Austrians were **cooked** too. If they got some Hun divisions they could do it. Did he think they would attack this fall? Of course they would. The Italians were **cooked**. Everybody knew they were **cooked**. The old Hun would come down through the Trentino an cut the railway at Vicenza and then where would the Italians be? They tried that in sixteen, I said. Not with Germans. Yes, I said.

But they probably wouldn't do that, he said. It was too simple. They'd try something complicated and get royally **cooked**. I had to go, I said. I had to get back to the hospital. "Good-by," he said. Then cheerily, "Every sort of luck!" There was a great contrast between his world pessimism and personal cheeriness. (133-134)

I went on to the hospital. There some letters, an official one, and some others. I was to have three weeks' convalescent leave and then return to the front. I read it over carefully. Well, that was that. The convalescent leave started October fourth when my course was finished. Three weeks was twenty-one days. That made October twenty-fifth. I told them I would not be in and went to the restaurant a little way up the street from the hospital for supper and read my letters and the *Corriere* Della Sera at the table. There was a letter from my grandfather, containing family news, patriotic encouragement, a draft for two hundred dollars, and a few clippings; a dull letter from the priest at our mess, a letter from a man I knew who was flying with the French and had gotten in with a wild gang and was telling about it, and a note from Rinalidi asking me how long I was going to skulk in Milano and what was all the news? (135-136)

I told her about my papers and leave.

"That's lovely," she said. "Where do you want to go?"

"Nowhere. I want to stay here."

"That's silly. You pick a place to go and I'll come too."

"How will you work it?"

"I don't know. But I will."

"You're pretty wonderful."

"No I'm not. But life isn't hard to manage when you're nothing to lose."

"How do you mean?"

"Nothing. I was only thinking how small obstacles seemed that once were so big."

"I should think it might be hard to manage."

"No it won't , darling. If necessary I'll simply leave. But it won't come to that."

"Where should we go?"

"I don't care. Anywhere you want. Anywhere we don't know people."

"Don't you care where we go?"

"No, I'll like any place."

She seemed upset and taut.

"What's the matter, Catherine?"

"Nothing. Nothing's the matter."

"Yes there is."

"No nothing. Really nothing."

"I know there is. Tell me, darling. You can tell me."

"It's nothing."

"Tell me."

"I don't want to. I'm afraid I'll make you unhappy or worry you."

"No it won't."

"You're sure? It doesn't worry me but I'm afraid to worry you."

"It won't if it doesn't worry you."

"I don't want to tell."

"Tell it."

"Do you have to?"

"Yes."

"I'm going to have a baby, darling. It's almost three months along."(136-137)

"You're not worried, are you? Please please don't. You mustn't worry."

"All right."

"Is it all right?"

"Of course."

"I did everything. I took everything but it didn't make any difference."

"I'm not worried."

"I couldn't help it, darling, and I haven't worried about it. You mustn't worry or feel badly."

"I only worry about you."

"That's it. That's what you musn't do. People have babies all the time. Everybody has babies. It's natural thing."(138)

We were quiet awhile and did not talk. Catherine was sitting on the bed and I was looking at her but we did not touch each other. We were apart as when some one comes into a room and people are self-conscious. She put out her hand took mine.

"You aren't angry are you, darling?"

"No."

"And you don't feel trapped?"

"Maybe a little. But not by you."

"I didn't mean by me. You musn't be stupid. I meant trapped at all."

"You always feel trapped biologically."

"She went away a long way without stirring or removing her hand."

"'Always' isn't a pretty word."

"I'm sorry."

"It's all right. But you see I've never had a baby and I've never even loved any one. And I've tried to be the way you wanted and then you talk about 'always.'"

"I could cut off my tongue," I offered.

"Oh, darling!" she came back from wherever she had been. "You musn't mind me." We were both together again and the self-consciousness was gone. "We really are the same one and we musn't misunderstand on purpose."

"We won't."

"But people do. They love each other and they misunderstand on purpose and they fight and then suddenly they aren't the same one."

"We won't fight."

"We musn't. Because there's only us two and in the world there's all the rest of them. If anything comes between us we're gone and then they have us."

"They won't get us," I said. "Because you're too brave. Nothing ever happens to the brave."

"They die of course."

"But only once."

"I don't know. Who said that?"

"The coward dies a thousand deaths, the brave but one?"(139)

"Of course. Who said it?"

"I don't know."

"He was probably a coward," she said. "He knew a great deal about cowards but nothing about the brave. The brave dies perhaps two thousand deaths if he's intelligent. He simply doesn't mention them."

"I don't know. It's hard to see inside the head of the brave."

"Yes. That's how they keep that way."

"You're an authority."

"You're right, darling. That was deserved."

"You're brave."

"No," She said. "But I would like to be."

"I'm not," I said. "I know where I stand. I've been out long enough to know. I'm like a ball-player that bats two hundred and thirty and knows he's no better."

"What is a ball-players that bats two hundred and thirty? It's awfully impressive."

"It's not. It means a mediocre hitter in baseball."

"But still a hitter," she prodded me.

"I guess we're both conceited," I said. "But you are brave."

"No. But I hope to be."

"We're both brave," I said. "And I'm very brave when I've had a drink."(140)

22장 (Chapter XXII)

■ 22장 주요 내용

- 황달로 인해 요양 휴가 갈 수 없음.

The whites of the eyes were yellow and it was the jaundice. I was sick for two weeks with it. For that reason we did not spend a convalescent leave together.

- 마조레 호수 근처에 있는 팔란차(Pallanza Lago Maggiore)에서 낚시 하면서 시간 보냄.

- 미스 밴 캠펀(Miss Van Campen)과 논쟁: 음낭을 걷어차서 불구가 되려고 하는 사람을 본 적이 있느냐? 그 고통은 황달과 가까운 고통인데 여자들은 경험하지 못하는 고통이라고 헨리가 주장함. "Miss van Campen," I said, "did you ever know a man who tried to disable himself by kicking himself in the scrotum?"(144)

■ Summary

헨리는 황달(Jaundice)이라는 진단을 받아서 요양 휴가를 떠날 수 없었다. 밴 캠펀(Van Campen)간호사가 옷장의 빈 술병을 찾았다. 캠펀 간호사는 술을 지나치게 마셔서 이 같은 질병에 걸렸고 그래서 휴가를 갈 자격이 없고 병원에 있어야 한다고 나물을 했다. 그 결과 캐서린과의 휴가 계획은 취소되었다.

■ 논평

캐서린이 임신 3개월이라는 사실을 말한 이후 비가 많이 왔고 많은 비가 상징하는 것은 부인할 수 없을 것 같다. 남자들이 전투를 피하려고 고통스러운 병에 걸릴 것이라는 캠펀 간호사의 생각은 남자들이 전투를 피하고자 고통스러운 병에 걸린다고 생각하는 캠펀 간호사의 생각이고 일부 사람들이 전투를 피하려고 실제로 얼마나 멀리 갈 것인지를 강조하는 것이다. 헨리 혼자만 전쟁에 대한 상반된 감정이 있는 것이 아니었다.

■ 22장 주요 작품 내용

It turned cold that night and the next day it was raining. Coming home from Ospedale Maggiore it rained very hard and I was wet when I came in. Up in my room the rain was coming down heavily outside on the balcony, and the wind blew it against the glass doors. I changed my clothing and drank some brandy but the brandy did not taste good. I felt sick in the night and in the morning after breakfast I was nauseated.

"There is no doubt about it," the house surgeon said. "Look at the whites of his eyes, Miss."

Miss Gage looked. They had me look in a glass. The whites of the eyes were yellow and it was the jaundice. I was sick for two weeks with it. For that reason we did not spend a convalescent leave together. We had planned to go to Pallanza on Lago Maggiore. It is nice there in the fall when the leaves turn. There are walks you can take and you can troll for trout in the lake. It would have been better than Stresa because there are fewer people at Pallanza. Stresa is so easy to get to from Milan that there are always people you know. There is a nice village at Pallanza and you can row out to the islands where the fishermen live and there is a restaurant on the biggest island. But we did not go.(142-143)

I suppose you can't be blamed for not wanting to go back to the front. But I should think you would try something more intelligent than producing jaundice with alcoholism.(144)

"Miss van Campen," I said, "did you ever know a man who tried to disable himself by kicking himself in the scrotum?"

Miss Van Campen ignored the actual question. She had to ignore it or the leave the room. She was not ready to leave. because she had disliked me for a long time and she was now cashing in.

"I have known many men to escape the front through self-inflicted wounds."

"That wasn't the question. I have seen self-inflicted wounds also. I asked you if you had ever known a man who had tried to disable himself by kicking himself in the scrotum. Because that is the nearest sensation to jaundice and it is a sensation that I believe few women have ever experienced. That was why I asked you if you had ever had the jundice, Miss Van Campen, because---" Miss Van Campen left the room. Later Miss Gage came in. "What did you say to Van Campen? She was furious."

"We were comparing sensation. I was going to suggest that she had never experienced childbirth----"

"You're a fool," Gage said. "She 's after your scalp."

"She has my scalp," I said. "She's lost me my leave and she might try and get me court-martialled. She's mean enough."

"She says I've drunk myself into jaundice so as not to go back to the front."

"Pooh," said Gage. "I'll swear you've never taken a drink. Everybody will swear you've never taken a drink."(144-145)

23장 (Chapter XXIII)

- **23장 주요 내용**

- 밀라노에서 마지막 저녁.

"I'm going to the front," I said.(149)

- **Summary**

밀라노에서의 마지막 저녁 헨리 중위와 캐서린 버클리는 권총을 구매한 후 호텔에 방을 잡았다.

- **논평**

우리는 앞서 캐서린 버클리가 전통적인 종교가 없다는 주제에 대해서 말한 적이 있다. 여기서 헨리 중위와 밀라노 대성당 진입 초대를 거부하는 것이 반복됩니다. 저자는 헨리와 캐서린을 교회의 피난처에 함께 서 있는 군인과 그 여자 친구와 비교합니다. 그러나 헨리와 캐서린을 보호할 관습적인 믿음 없습니다. 전방의 장교들이 매춘 굴로 피신했다는 사실을 기억하면 분명히 헨리와 캐서린에게는 선택사항이 아닙니다. 그들이 가진 것은 오로지 서로에 대한 사랑입니다. 헨리는 그가 다칠 때 잃어버린 권총을 대신하기 위해 권총을 산다. 우리의 관심이 헨리의 권총에 쏠린 것은 이번이 두 번째이기 때문에 우리는 그것이 어떤 중요한 물건이라고 추측할 수밖에 없다.

헨리가 "중고, 매우 저렴한"(used, very cheap) 검의 제안을 거부하는 것들 주목해야 한다.

"I have some used swords very cheap."(149)

"나는 전선에 갈 겁니다." 내가 말했다.
"I'm going to the front," I said.(149)

그러자 갑옷 가게 주인은 "아, 그럼 검은 필요 없을 것이다."라고 대답합니다.

헤밍웨이가 소설의 첫 장면에서 분명히 밝혔듯이 이것은 전투원들이 칼을 들고 다니는 이야기책 전쟁이 아닙니다. 하물며 칼을 사용하는 것은 더더욱 그렇습니다. 1차 세계대전은 현대적이고 낭만적이지 않으며 잔인한 전쟁입니다.

헨리와 캐서린이 무기고에서 기차역 근처의 호텔로 가는 동안 23장 초반부터 도시를 뒤덮었던 안개가 소설의 죽음 상징은 비로 변한다. 남편이 아닌 남자와 함께 호텔 방에 하룻밤 묵는 것은 캐서린을 창녀처럼 느끼게 한다. 여기서 우리는 소설 초반에 헨리가 전방에서 떠난 것을 상기시키는데, 그는 성매매 여성들과 흥미진진하지만 만족스럽지 못한 만남에서 가장 많은 부분을 할애했고 우리는 그가 그 이후로 얼마나 성숙해졌는지를 깨닫게 된다.

헤밍웨이 스타일과 관련하여 헨리는 몇 달 동안 친밀한 관계를 유지한 후에야 캐서린에게 아버지가 있다는 것을 알게 되고 헨리는 아버지가 없다는 것을 알게 된다. 다시 말하자면 헤밍웨이 소설과 이야기는 설명이 부족하므로 주목할 만하고 독특하게 현대적이다. 이 작품을 통해 헨리의 전쟁 전 삶에 대한 정보는 거의 없으며 캐서린의 정보는 말할 것도 없고 현재의 행동이 매우 설득적이기 때문에 우리는 특별히 그것을 놓치지 않는다.

■ 23장 주요 작품 내용

The night I was to return to the front I sent the porter down to hold a seat for me on the train when it came from Turin. The train was to leave at midnight. It was made up at Turin and reached Milan about half-past ten at night and lay in the station until time to leave. You had to be there when it came in, to get a seat. The porter took a friend with him, a machine-gunner on leave who worked in a tailor shop, and was sure that between them they could hold a place. I gave them money for platform tickets and had them take my baggage. There was a big rucksack and two musettes.(146)

There were streetcar tracks and beyond them was the cathedral. It was white and wet in the mist. We cross the tram tracks. On our left were the shops, their windows lighted, and the entrance to the galleria. There was a fog in the square and when we came close to the front of the cathedral it was very big and the stone was wet.

"Would you like to go in?"

"No," Catherine said. We walked along. There was a soldier standing with his girl in the shadow of one of the stone buttresses ahead of us and we passed them. They were standing tight up against the stone and he had put his cape around her.

"They're like us," I said.

"Nobody is like us," Catherine said. She did not mean it happily.

"I wish they had some place to go."

"It mightn't do them any good."

"I don't know. Everybody ought to have some place to go."

"They have the cathedral," Catherine said. We were past it now. We crossed the far end of the square and looked back at the cathedral. It was fine in the mist. We were standing in front of the leather goods shop. There were riding boots, a rucksack and ski boots in the window. Each article was set apart as an exhibit; the rucksack in the centre, the riding boots on one side and the ski boots on the other. The leather was dark and oiled smooth as a used saddle. The electric light made high lights on the dull oiled leather.

"We'll ski some time."

"In two months there will be ski-ing at Murren," Catherine said.(147)

"Let's go there."

"All right," she said. We went on past other windows and turned down a side street.

"I've never been this way."

"This is the way I go to the hospital," I said. It was a narrow street and we kept on the right-hand side. There were many people passing in the fog. There were shops and all the windows were lighted. We looked in a window at a pile of cheeses. I stopped in front of an armorer's shop.

"Come in a minute. I have to buy a gun."

"What sort of gun?"

"A pistol." We went in and I unbuttoned my belt and laid it with the empty holster on the counter. Two women were behind the counter. The women brought out several pistols.

"It must fit this," I said, opening the holster. It was a gray leather holster and I had brought it second-hand to wear in the town.

"Have they good pistols?" Catherine asked.

"They're all about the same. Can I try this one?" I asked the woman.

"I have to place now to shoot," she said. "But it is very good. You will not make mistake with it."

I snapped it and pulled back the action. The spring was rather strong but it worked smoothly. I sighted it and snapped it again.

"It is used," the woman said. "It belonged to an officer who was an excellent shot."

"Did you sell it to him?"

"Yes."

"How did you get it back?"

"From his orderly."

"Maybe you have mine," I said. "How much is this?"

"Fifty lire. It is very cheap."

"All right. I want two extra clips and a box of cartridges."(148)

She brought them from under the counter.

"Have you any need for a sword?" she asked. "I have some used swords very cheap."

"I'm going to the front," I said.

"Oh yes, then you won't need a sword," she said.

I paid for the cartridges and the pistol, filled the magazine and put it in place, put the pistol in my empty holster, filled the extra clips with cartridges and put them in the leather slots on the holster and then buckled on my belt. The pistol felt heavy on the belt. Still, I thought, it was better to have a regulation pistol. You could always get shells.(149)

"Have you any need for a sword?" she asked.

"I have some used swords very cheep."

"I'm going to the front," I said.

"Oh yes, then you won't need a sword," she said.(149)

The fog was turning to rain.(150)

It was raining and I could smell the wet street and the horse steaming in the rain. She came back with a package and got in and we drove on.(151)

I went to the window and looked out, then pulled a cord that shut the thick plush curtains. Catherine was sitting on the bed, looking at the cut glass chandelier. She had taken her hat off and her hair shone under the light. She saw herself in one of the mirrors and put her hands to her hair. I saw her in three other mirrors. She did not look happy. She let her cape fall on the bed.

"What's the matter, darling?"

"I never felt like a whore before," she said. I went over to the window and pulled the curtain aside and looked out. I had not thought it would be like this.

"You're not a whore."

"I know it, darling. But it isn't nice to feel like one." Her voice was dry and flat.(152)

"Wine is a grand thing." I said. "It makes you forget all the bad."

"It's lovely," said Catherine. "But it's given my father gout very badly."

"Have you a father?"

"Yes," said Catherine. "He has gout. You won't ever have to meet him. Haven't you a father?"

"No," I said. "A step-father."

"Will I like him?"

"You won't have to meet him."(154)

24장 (Chapter XXIV)

- **24장 주요 내용**

- 헨리는 전선에 복귀하기 위해 캐서린과 헤어짐.
- 2부 마지막 장.

- **Summary**

헨리와 캐서린은 밀라노역에서 작별한다. 헨리는 어려움을 덜기 위해서 군인에게 자리를 잡아달라고 돈을 지급한다. 헨리는 대위에게 자리를 양보한다. 기차는 전선을 향해 출발한다.

- **논평**

헨리와 캐서린의 평화로운 시간이 끝나는 것을 고려해 보면 제2부의 마지막 장인 24장은 매우 짧고 감성적이지 않다: 헨리는 전선으로 돌아가고 그들의 사랑도 어떻게 될 줄 모르는 상황을 고려해 봐도 매우 짧다.

작가는 사랑하는 사람의 이별을 앞에 두고서 달콤한 멜로드라마(milk melodrama)를 펼치려는 욕구를 자제했다. 이 같은 작가의 태도는 인물이나 절제된 행동에서 일관적으로 나타난 현상이다. 또한, 서로 작별할 때 계속 비가 오는 것도 주목해야 할 점이다. 이 소설의 24장에서 캐서린의 마지막 행동은 헨리가 비를 피해 들어와야 한다는 신호를 보내는 것이다.

　캐서린은 아치형 통로 쪽을 손짓으로 가리켰다. 돌아보니 헌병 두 명과 아치형 통로가 보였다. 비를 피해 거리로 들어가라는 뜻 같았다.(158)

　Catherine pointed in toward the archway. I looked, there were only the two carabinieri and the archway. I realized she meant for me to get in out of the rain.(158)

■ 24장 주요 작품 내용

We walked down the stairs instead of taking the elevator. The carpet on the stairs was worn. I had paid for the dinner when it came up and the waiter, who had brought it, was sitting on a chair near the door. He jumped up and bowed and I went with him into the side room and paid the bill for the room. The manager had remembered me as a friend and refused payment in advance but wnen he retired he had remembered to have the waiter stationed at the door so that I should not get out without paying. I suppose that happened; even with his friends. One had so many friends in a war.(156)

I asked the waiter to get us a carriage and he took Catherine's package that I was carrying and went out with an umbrella. Outside through the window we saw him crossing the street in the rain. We stood in th side room and looked out the window.

"How do you feel, Cat?"

"Sleepy."

"I feel hollow and hungry."

"Have you anything to eat?"(156)

"Yes, in my musette."

I saw the carriage coming. It stopped, the horse's head hanging in the rain, and the waiter stepped out, opened his umbrella, and came toward the hotel. We met him at the door and walked out under the umbrella down the wet walk to the carriage at the curb. Water was running in the gutter.(157)

"No," I said. "Thanks. I don't need thee."

He went back under the shelter of the archway. I turned to Catherine. Her face was in the shadow from the hood of the carriage.

"We might as well say good-by."

"I can't go in?"

"No."

"Good-by Cat."

"Will you tell him the hospital?"

"Yes."

I told the driver the address to drive to. He nodded.

"Good-by," I said. "Take good care of yourself and young Catherine."

"Good-by, darling."

"Good-by," I said. I stepped out into the rain and the carriage started. Catherine leaned out and I saw her face in the light.(157)

She smiled and waved. The carriage went up the street, Catherine pointed in toward the archway. I looked, there were only the two carrabinieri and the archway. I realized she meant for me to get in out of the rain. I went in and stood and watched the carriage turn the corner. Then I started through the station and down the runway to the train.(158)

"More will get on at Brescia," said the machine-gunner. I said good-by to them and we shook hands and they left. They both felt badly. Inside the train we were all standing in the corridor when the train started. I watched the lights of the station and the yards as we went out. It was still raining and soon the windows were wet and you could not see out. Later I slept on the floor of the corridor; First putting my pocket-book with my money and papers in it inside my shirt and trousers so that it was inside the leg of my breeches. I slept all night, waking at the Brescia and Verona when more men got on the train, but going back to sleep at once. I had my head on one of the musettes and my arms around the other and I could feel the pack and they could all walk over me if they wouldn't step on me. Men were sleeping on the floor all down the corridor. Others stood holding on to the window rods or leaning against the doors. That train was always crowded.(159)

3부(Book Three)

25장 (Chapter XXV)

■ 25장 주요 내용

- 헨리의 전선에 복귀 리날디와 재회
- 가을이 왔다.

Now in the fall the trees were all bare and the roads were muddy.

- 전쟁에 지쳐 있고 전쟁을 증오하면서 계속 수술만 해서 훌륭한 외과 의사가 되었다는 리날디의 자조 섞인 대화를 통해 리날디의 상황과 전쟁의 상황을 추측.
- 그래도 헨리와 리날디는 가장 좋은 친구.

"He very tired and overworked."

This is a terrible war, baby.

"You are my best friend and my war brother."

■ Summary

헨리가 전선에 복귀했다. 그는 소령으로부터 여름에 이탈리아 군이 매우 불리하다는 소식을 들었다. 리날디와 다시 만나서 둘은 장교 식당에서 식사했고 그곳에서 리날디는 신부를 화나게 했다.

■ **논평**

여러 가지로 3부(Book Three) 시작인 25장에서는 이 소설의 시작을 알리는 개요를 말해준다. 다시 가을이 왔고 "나무 들은 헐벗고 길은 진흙탕이 되었다."(163) Now in the fall the trees were all bare and the roads were muddy. (163)

리날디는 여전히 신부를 괴롭힌다. 그러나 이 시점에서 두 가지 것이 변했다. 이탈리아 군대의 운명과 헨리 자신이다. 리날디는 헨리의 몸 상태를 확인한 후에 "마치 결혼한 사람처럼 구는군." "You are like a married man," he said. (167)

헤밍웨이는 리날디라는 인물을 헨리와 대조적인 인물로 묘사하고 있다. 헨리는 부상 때문에 전선으로 떠났으며 치료를 받는 중에 캐서린과의 사랑의 결과로 매우 성숙해졌다.

"이놈의 전쟁 때문에 죽을 맛이지" This war is killing me, "Rinaldi said."(167)라고 리날디가 말했다. 이 말은 은유 이상의 많은 의미를 내포하고 있다. 리날디는 매춘부와의 성관계로 인해서 자신이 매독에 걸렸다고 믿고 있다. 작가는 다시 한번 전쟁으로 인한 죽음과 성을 연결했다.

전쟁으로 인해 좋지 않은 일들이 부대에서 많이 발생하는데 그중에서 젊은이들이 매춘부와의 성관계를 작가는 지적하고 있다. 전쟁터에 젊은 이들이 참전하지 않았다면 그들은 자유롭게 사랑을 키우고 나눌 수 있었을 텐데 전쟁터인 곳에 가둬 두다 보니 젊은이들의 성적인 욕구를 사창가에서 해결하는 현상을 지적한다. 이 같은 일을 젊은이들만의 문제가 아니고 그곳에 온 매춘부인 여성들도 전쟁의 피해자이다. 다시 한번 당시의 젊은이들이 기성세대와 제도 가치관 등등을 배격한 이유를 알 수 있다. 전쟁이 없으면 이곳에 우리도 오지 않았다. 이 말이 그 당시 젊은이들의 마음을 대변한다.

■ 25장 주요 작품 내용

"You act like a married man," he said. "What's the matter with you?"

"Nothing," I said. "What's the matter with you?"

"This war is killing me," Rinaldi said. "I am very depressed by it." He folded his hands over his knee.

"Oh," I said.

"What's the matter? Can't I even have human impulses?"

"No, I can see you've been having fine time. Tell me."

"All summer and all fall I've operated. I work all the time. I do everybody's work. All the hard ones they leave to me. By God, baby, I am becoming a lovely surgeon."(167)

"There's nothing to tell," I said. "I've led a quiet life."

"You act like a married man," he said. "What's the matter with you?"

"Nothing," I said. "What's the matter with you?"

"This war is killing me," he said. "I'm very depressed by it." He folded his hands over his knee.

"Oh," I said.

"What's the matter? Can't I even have human impulses?"

"No. I can see you've been having a fine time. Tell me."

"All summer and all fall I've operated. I work all the time. I do everybody's work. All the hard ones they leave to me. By God, baby, I am becoming a lovely surgeon."

"That sounds better."

"I never think. No, by God. I don't think; I operate."

"That's right."

"But now, baby, it's all over. I don't operate now and I feel like hell. This is a terrible war, baby. You believe me when I say it. Now you cheer me up. Did you bring the phonograph records?"

"Yes."

They were wrapped in paper in a cardboard box in my rucksack. I was too tired to get them out. "Don't you feel good yourself, baby?"

"I feel like hell."(167)

"This war is terrible," Rinaldi said. "Come on. We'll both get drunk and be cheerful. Then we'll go get the ashes dragged. Then we'll feel fine."

"I've had the Jaundice," I said. "and I can't get drunk."

"Oh, baby, how you've come back to me. You come back serious and with a liver. I tell you this war is a bad thing. Why did we make it anyway."

"We'll have a drink. I don't want to get drunk but we'll have a drink."

Rinaldi went across the room to the washstand and brought back two glasses and a bottle of cognac.

"It's an Austrian cognac," he said. "Seven stars. It's all they captured on San Gabriele."

"Were you up there?"

"No. I haven't been anywhere. I've been here all the time operating. Look, baby, this is your old tooth-brushing glass. I kept it all the time to remind me of you."

"To remind you to brush your teeth."

"No. I have my own too. I kept this to remind me of you trying to brush away the Villa Rosa from your teeth in the morning, swearing and eating aspirin and cursing harlots. Every time I see that glass I think of you trying to clean your conscience with a toothbrush." He came over to the bed. "Kiss me once and tell me you're not serious."

"I never kiss you. You're an ape."

"I know, you are the fine good Anglo-Saxon boy. I know. You are the remorse boy, I know. I will wait till I see the Anglo-Saxon brushing away harlotry with a toothbrsuh."

"Put some cognac in the glass."

We touched glasses and drank. Rinaldi laughed at me.

"I will get you drunk and take out your liver and put you in a good Italian liver and make you a man again."

I held the glass for some more cognac. It was dark outside now.(168)

Holding the glass of cognac, I went over and opened the window. The rain had stopped falling. It was colder outside and there was a mist in the trees.

"Don't throw the cognac out of window," Rinaldi said. "If you can't drink it give it to me."

"Go something yourself," I said. I was glad to see Rinaldi again. He had spent two years teasing me and I had always liked it. We understood each other very well.(169)

"I am the snake. I am the snake of reason."

"You're getting it mixed. The apple was reason."

"No, it was the snake." He was more cheerful.(170)

"You are my best friend and my war brother."(171)

I saw the major look at him and notice that he was drunk. His thin face was white. The line of his hair was very black against the white of his forehead.

"It's all right, Rinaldi," said the priest. "It's all right."

"To hell with you," said Rinaldi. "To hell with the whole damn business." He sat back in his chair. "He's been under a strain and he's tired," the major said to me. He finished his meat and wiped up the gravy with a piece of bread. "I don't give a damn," Rinaldi said to the table. "To hell with the whole business." He looked defiantly around the table, his eyes flat, his face pale.

"All right," I said. "To hell with the whole damn business."

"No, no," said Rinadli. "You can't do it. I say you can't do it. You are dry and you're empty and there's nothing else. There's nothing else I tell you. Not a damned thing. I know, when I stop working."(174)

The priest shook his head. The elderly took away the stew dish. "What are you eating meat for?" Rinaldi turned to the priest. "Don't you know it's Friday?"

"It's Thursday,"the priest said.

"It's a lie. It's Friday. You're eating the body of our Lord. It's God-meat. I know. It's dead Austrian. That's what you're eating."

"The white meat in from officers," I said, completing the old joke.(174)

"To hell with you," Rinaldi said. "They try to get ride of me. Every night they try to get ride of me. I fight them off. What if I have it. Everybody has it. The whole world's got it. First," he went on, assuming the manner of a lecturer, "It's a little pimple. Then we notice a rash between the shoulders. Then we notice nothing at all. We put our faith in mercury."

"Or salvarsan," the major interrupted quietly.

"A mercurial product," Rinaldi said. He acted very elated now. "I know something worth two of that. Good old priest," he said. "You'll never get it. Baby will get it. It's an industrial accident. It's a simple industrial accident."(175)

"Yes." I said. "Come in early." He made a face and went out the door. "The major was standing with us." He's very tired and overworked. he said. "He thinks too he has syphilis. I don't believe it but he may have. He is treating himself for it. Good-night. You will leave before daylight, Enrico?"(175)

26장(Chapter XXVI)

■ 26장 주요 내용

- 헨리와 신부의 재회. 변화된 신부의 모습과 장교들.

- 그는 내가 이곳을 떠나기 전보다 훨씬 확신에 차 있었다.

He was surer of himself now than when I had gone away(178)

- 깨닫지 못할 것 같던 장교들도 이제는 깨달았죠.

Officers whom I thought could never realize it realize it now.(178)

- 전쟁에 관해 헨리와 신부의 대화

잠자는 것을 제외하고는 헨리와 신부 모두 현실에서 발생하는 어떤 것도 믿지 못하는 상태가 되었다. 전쟁이 오래 지속하면서 일어난 현상이다.

■ summary

저녁 식사 후 헨리의 방으로 돌아온 헨리와 신부는 전쟁에 관해서 여러 가지 이야기를 했다.

"끔찍한 여름이었죠." 신부가 말했다. 그는 내가 이곳을 떠나기 전보다 훨씬 확신에 차 있었다. "얼마나 끔찍했는지 믿기지 않을 겁니다. 현장에서 실체를 보지 않았다면요. 많은 사람이 이번 여름에 전쟁을 제대로 깨달았습니다. 절대로 깨닫지 못할 것 같던 장교들도 이제는 깨달았죠."(177-178)

"It has been a terrible summer," said the priest. He was surer of himself now than when I had gone away. "You cannot believe how it has been there and you know how it can be. Many people have realized the war this summer. Officers whom I thought could never realize it realize it now."(178)

"이기고 있는 싸움을 멈추는 사람은 없습니다."(178)
"No one ever stopped when they were winning."(178)

■ 논평

주로 태그 없는 대화로(부사구가 없는 대화) 작성된 이 장은 주로 헨리 중위 성장의 지표 역할을 한다. 그들의 이야기가 거의 끝나갈 무렵 헨리는 신부가 "나는 이제 더 이상 승리를 믿지 않습니다."(179) "I don't believe in victory any more."라고 말했을 때 신부 말에 동의했다. 헨리는 여전히 패배를 믿지 않는다고 주장한다. "I don't. But I don't believe in defeat. Though it may be better." 그런데도 그는 철학적으로 패배가 "더 나을 수도 있다고"("defeat may be better.")라고 말하자 그럼 뭘 믿습니까? (What do you believe in?)이라고 하자 "잠자는 거요."(In sleep)이라고 말하는 것으로 봐서 잠자는 것 이외에 나를 믿을 수 없는 절박한 상황을 말해 준다. 소설의 시작 부분에서 헨리는 그런 진술을 할 수 없었다. 신부 역시 헨리가 전선에 떠났을 때보다 지금은 "자신을 확신한다."(surer of himself)고 바뀌었다.

전쟁에 관해 헨리와 신부의 대화는 고통스러우면서도 전쟁터에서 군인과 종교인의 고뇌를 들여다볼 수 있는 장이다. 끔찍한 여름, 믿기지 않을 정도의 심각한 전쟁터라는 신부의 말을 통해서 전쟁의 실상을 말해 준다. 또한, 제대로 깨닫지 못했던 장교들이 이제는 알게 됐다는 대목은 더욱 그렇다. 젊은 장교가 전쟁에서 누구든 이길 수 있을 것이라는 젊은 패기가 전쟁이 계속 지속되다 보면 젊은 패기는 온데간데없고 이기고 지고의 관계없이 이제 전쟁이 끝났으면 하는 현실을 파악한 장교들의 현실 인식을 말해 준다. 소설이 시작되는 부분에서 헨리와 26장에서 헨리의 모습은 달라도 너무 다르다. 차라리 패배가 더 나을 수 있다는 말에서 헨리의 많은 변화를 찾아볼 수 있다. 즉 전쟁이 더 지속하면 우군이든 적군이든 희생자만 늘어나는 전쟁터의 현실 인식을 한 것이다. 더 이상 총에 의한 인간의 파괴를 볼 수 없다는 인식이다. 사람이 쉽게 변하지 않는다고 한다. 그렇지만 심각하고 충격적인 급격한 사건이나 상황을 경험하면 사람은 변화한다. 전쟁터에 있는 젊은이들과 그들을 후방에서 돕는 모든 이들과 심지어는 매춘부에 이르기까지 충격적이고 슬픈 현장이다. 그래서 전쟁에서 패배하더라도 빨리 끝나는 게 좋겠다는 헨리와 신부의 생각을 알 수 있다.

■ 26장 주요 작품 내용

"What about the war?"

"I think it will be over soon. I don't know why, but I feel it."

"How do you feel it?"

"You know how your major is? Gentle? Many people are like that now."

"I feel that way myself," I said.

"It has been a terrible summer," said the priest. He was surer of himself now than when I had gone away. "You cannot believe how it has been there and you know how it can be. Many people have realized the war this summer. Officers whom I thought could never realize it realize it now."(177-178)

"What will happen?" I stroked the blanket with my hand.

"I do not know but I do not think it can go on much longer."

"What will happen?"

"They will stop fighting."

"Who?"

"Both sides."

"I hope so," I said.

"You don't believe it?"

"I don't believe both sides will stop fighting at once."

"I suppose not. It is too much to expect. But when I see the changes in men I do not think it can go on."

"Who won the fighting this summer?"

"No one."

"The Austrians won," I said. "They kept them from taking San Gabriele. They've won. They won't stop fighting."

"If they feel as we feel they may stop. They have gone through the same thing."

"No one ever stopped when they were winning."(178)

"You discourage me."

"I can only say what I think."

"Then you think it will go on and on? Nothing will ever happen?"

"I don't know. I only think the Austrians will not stop when they have won victory. It is in defeat that we become Christian."

"The Austrians are Christians---- except for the Bosnians."

"I don't mean technically Christian. I mean like Our Lord."

He said nothing.

"We are all gentler now because we are beaten. How would Our Lord have been if Peter had rescued him in the Garden?"(178)

"Many of the soldiers have always felt this way. It is not because they were beaten."

"They were beaten to start with. They were beaten when they took them from their farms and put them in the army. That is why the peasant has wisdom, because he is defeated from the start. Put him in power and see how wise he is."

He did not say anything. He was thinking. "Now I am depressed myself," I said. "That is why I never think about these things. I never think and yet when I begin to talk I say the things I have found out in my mind without thinking."

"I had hoped for something."

"Defeat?"

"No, something more."

"There isn't anything more. Except victory. It may be worse."

"I hoped for a long time for victory."

"Me too."

"now I don't know."

"It has to be one or the other."

"I don't believe in victory any more."

"I don't. But I don't believe in defeat. Though it may be better."

"What do you believe in?"

"In sleep," I said. He stood up.(179)

27장(Chapter XXVII)

■ 27장 주요 내용

- 영광, 명예, 신성, 용기라는 추상적인 말은 강 이름과 같은 구체적인 말 옆에서 외설스럽다.
- 27장의 퇴각일지
  △ 전우(war brother)인 리날디와 서로 말도 못 하고 헨리는 전선으로 떠남.
  △ 코로아티아인(Croatins)의 공격 시작: 포격을 퍼붓고 로켓을 발사하고 기관총과 소총을 쏴댔다.

There was a bombardment and the Croatians came over across the mountain meadows and through patches of woods and into the front line. They fought in the dark in the rain and a counter-attack of scared men from the second line drove them back. There was much shelling and many rockets in the rain and machine -gun and rifle fire all along the line.(186)

  △ 북쪽 전선이 뚫렸다는 소식에 밤중에 퇴각 지시가 떨어짐

They did not attack that night but we heard that they had broken through to the north. In the night word came that we were to prepare to retreat.(186)

△ 바인시차(Bainsizza) 전선을 사수하라는 명령이 떨어짐

The Brigade had received orders that the line of the Bainsizza should be held no matter what happened.(187)

△ 오스트리아 군이 카포레토(Caporetto) 쪽에 있던 27군단(Twenty-seventh army corps)을 정복했다.

he said that he had heard at the Brigade that Austrians had broken through the twenty-seven army corps up toward Caporetto.(187)

△ 여단 사령부는 이 전선을 사수하라고 지시했다. 그렇지 않으면 우리가 고립된다.

"There are fifteen divisions of German," the medical officer said. "They have broken through and we will be cut off."
"At the Brigade, they say this line is to be held. They say they have not broken through badly and that we will hold a line across the mountains from Monte Maggiore."(187)

△ 다음 날 퇴각이 시작된다. (The next night the retreat starts)
△ 탈리아멘토 강(Tagliamento River) 너머의 포르테노네(Pordenome)로 퇴각.

"Where will they retreat to, Tenente?"

"Beyond the Tagliamento, they say. The hospital and the sector are to be at Pordenome."(193)

■ Summary

헨리가 지역을 순찰했다. 그날 밤 나중에 독일군과 오스트리아군은 공격하기 시작했고 이탈리아 부대에 포격을 가하기 시작했다. 그래서 결국 카포레토(Caporetto)근처에 있는 이탈리아 전선이 무너졌다. 이탈리아 군은 퇴각하기 시작했다. 그리고 앰블런스 운전병들은 탈리아멘토 강(Tagliamento River)너머의 포르테노네(Pordenome)로 떠날 준비를 하고 있었다.

■ 논평

이 소설에서 독일군의 등장은 전환점(a turning point)이 된다. 헨리는 우리에게 다음과 같이 말했다.

"독일군이라는 말만으로도 두려웠다. 독일군과는 절대로 엮이고 싶지 않았다."(187)

"The word Germans are something to be frightened of. We did not want to have anything to do with the Germans."(187)

헨리는 지노(Gino)라고 불리는 운전병에게 그는 전쟁은 산에서 싸워서 승리하는 것이라고 믿지 않았다고 말할 때 산과 평지라는 이분법이 전개된다. 여기서 평지는 부패한 장소지만 산은 순수한 장소일 뿐만 아니라 은신처(피난처)의 장소를 나타낸다. 이것은 이야기의 후반부에 중요해진다. 지노가 헨리에게 "우리가 올여름에 했던 일이 헛된 일이었을 리 없습니다."(184)라고 말했다. "What has been done this summer can not have been done in vain." 그는 싸움을 지칭했다. 그러나 그 말은 독자들에게 중의적인 의미가 있다. 즉 헨리와 캐서린이 여름에 나누었던 사랑에 적용되기도 했다. 긴 27강은 헨리의 인물과 소설의 주제를 말해준다.

"나는 신성이니 영광이니 희생이니 하는 말과 헛되다는 말을 들을 때마다 늘 곤혹스러웠다."(185)

헨리는 또 우리에게 다음과 같이 말했다.

나는 신성한 것은 아무것도 보지 못했고 영광스럽다고 하는 그것들에는 영광이 없었으며, 희생은 고깃덩어리를 땅속에 파묻는 그것 말고는 할 일이 없는 시카고 도축장에서 벌어지는 살육이나 다름없었다.(185)

"영광이니 명예니 용기니 신성이니 하는 추상적인 말들은 마을 이름이나 도로 번호 강 이름 연대번호 날짜 같은 구체적인 말 앞에서 외설스럽게 느껴졌다."(185)

I was always embarrassed by the words scared, glorious, and sacrifice and the expression in vain. We had heard them, sometimes standing in the rain almost out of earshot, so that only the shouted words came through, and had read them, on proclamations that were slapped up by billposters over other proclamations, now for a long time, and I had seen nothing sacred, and the things that were glorious had no glory and sacrifices were like the stockyards at Chicago if nothing was done with the meat except to bury it.(185)

There were many words that you could not stand to hear and finally only the names of places had dignity. Certain numbers were the same way and certain dates and these with the names of the places were all you could say and have them mean anything.

Abstract words such as glory, honor, courage, or hallow were obscene beside the concrete names of villages, the numbers of roads, the name of rivers, the numbers of regiments and the dates.(185)

작가는 전쟁터에서 벌어지는 젊은이들의 죽음이 헛된 것임을 말하고 있다. 조국을 위해서 싸우는 것은 개인의 영광이며 동시에 조국을 위한 위대한 희생이라고 정치인들이 전쟁과 전쟁에 참여한 사람들을 미화하지만, 사실 전쟁터에 있는 젊은이들은 그렇게 생각하지도 않고 현실이 그렇지도 못하다. 희생이란 거창한 말은 도축장에 죽은 고기를 땅속에 묻는 것과 같다. 즉 도축장에서처럼 전쟁터에서 젊은이들이 죽어서 그곳에서 묻히는 현장의 모습을 아주 신랄한 비판을 하고 있다. 헤밍웨이를 포함해서 그 당시의 작가들을 거트루드 스타인 여사는 "잃어버린 세대"(lost generation)라 말했지만, 그 젊은 작가들은 그럴 수밖에 없었던 시대적인 상황이었다. 전쟁에 참전하여 죽고 아무 곳이나 땅속에 묻고 그렇게 땅속에 묻히면 그나마 다행이고 땅속에 묻히지도 못하고 이국땅에서 죽은 채 버려진 젊은이들이 많다. 아니면 다치고 정신적으로 육체적으로 부실한 몸을 가지고 고국에 돌아온 그들의 정신이 온전한 것이 더 이상할 것이다. 그래서 기존의 제도 관습 가치관을 모두 무시하고 자신들이 경험한 것 이외에는 어느 것도 믿지 않는 세대의 특징을 말해준다. 젊은이들의 문제가 아니고 전쟁을 만든 기성세대 정치 지도자들의 잘못으로 젊은이들이 희생당한 것이다.

헨리가 작품 초반에 자신에게 사용해 왔던 단어를 헨리가 언급한 것은 지금은 자신의 실질적인 전쟁 경험의 결과로써 공허하게 들린다. 헤밍웨이는 이 작품에서 새로운 종류의 전쟁 이야기를 쓰고자 노력했다. 27장에서 자신의 노력을 분명히 했다. 이번 장에서 작가의 문체적인 신조(credo)를 분명히 드러냈다. 자신의 글쓰기 경력을 통해서 헤밍웨이는 추상적인 것보다 구체적인 것 모호한 것보다 구체적인 것을 항상 선호해 왔다. 구체적인 것에 대한 그의 극단적인 선호도는 그의 가장 위대한 문체의 유산으로 남았다. 헤밍웨이만의 고유한 문체의 특징으로 알려진 것은 복문이나 복잡한 문장보다 and 나 or로 이끄는 단문 아니면 제한된 중문을 상용한다. 더 중요한 것은 이 같은 표면적인 문자의 길이나 특징보다는 그 문장을 구성하는 단어, 특히 상황을 직접 잘 묘사하는 구체적인 단어가 더 큰 영향을 준다.

27장에서 계속해서 비가 왔다는 것에 주목해 보자.

이 장에서 분위기가 바뀌어서 오스트리아와 독일의 맹공격에 직면한 이탈리아 군은 퇴각했다. 저녁에 비가 눈으로 바뀌어서 공격이 멈출 것이라고 희망을 품어본다. 그러나 바로 눈이 녹고 다시 비가 내리기 시작했다. 운전병들이 저녁에 와인을 마시면서 이야기하는 동안 아이모 (Aymo)라고 불리는 운전병은 "하지만 내일은 빗물을 마시게 될지도 몰라."(191)라고 말했다. "To-morrow may we drink rainwater." Aymo said. 우리도 죽을지 모른다는 의미이다. 이때까지 헤밍웨이는 독자들이 불길한 예감의 진정한 느낌을 느낄 정도까지 비의 상징을 전개해 왔다.

■ 27장 주요 작품 내용

I woke when Rinaldi came in but he did not talk and I went back to sleep again. In the morning I was dressed and gone before it was light. Rinaldi did not wake when I left.(181)

"I don't suppose they are so effective," Gino said. "But they scare me, They all sound as though they came directly for you. There is the boom, then instantly the shriek and burst. What's the use of not being wounded if they scare you to death."(182)

"I myself have never had enough to eat but I am a big eater and I have not starved. The mess is average. The regiments in the line get pretty good food but those in support don't get so much. Something is wrong somewhere. There should be plenty of food."
"The dogfish are selling it somewhere else."(184)

"We won't talk about losing. There is enough talk about losing. What has been done this summer cannot have been done in vain."
I did not anything. I was always embarrassed by the words sacred, glorious, and sacrifice and the expression in vain. We had heard them, sometimes standing in the rain almost out of earshot, so that only the shouted words came through, and had read them, on proclamations that were slapped up by billposters over

other proclamations, now for a long time, and I had seen nothing sacred, and the things that were glorious had no glory and sacrifices were like the stockyards at Chicago if nothing was done with the meat except to bury it.(184-185)

There were many words that you could not stand to hear and finally only the names of places had dignity. Certain numbers were the same way and certain dates and these with the names of the places were all you could say and have them mean anything. Abstract words such as glory, honor, courage, or hallow were obscene beside the concrete names of villages, the numbers of roads, the name of rivers, the numbers of regiments and the dates.(185)

The wind rose in the night and at the three o'clock in the morning with the rain coming in sheets there was bombardment and the Croatians come over across the mountain meadows and through patches of woods and into the front line. They fought in the dark in the rain and a counter-attack of scared men from the second line drove them back. There was much shelling and many rockets in the rain and machine-gun and rifle fire all along the line. They did not come again and it was quieter and between the gusts of wind and rain we could hear the sound of a great bombardment far to the north.(186)

We heard that the attack to the south had been unsuccessful. The did not attack that night but we heard that they had broken through to the north. In the night word came that we were to prepare to retreat. The captain at the post told me this. He had it from the Brigade. A little while later he came from the telephone and said it was a lie. The Brigade had received orders that the line of the Bainsizza should be held no matter what happened. I asked about the break through and he said that he had heard at the Brigade that the Austrians had broken through the twenty-seventh army corps up toward Caporetto. There had been a great battle in the north all day.(186-187)

I went out then through the dinning-room and the hall and up the marble stairs to the room where I had lived with Rinaldi. It was raining outside. I went to the window and looked out. It was getting dark and I saw the three cars standing in line under the trees. The trees were dripping in the rain. It was cold and the drops hung to the branches. I went back to Rinaldi's bed and lay down and let sleep take me.

We ate in the kitchen before we started. Aymo had a basin of spaghetti with onions and tinned meat chopped up in it. We sat around the table and drank two bottles of the wine that had been left in the cellar of the villa. It was dark outside and still raining. Piani sat the table very sleepy.

"I like a retreat better than an advance," Bonello said. "on a retreat we drink barbera."

"We drink it now. To-morrow maybe we drink rainwater," Aymo said.(191)

28장 (Chapter XXVIII)

■ 28장 주요 내용

- 퇴각행렬에 대한 구체적인 묘사.

"다리에서 작업하느라 남아 있었답니다."
"They were left to do something to a bridge," Bonello said.
"자기들 부대를 찾지 못한다고 해서 태워줬습니다."(195)
"They an't find their unit so I gave them a ride."(195)

- 그들은 이탈리아 군의 두 공병(engineer sergeants)과 십 대 두 명의 여자.

■ Summary

앰블런스 운전병들은 적의 공격으로부터 퇴각(retreat)한다. 차량의 행렬과 짐마차 등의 합류와 비로 인한 길이 진흙탕이 되어서 매우 느리게 움직였다.

"다리에서 작업하느라 남아 있었답니다." 보넬로(Bonello)가 말했다. "자기들 부대를 찾지 못한다고 해서 태워 줬습니다."(195)

공사하다 부대를 찾지 못한 공병 두 명과 두 명의 소녀도 함께 태웠다.

그들은 이탈리아 군의 두 공병(engineer sergeants)과 십 대 두 명의 여자를 태웠다. 차에서 잠든 헨리는 캐서린을 꿈꾸었다. 결국 앰블런스는 주요 도로에서 벗어나 버려진 농가에서 멈추었다. 그리고 그곳에서 남아 있는 것이 없지만 겨우 먹을 것을 찾아서 아침을 먹었다.

■ 논평

카포레토(Caporetto)에서 퇴각하는 모습의 묘사를 통해서 작가는 구체적이며 명확한 것에 초점을 맞췄다. 예를 들면 빗속에서 우리 앞에 가던 짐마차에는 재봉틀이 실려 있었다.(198) 등과 같이 구체적으로 기술했다.

In the night many peasants had joined the column from the roads of the country and in the column there were carts loaded with household goods; there were mirrors projecting up between mattresses, and chickens and ducks tied to carts. There was a sewing machine on the cart ahead of us in the rain.(198)

서술적인 관점에서 엠블런스 운전병 중의 한 명이 태운 두 명의 이탈리아 공병은 앞으로 일어날 이야기 속에서 중심이 된다는 것을 입증할 것이다. 처음에는 악의 없는 것처럼 보인다. 28장이 끝나갈 무렵에서는 악의적인 면을 보이기 시작한다. 버려진 농가에서 다른 사람들과 아침을 같이 나눠 가지지 않을 때 대의명분에서 헨리 중위는 소외는 그가 이탈리아계 미국인(Italian American) 아니라는 두 공병의 잘못된 믿음에서 시작된다. 대신 헨리 중위는 독자들에게 캐서린과의 관계를 강력하게 연상시키는 북미 영어(North American English)로 묘사되었다.

실제로 헤밍웨이가 주기적으로 조이스 적 기법(Joycean) 의식의 흐름 재현뿐만 아니라 이 소설 사랑의 관점을 상기시키는 것으로 헨리는 캐서린을 생각하고 꿈을 꾼다. 이 같은 기법은 『노인과 바다』에서 노인이 잠을 잘 때 또는 바다에서 고기와 사투를 벌일 때 사자의 꿈을 꾸는 것과 같은 기법이라 할 수 있다.

헨리는 헤밍웨이의 사랑, 섹스, 전쟁, 죽음(love-sex-war-death) 연속체를 미묘하게 상기시키면서 독자에게 "이런 퇴각행렬은 처녀애들이 있을 곳이 못 된다."(197) 라고 말한다. 특별히 성적인 경험이 없는 사람은 전쟁 기간에 매우 취약하다는 것을 작가는 우리에게 말한다. 물론 이 장의 중간에 헨리가 독자들에게 상기시킨 것처럼 모든 사람이 전쟁 기간에는 취약하다. 그렇지만 젊은 여자의 등장은 작가가 더 강조한 점으로 짐작된다. 날씨가 맑으면 천천히 움직이는 차량 행렬은 적군의 비행기 포탄에 의해서 치명적으로 보호받을 수 없다. 밀라노에 있는 안전하고 보안이 보장된 미국병원에서 삶과 죽음(life and death) 즉 생사가 걸린 상황으로 우리는 이송되었다.

■ 퇴각행렬 및 28장 주요 내용

There are many trucks too and some carts going through on other streets and converging on the main road. when we were out past the tanneries onto the main road the troops, the motor trucks, the horse-drawn carts and the guns were in one wide slow-moving column. We moved slowly but steadily in the rain, the radiator cap of our almost against the tailboard of a truck that was loaded high, the load covered with wet canvas.(194)

비가 계속 오는 중에 퇴각행렬이 움직이다 멈추기를 반복했다. 공병병장(two sergeants engineers) 둘과 두 여자아이를 태웠다.

Piani was asleep over the wheel. I climbed up beside him and went to sleep too. Several hours later I heard the truck ahead of us grinding into gear. I woke Piani and we started, moving few yards, then stopping, then going on again. It was still raining.

The column stalled again in the night and did not start. I got down and went back to see Aymo and Bonello. Bonello had two sergeants of engineers on the seat of his car with him. They stiffened when I came up.

"They were left to do something to a bridge" Bonello said. "They can't find their unit so I gave them a ride."

"With the Sir Lieutenant's permission."

"With permission," I said.

"The lieutenant is an American," Bonello said. "He'll give anybody a ride."

One of the sergeants smiled. The other asked Bonello if I was an Italian from North or South America.

"He's not an Italian. He's North American English."

The sergeants were polite but did not believe it. I left them and went back to Aymo. He had two girls on the seat with him and was sitting back in the corner and smoking.(195)

"Barto, Barto," I said. He laughed.

"Talk to them, Tenente," he said. "I can't understand them. Hey!" He put his hand on the girl's thigh and squeezed it in a friendly way. The girl drew her shawl tight around her and pushed his hand away. "Hey!" he said. "Tell the Tenente your name and what you're doing here."

The girl looked at me fiercely. The other girl kept her eyes down. The girl who looked at me said something in a dialect I could not understand a word of. She was plump and dark and looked about sixteen.

"Sorella?" I asked and pointed at the other girl.

She nodded her hand smiled.

"All right," I said and patted her knee. I felt her stiffen away when I touched her. The sister never looked up. She looked perhaps a year younger. Aymo put his hand on the elder girl's thigh and she pushed it away. He laughed at her.

"Good man," he pointed at himself. "Good man," he pointed at me. "Don't you worry." The girl looked at him fiercely. The pair of them were like two wild birds.(195-196)

"I guess I scared her," Aymo said. "I didn't mean to scare her."

Bartolomeo brought out his knapsack and cut off tow pieces of cheese. "Here," he said. "Stop crying."

The older girl shook her head and still cried, but the younger girl took the cheese and commenced to eat. After a while the younger girl gave her sister the second piece of cheese and they both ate. The older sister still sobbed a little.

"She'll be all right after a while," Aymo said.

An idea came to me. "Virgin?" he asked the girl next to him. She nodded her head vigorously. "Virgin too?" he pointed to the sister. Both the girls nodded their heads and elder said something in dialect.

"That's all right," Bartolomeo said. "That's all right."

Both the girls seemed cheered.(196)

I left them sitting together with Aymo sitting back in the corner and went back to Piani's car. The column of vehicles did not move but the troops kept passing alongside. It was still raining hard and I thought some of the stops in the movement of the column might be from cars with wet wiring. More likely they were from horses or men going to sleep. Still traffic could tie up in cities when every one was awake. It was combination of horse and motor vehicles. They did not help each other any. The peasants' carts did not help much either. Those were a couple of fine girls with Barto.(197)

A retreat was no place for two virgins. Real virgins. Probably very religious. If there were no war we would probably all be in bed. In bed I lay me down my head. Bed and board. Stiff as a board in bed. Catherine was in bed now between two sheets, over her and under her. Which side did she sleep on? Maybe she wasn't asleep. Maybe she was lying thinking about me. Blow, blow, ye western wind. Well, it blew and it wasn't the small rain but the big rain down that rain. It rained all night. You knew it rained down that rained. Look at it. Christ, that **my love were in my arms** and I in my bed again. That my love Catherine. That my sweet love Catherine down might rain. Blow her again to me. Well, we were in it. Every one was caught in it and the small rain would not quiet it. "Good night, Catherine," I said out loud. "I hope you sleep well." Good night Catherine, "I said out loud. If it's too uncomfortable, darling, lie on the other side," I said. "I'll get you some cold water. In a little while it will be morning and then it won't be so bad. I'm sorry he makes you so uncomfortable. Try and go to sleep, sweet."

I was asleep all the time, she said. "You've been talking in your sleep. Are you all right?"

Are you really there?

Of course I'm here. I wouln't go away. This doesn't make any difference between us.

You're lovely and sweet. You wouldn't go away in the night, would you?

Of course I wouldn't go away. I'm always here. I come whenever you want me.(197-198)

『A Farewell to Arms』제목에서 arms에 대한 여러 가지 해석이 가능하다. 위에서처럼 '내 사랑을 나의 품에 안고'라고 말할 수 있다. 대부분 무기라고 보지만 굳이 다른 쪽으로 본다면 나의 품으로 생각할 수 있다. 왜냐하면 결국에는 캐서린은 아이를 낳다가 죽게 되고 헨리는 그 아이와 캐서린과 작별을 하게 된다. 어떤 의미에서는 나의 사랑(품)과의 이별이라고 볼 수도 있다.

전진하는 속도로 봐서는 우디네(Udine)에 도착하려면 간선도로(Main road)를 벗어나 들판을 가로질러 가야 할 것 같다.

I knew we were going to have to get off that main road some way and go across country if we were hoped to reach Udine.(198)

밤에 많은 농부가 행렬에 합류해서 더욱 늦어졌다. 도로가 막혀서 트럭을 버리고 도망가거나 아니면 말 몇 마리만 길에서 죽어도 도로는 완전히 마비될 상황.

In the night many peasants had joined the column from the road of the country and in the column there were carts loaded with household goods; there were mirrors projecting up between mattresses, and chickens and ducks tied to carts. There was a sewing machine on the cart ahead of us in the rain.(198)

부대 이탈과 탈영을 하게 되는 원인이 되는 매우 중요한 장면 북쪽으로 뻗은 작은 길을 보고 샛길로 빠지라고 했다.

I got down from the car and worked up the road a way, looking for a place where I could see ahead to find a side-road we could take across country. I knew there were many side-roads but did not want one that would lead to nothing. I could not remember them because we had always passed them bowling along in the car on the main road and they all looked much alike. Now I knew we must find one if we hoped to get through. No one knew where the Austrians were nor how things were going but I was certain that if the rain should stop and planes come over and get to work on that column that it would be all over. All that was needed was for a few men to leave their trucks or a few horses be killed to tie up completely the movement on the road.(198-199)

29장 (Chapter XXIX)

■ 29장 주요 내용

- 공병 두 명이 탈출하는 것에 총을 쏴서 한 명을 죽였다.

Then they started off down the road without a word. I went after them. "Come on," I said. "Cut some brush." "We have to go," one said. "Get busy," I said, "and cut brush."(203)

I shot three times and dropped one.(204)

■ Summary

앰블런스 차량 중 한 대가 진흙에 빠져서 움직이지 못할 때 두 명의 공병은 차량을 꺼내는 일을 도와주는 것을 거부했다. 대신 그들 스스로 탈출하려고 노력했고 도망치기 시작했다. 그러더니 말도 없이 길 아래쪽으로 내려가기 시작했다. 나는 그들을 뒤따라갔다.

"이봐." 내가 말했다. "나뭇가지를 꺾어와."
"우리는 가야 합니다." 한 병장이 말했다.
"어서." 내가 말했다. "나뭇가지를 꺾어와."
"우리는 가야 합니다." 한 병장이 말했다.(203-204)

나는 권총집을 열고 권총을 꺼내, 말수가 없는 놈을 겨누었다. 발사했다. (204) 나는 세 발을 쏴서 한 명을 쓰러뜨렸다. (204) 헨리는 그들에게 멈추라고 명령했다. 그런데도 계속 이탈할 때 총을 쏴 한 명을 쓰러뜨렸다.

그때 보넬로가 다가와서 "제가 끝내게 해 주십시오." 그가 말했다. "Let me go to finish him." he said. (204) 그가 그 일을 끝냈다. 그들은 더 차량으로 이동할 수 없다는 것을 알고 차를 버리고 걸어서 출발했다.

■ 논평

29장은 헨리 중위가 탈영하는 이탈리아 공병을 저격하는 이야기에서 가장 극적이고 중요한 전환점 중 하나를 보여 준다. 전쟁소설에서 캐서린과 휴가 마지막 날 구매한 권총으로 주동 인물이 총을 쏜 것이 처음 일이다. 그런데도 그는 적보다는 자신의 편에 있는 사람에게 총을 발사했다. 헨리 자신이 탈주로 인해서 총살당할 직전에 이 같은 아이러니가 다음 장에서 더 강화된다. 전선의 규율은 거친 후퇴로 대체되었고 이제 상황은 완전히 무질서에 가깝습니다. 헤밍웨이는 이번 전쟁은 신화나 전설의 전쟁 차이점을 강조했다. 앰블런스 운전병 피아니가 (Piani) "우리가 처음으로 만난 건 아마도 기병일 겁니다." "The first thing we will see will be the cavalry," Piani said. (207)라고 말했다. 이때 헨리는 "적군에게는 기병이 없을 텐데." "I don't think they've got any cavalry."(207)라고 답했다.

이 소설의 첫 번째 장에서 도입된 진흙(진창)(mud)이 여기에서는 일종의 반동 인물(antagonist)로 되살아난다는 점을 특별히 주목해야 한다. 헨리와 운전병들은 차를 가지고 후퇴하려고 하지만 날씨로 인해 도로가 진흙투성이가 되어서 결국에는 다른 길을 찾아 떠나게 된다. 이에 따라서 근무지 이탈이 되고 헨리는 자신이 탈영병이 되게 된다. 총살을 받게 되는 상황에 부닥치게 된다. 소설에서 진흙이 반동 인물인 경우는 그렇게 흔치 않은 경우이다. 본인의 의지와는 상관없이 근무지를 벗어나게 된 상황 그런 상황의 원인이 날씨에 의한 진흙탕으로 변한 도로는 인간이 어쩔 수 없는 경우이다. 그러나 헨리는 주어진 상황에서도 최선을 다해서 자신을 방어하고 설명하려고 노력하지만, 도저히 설득이 안 되는 극한의 상황을 맞이하게 되고 어쩔 수 없이 부대를 이탈하는 선택을 하게 된다. 등장인물 한 명도 등장시키지 않고 작가는 주인공이 곤경에 빠지게 하는 아주 효과적인 수단을 찾아서 주인공은 한쪽으로 효과적으로 몰아가고 있다. 탈영한 장교를 죽음으로 몰고 오게 되는 것은 엠블런스가 진흙과 사람과 마차들의 집중으로 인해서 움직일 수 없는 것이 원인이 된다. 이 같은 이야기는 옛날의 영웅담이 없다 하더라도 매우 흥미롭다. 적군의 비행기가 퇴각행렬들이 이동하는 도로에 폭탄을 머리 위에 투하한다고 우리에게 말함으로써 작가는 다음 장에서 긴장을 고조시킨다. 헨리는 멀리서 발포하는 소리가 들린다는 생각을 말했다.

■ 29장 주요 작품 내용

At noon we were stuck in muddy road about, as nearly as we could figure, ten kilometres from Udine. The rain had stopped during the forenoon and three times we had heard planes coming, seen them pass overhead, watched them go far to the left and heard them bombing on the main highroad. We had worked through a network of secondary roads and had take many roads that were blind, but had always, by backing up and finding another road, gotten closer to Udine.

Now, Aymo's car, in backing so that we might get out of a blind road had gotten into the soft earth at the side and the wheels, spinning, had dug deeper and deeper until the car rested on it differential. The thing to do now was to dig out in front of the wheels put in brush so that the chains could drip, and then push until the car was on the road. We were all down on the road around the car.

The two sergeants looked at the car and examined the wheels. Then they started off down the road without a word. I went after them. "Come on," I said. "Cut some brush." "We have to go," one said.(203)

"Get busy," I said, "and cut brush."

"We have to go," one said. The other said nothing. They were in a hurry to start. They would not look at me. "I order you to come back to the car and cut brush," I said. The one sergeant turned. "We have to go on. In a little while you will be cut off. You can't order us. You're not our officer."(204)

"I order you to cut brush," I said. They turned and started down the road.

"Halt," I said. They kept on down the muddy road, the hedge on either side. "I order you to halt," I called. They went a little faster. I opened up my holster, took the pistol, aimed at the one who had talked the most, and fired. I missed and they both started to run. I shot three times and dropped one. The other went through the hedge and was out of sight. I fired at him through the hedge as he ran across the field. The pistol clicked empty and I put in another clip. I saw it was too far to shoot at the second sergeant. He was far across the field, running, his head held low. I commenced to reload the empty clip. Bonello came up.

"Let me go finish him," he said. I handed him the pistol and he walked down to where the sergeant of engineers lay face down across the road. Bonello leaned over, put the pistol against the man's head and pulled the trigger. The pistol did not fire.

"You have to cock it," I said. He cocked it and fired twice. He took hold of the sergeant's legs and pulled him to the side of the road so he lay beside the hedge. He came back and handed me the pistol.(204)

"What do you say, Tenente?" Bonello asked. "We'll dig out and try once more with the brush," I said. I looked down the road. It was my fault. I had led them up here. The sun was almost out from behind the clouds and the body of the sergeant lay beside the hedge.

"We'll put his coat and cape under," I said. Bonello went to get them. I cut brush and Aymo and Piani dug out in front and between the wheels. I cut the cape, then

3부(Book Three)

ripped it in two, and laid it under the wheel in the mud, then pile brush for the wheels to catch. We were ready to start and Aymo got up on the seat and started the car. he wheels spun and we pushed and pushed. But it wasn't any use.(205)

"Come on," I said. "Get in," The two girls climbed in and sat in the corner. They seemed to have taken no notice of the shooting. I looked back up the road. The sergeant lay in his dirty long-sleeved underwear. I got up with Piani and we started. We were going to try to cross the field. When the road entered the field I got down and walked ahead. If we could get across, there was a road on the other side. We could not get across. It was too soft and muddy for the cars. When they were finally and completely stalled, the wheels dug in to the hubs, we left them in the field and started on foot for Udine.(206)

"You certainly shot that sergeant, Tenente," Piani said. We were walking fast. "I killed him," Bonello said. "I never killed anybody in this war, and all my life I've wanted to kill a sergeant."

"You killed him on the sit all right," Piani said. "He wasn't flying very fast when you killed him."

"Never mind. That's one thing I can always remember. I killed that----- of a sergeant."(207)

30장 (Chapter XXX)

■ 30장 주요 내용

- 단독강화(Separate Peace) 실행.

■ Summary

우디네(Udine)로 걷고 있을 때 헨리, 엠블런스 운전병, 아이모(Aymo), 보넬로(Bonello), 피아니(Piani)는 독일군을 발견했다. 아이모는 총을 맞아 죽었다. 아마도 독일군이 아니라 이탈리아 군의 실수로 쏜 총에 맞아 죽은 것 같다. 보넬로는 독일군에게 항복하기 위해 도망쳤다. 드디어 탈리아멘토 강(Tagliamento River)을 건넜는데 헨리는 부대를 이탈했다는 이유로 헌병들에 의해서 이탈리아 장교들이 사살되는 것을 목격했다. 그는 독일 정보원(spy)으로 몰릴지 걱정이 되었다. 그래서 그는 강으로 뛰어들어서 결국 이탈리아 부대를 버리고 강으로 뛰어 들어간다.

I ducked down, pushed between two men, and ran for the river, my head down. I tripped at the edge and went in with a splash. The water was very cold and I stay under as long as I could.(225)

■ 논평

  이 장은 모든 행동이 어떤 의미에서는 내리막인 반환점이 없는 소설의 클라이맥스 역할을 한다. 먼저 우리는 이탈리아 군인들이 탈영하고 있었기 때문에 그들의 상관(헨리 중위)이 쏜 총을 맞은 것을 보았다. 여기서 아이모는 두려움과 무능함으로 동료들이 쏜 총에 맞아 죽는다. 30장이 끝날 무렵 이탈리아 군인들이 장교라는 이유만으로 이탈리아 군인들은 다른 이탈리아 군인들을 무작위로 쏘고 있다. 혼란 속으로 빠져든다.

  그래서 헤밍웨이는 소설 초반에 영국 간호사가 이탈리아 군대에 간 것을 보고 어리둥절하게 하는 장면에서부터 지금, 이 순간을 준비해 왔기 때문에 헨리 중위의 탈영 결정에 의문을 품지 않는다. 그가 보넬로에게 말했듯이 "우리는 독일인보다 이탈리아인들로부터 더 위험에 처해있습니다." "We are in more danger from Italians than Germans," I said(214) 사실 30장의 마지막 부분에서 그가 도망치지 않는다면 헨리는 이탈리아 헌병대에 의해서 처형될 것이 확실합니다. 그는 선택의 여지가 없습니다.

  또한, 헨리의 충성심은 이탈리아 군대 전체에 대한 것이 아니고 오히려 그와 함께 살고 일한 사람들에 대한 것이었다. 앰블런스 그룹이 해체된 후 결국 그는 추상적인 대의를 위해 계속할 의무가 없다고 생각합니다. 단독강화(separate peace)를 선언하는 주제를 주목해 보자. 총을 버림으로써 전쟁을 끝낼 수 있다고 생각하는 이탈리아 병사들에 의해 언어화된 것처럼 그것은 순진하고 어리석게 들린다. 소설이 끝날 때쯤이면 그렇게 될 것이다.

  또한, 다음과 같은 단어에 대한 헌병의 의존도를 주목해 보자.

"신성한 토양"(sacred soil)과 "승리의 열매"(fruits of victory)와 같은 헨리가 몇 장 전에 언급했지만 신뢰하지 않는 추상적인 단어들을 생각해 보자. 총살을 앞둔 중령이 "후퇴를 해본 적이 있습니까?"라고 묻습니다.("Have you ever been in a retreat?"(223) 후퇴(retreat)는 구체적이고 구체적입니다. 그것은 진짜입니다. 헌병에 의해서 사용된 고상한 용어들은 헨리가 소설의 과정에서 얻은 그런 종류의 경험을 갖지 못했다는 증거입니다. 실제 전선에서 싸워 보지도 싸움의 현장에서 어려움을 겪어 보지도 못한 헌병들이 그런 질문을 하는 것 자체가 모순이고 부조리한 현장을 말해 준다. 목숨을 걸고 부상병들을 치료하기 위해서 적들의 포탄이 날아오는 전장에서 운전하다가 명령에 따라 후퇴한 군인들을 아무 일도 하지 않고 후방에서 이들에게 후퇴니, 뭐니 하면서 총살을 명한다는 사실이 너무 부조리한 현장이 아닐 수 없고 헤밍웨이는 너무 기가 막혀서 작품을 통해서 전쟁 속에서 부조리한 현장을 고발하고 있다. 적군과 대치하고 있는 군인이 살기 위해서 후퇴하는 것이 아니고 더더욱이 개인 혼자서 후퇴한 것이 아닌 이상 이 들을 따뜻하게 맞이하고 다시 적군들과 싸울 힘을 불어넣어 줘야 하는 상황에 그렇지 못한 헨리는 탈출을 선택한다. 무기와의 결별을 선택한다. 자원해서 입대한 자신이 자원해서 그곳에서 탈출하게 된다. 어찌 보면 헨리는 어쩔 수 없이 타인에 의한 단독강화를 선택한 것이다. 앞서 말한 것처럼 오히려 독일인보다 이탈리아인에 의해서 더 위험에 처한 상황이라니 헨리는 너무도 절체절명의 위기에서 자신을 강에 던진다. 자신이 군대에 자원입대해서 적과 싸움에 동참하면 자신이 원하는 어떤 것을 얻을 것으로 믿고 생각하고 자원한 군대에서 오히려 자기 생각과는 정 다른 방향으로 진행되는 상황에 부닥친 헨리는 무기와의 결별은 자기 생각이 잘못되었다는 자성 어린 행동으로 봐야 한다.

■ 30장 주요 작품 내용

Later we were on a road that led to a river. There was a long line of abandoned trucks and carts on the road leading up to the bridge. No one was in sight. The river was high and the bridge had been blown up in the centre; the stone arch was fallen into the river and the brown waster was going over it. We went on up the bank looking for a place to cross. Up ahead I knew there was a railway bridge and I thought we might be able to get across there. The path was wet and muddy. We did not see any troops; only abandoned trucks and stores. Along the river bank there was nothing and no one but the wet brush and muddy ground. We went up to the bank and finally we saw the railway bridge.

"What a beautiful bridge," Aymo said. It was a long plain iron bridge across what was usually a dry river-bed.

"We'd better hurry and get across before they blow it up," I said.

"There is nobody to blow it up," Piani said. "They're all gone."

"It's probably mined," Bonello said. "You cross first, Tenente."

"Listen to the anarchist," Aymo said. "Make him go first."(209)

"I'll go," I said. "It wouldn't be mined to blow up with one man."

"You see," Piani said. "That is brains. Why haven't you brains, anarchist?"

"If I had brains I wouldn't be here," Bonello said.

"That's pretty good, Tenente," Aymo said.

"That's pretty good," I said. We were close to the bridge now. The sky had clouded over again and it was raining a little. The bridge looked long and solid. We climbed up the embankment.

"Come on at a time," I said and started across the bridge. I watched the ties and the rails for any trip-wires or signs of explosive but I saw nothing. Down below the gaps in the ties the river ran muddy and fast. Ahead across the wet countryside I could see Udine in the rain. Across the bridge I looked back. Just up the river was another bridge. As I watched, a yellow mud-colored motor car crossed it. The sides of the bridge were high and the body of the car, once on, was out of sight. But I saw heads of the driver, the man on the seat with him, and the two men on the rear seat. They all wore German helmets. The the car was over the bridge and out of sight behind the trees and the abandoned vehicles on the road. I waved to Aymo who was crossing and to the others to come on. I climbed down and crouched beside the railway embankment. Aymo came down with me.

"Did you see the car?" I asked.

"No. We were watching you."

"A German staff car crossed on the upper bridge."

"A staff car?"

"Yes."

"Holy Mary."

The others came and we all crouched in the mud behind the embankment, looking across the rails at the bridge, the line of trees, the ditch and the road.

"Do you think we're cut off then, Tenente?"(210)

"I don't know. All I know is German staff car went along that road."

"You don't feel funny, Tenente? You haven't got strange feelings in the head?"

"Don't be funny, Bonello."

"What about a drink?" Piani asked. "If we're cut off we might as well have a drink." He unhooked his canteen and uncorked it.

"Look! Look!" Aymo said and pointed toward the road. Along the top of the stone bridge we could see German helmets moving. They were bent forward and moved smoothly , almost supernaturally, along. As they came off the bridge we saw them. They were bicycle troops. I saw the faces of the first two. They were ruddy and healthy looking. Their helmets came low down over their foreheads and the side of their faces. Their carbines were clipped to the frame of the bicycles. Stick bombs hung handle down from their belts. Their helmets and their gay uniforms were wet and they road easily, looking ahead and to both sides. There were two-- then four in line, then two, then almost a dozen; then another dozen- then one alone. They did not talk but we could not have heard them because of the noise from the river. They were gone out of sight up the road.

"Holy Mary," Aymo said.

"They were Germans," Piani said. Those weren't Austrians.

"Why isn't there somebody here to stop them?" I said. "Why haven't they blown the bridge up?" "Why aren't there machine-guns along this embankment?"

"You tell us, Tenete," Bonello said.

I was very angry.

"The whole bloody thing is crazy. Down below they blow up a little bridge. Here they leave a bridge on the main road. Where is everybody? Don't they try and stop them at all?"

"You tell us, Tenente," Bonello said. I shut up.(211)

It was none of my business; all I had to do was to get to Pordenone with three ambulances. I had failed at that. All I had to do now was get to Pordenone. I probably could not even get to Udine. The hell I couldn't. The thing to do was to be calm and not get shot or captured.

"Didn't you have a canteen open?" I asked Piani. He handed it to me. I took a long drink. "we might as well start," I said. "There's no hurry though. Do you want to eat something?"

"This is no place to stay," Bonello said.

"All right. We'll start."

"Should we keep on this side- out of sight?"

"We'd be better off on top. They may come along this bridge too. We don't want them on top of us before we see them."

We walked along the railroad track. On both sides of us stretched the wet plain. Ahead across the plain was the hill of Udine. The roofs fell away from the castle on the hill. We could see campanile and the clock-tower. There were many mulberry trees in the fields. Ahead I saw a place where the rails were torn up. The ties had been dug out too and thrown down the embankment.

"Down! down!" Aymo said. We dropped down beside the embankment. There was another group of bicyclists passing along the road. I looked over the edge and saw them go on.

"They saw us but they went on," Aymo said.

"We'll get killed up there. Tenente," Bonello said.

"They don't want us," I said. "They're after something else."

"We're in more danger if they should come on us suddenly."

"I'd rather walk here out of sight," Bonello said.

"All right. We'll walk along the tracks."

"Do you think we can get through?" Aymo said.

"Sure. There aren't very much of them yet. We'll go through in the dark."

"What was that staff car doing?"

"Christ knows," I said. We kept on up the tracks.(212)

Bonello tired of walking in the mud of the embankment and came up with the rest of us. The railway moved south away from highway now and we could not see what passed along the road. A short bridge over a canal was blown up but we climbed across on what was left of the span. We heard firing ahead of us.(212-213)

We came up on the railway beyond the canal. It went on straight toward the town across the low fields. We could see the line of the other railway ahead of us. To the north was the main road where we head seen the cyclists; to the north there was a small branch-road across the fields with thick trees on each side. I thought we had better cut to the south and work around the town that way and across country toward Campoformio and the main road to the Tagliamento. We could avoid the main line of the retreat by keeping to the secondary roads beyond Udine. I knew there were plenty of side-roads across the plain. I started down the embankment.

"Go on back," I shouted. I started up the embankment, slipping in the mud. The drivers were ahead of me. I went up the embankment as fast as I could go. Two more shots came from the thick brush and Aymo, as he was crossing the tracks, lurched, tripped and fell face down. We pulled him down on the other side and turned him over. "His head ought to be uphill," I said. Piani moved him around. He lay in the mud on the other side of the embankment, his feet pointing downhill, breathing blood irregularly. The three of us squatted over him in the rain. He was hit low in the back of the neck and the bullet had ranged upward and come out under the right eye. He died while I was stopping up the two holes. Piani laid his head down, wiped at his face, with a piece of emergency dressing, then let it alone.(213)

"They weren't German," I said. "There can't be any Germans over there." "Italians," Piani said, using the word as an epithet, "Italiani!" Bonello said nothing. He was sitting beside Aymo, not looking at him. Piani picked up Aymo's cap where it had rolled down the embankment and put it over his face. He took out his canteen. "Do you want to a drink?" Piani handed Bonello the canteen. "No," Bonello said. He turned to me. "That might have happened to us any time on the railway tracks."

"No," I said. "It was because we started across the field."

Bonello shook his head. "Aymo's dead," he said. "Who is dead next, Tenente? Where do we go now?"

"Those were Italians that shot," I said. "They weren't Germans."

"I suppose if they were Germans they'd have killed all of us," Bonello said. "We are in more danger from Italians than Germans," I said. "The rear guard are afraid of everything. The Germans know what they're after."(214)

"Let's go then," Bonello said. We went down the north side of embankment. I looked back. Aymo lay in the mud with the angle of the embankment. He was quite small and his arms were by his side, his puttee-wrapped legs and muddy boots together, his cap over his face. He looked very dead. It was raining. I had liked him as well as any one I ever knew. I had his papers in my pocket and would write to his family.(214)

Last night on the retreat we had heard that there had been many Germans in Italian uniforms mixing with the retreat in the north. I did not believe it. That was one of those things you always heard in the war. It was one of the things the enemy always did to you. You did not know any one who went over in German uniform to confuse them. Maybe they did but it sound difficult. I did not believe the Germans did it. I did not believe they had to. There was no need to confuse our retreat.(216)

That was a very strange night. I do not know what I had expected, death perhaps and shooting in the dark and running, but nothing happened. We waited, lying flat beyond the ditch along the main road while a German battalion passed, then when they were gone we crossed the road and went on to the north. We were very close to Germans twice in the rain but they did not see us. We got past the town to the north without seeing any Italians, then after a while came on the main channels of the retreat and walked all night toward the Tagliamento. I had not realized how gigantic the retreat was. The whole country was moving, as well as the army. We walked all night, making better time than the vehicles My leg ached and I was tired but we made good time. It seemed so silly for Bonello to have decided to be taken prisoner. There was no danger. We had walked through two armies without incident. If Aymo had not been killed there would never have seemed to be any danger. No one had bothered us when we were in plain sight along the railway. The killing came suddenly and unreasonably. I wondered where Bonello was.(218)

We were almost across. At the far end of the bridge there were officers and carabinieri standing on both sides flashing lights. I saw them silhouetted against the sky-line. As we came close to them I saw one of the officers point to a man in the column. A carabiniere went in after him and came out holding the man by the arm. He took him away from the road. We came almost opposite them. The officers were scrutinizing every one in the column, sometime speaking to each other, going forward to flash a light in some one's face. They took some one else out just before we came opposite. I saw the man. He was a lieutenant-colonel. I saw the stars in the box on his sleeve as they flashed a light on him. His hair was gray and he was short and fat. The carabiniere pulled him in behind the line of officers.(221-222)

"Don't you know you can touch an officer?"

The other one grabbed me from behind and pulled my arm up so that it twisted in the socket. I turned with him and the other one grabbed me around the neck. I kicked his shins and got my left knee into his groin.

"Shoot him if he resists," I heard some one say.

"What's the meaning of this?" I tried to shout but my voice was not very loud. They had me at the side of the road now.

"Shoot him if he resist," an officer said. "Take him over back."

"Who are you?"

"You'll find out."

"Who are you?"

"Battle police," another officer said.

"Why don't you ask me to step over instead of having one of these airplane grab me?"

They did not answer. They did not have to answer. They were battle police.

"Take him back there with the others," the first officer said. "You see. He speaks Italian with an accent."(222)

"So do you, you＿＿＿," I said.

"Take him back with the others," the first officer said. They took me down behind the line of officers below the road toward a group of people in a field by the river bank. As we walked toward them shot were fired. I saw flashes of the rifles and heard the reports. We came up to the group. There were four officers standing together, with a man in front of them with a carabiniere on each side of him. A group of men were standing guarded by carabinieri. Four other carabinieri stood near the questioning officers, leaning on their carbines. They were wide-hatted carabinieri. The two who had me shoved me in with the group waiting to be questioned. I looked at the man the officers were questioning. He was the fat gray -haired little lieutenant-colonel they had taken out of the column. The questioners had all the efficiency, coldness and command of themselves of Italians who are firing and are not being fired on.

"Your brigade?"

He told them.

"Regiment?"

He told them.

"Why are you not with your regiment?"

He told them.

"Do you not know that an officer should be with his troops?"

He did.

That was all. Another officer spoke.

"It is you and such as you that have let the barbarians onto the sacred soil of the fatherland."

"I beg your pardon," said the lieutenant-colonel.

"It is because of treachery such as yours that we have lost the fruits of victory."

"Have you ever been in a retreat?" the lieutenant-colonel asked. "Italy should never retreat."(223)

We stood there in the rain and listened to this. We were facing the officers and the prisoner stood in front and a little to one side of us.

"If you are going to shoot me," the lieutenant-colonel said, "please shoot me at once without further questioning. The questioning is stupid." He made the sign of the cross. The officers spoke together. One wrote something on a pad of paper.

"Abandoned his troops, ordered to be shot," he said.

Two carabinieri took the lieutenant-colonel to the river bank. He walked in the rain, an old man with his hat off, a carabinieri on either side. I did not watch them shoot him but I heard the shots. They were questioning some one else. This officer too was separated from his troops. He was not allowed to make an explanation. He cried when they read the sentence from the pad of paper, and they were questioning another when they shot him. They made a point of being intent on questioning the next man while the man who had been questioned before was being shot. In this way there was obviously nothing they could do about it. I did not know whether I should wit to be questioned or make a break now. I was obviously a German in Italian uniform. I saw how their mind worked; if they had minds and if they worked. They were all young men and they were saving their country. The second army was being re-formed beyond the Tagliamento. They were executing officers of the rank of major and above who were separated from their troops. They were also dealing summarily with German agitators in Italian uniform. They were steel helmets. Only two of us had steel helmets. Some of carabinieri had them. The other carabinieri wore wide hat. Airplanes we called them. We stood in the rain and were taken out one at a time to be questioned and shot. So far they had shot every one they had questioned. The questioners had that beautiful detachment and devotion to stern justice of men dealing in death without being in any danger of it. They were questioning a full colonel of a line regiment. Three more officers had just been put in with us.(224-225)

"Where was his regiment?"

I look at the carabinieri. They were looking at the newcomers. The others were looking at the colonel. I ducked down, pushed between two men, and ran for the river. my head down. I tripped at the edge and went in with a splash. The water was very cold and I stay under as long as I could. I could feel the current swirl me and I stay under until I thought I could never come up. The minute I came up I took a breath and went down again. It was easy to stay under with so much clothing and my boots. When I came up the second time I saw a piece of timber ahead of me and reached it and held on with one hand. I kept my head behind it and did not even look over it. I did not want see the bank. There were shots when I ran and shots when I came up the first time. I heard them when I was almost above water. There were no shots now. The piece of timber swung in the current and I held it with one hand. I look at the bank. It seemed to be going by very fast. There was much wood in the stream. The water was very cold. We passed the brush of an island above the water. I held onto the timber with both hands and let it take me along. The shore was out of sight now.(225)

31장(Chapter XXXI)

■ 31장 주요 내용

- 군인이 아닌 민간인 헨리. (헨리 중위가 아닌 민간인 헨리)

I cut the cloth stars off my sleeves.

■ Summary

이제 더 이상 헨리 중위가 아닌 헨리는 강한 조류에도 불구하고 수영해서 해안가에 도착했다. 그는 걸어서 베니스의 평원지역을 넘어갔다. 그리고 그는 달리는 기차에 가까스로 올라탔다. 방수포 아래에 저장된 총기들 사이에서 숨어 갔다.

■ 논평

이장은 행동들이 매우 연계성이 높다. 헨리의 탈주는 매우 구체적인 세부 사항들로 묘사되었다. 이젠 총이 없다. (gunless) 그리고 군복의 소매에 있는 헝겊으로 된 별을 떼어냈다.

"외투를 입기 전에 소매에서 헝겊 별을 떼어내…"(227)

Before I put on my coat I cut the cloth stars off my sleeves and put them in the inside pocket with my money. (227)

행동을 보여 주는 헤밍웨이만의 능숙한 방법이 31장에서 시작하면서 나타나기 시작했다. 특히 헨리가 기차에 올라탔을 때 그렇다. 특히 주목해야 할 점은 일인칭 단수(I)를 사용하지 않고 "You"와 "We"를 상용한다는 점이다. 수영하는 동안 헨리는 자기 자신을 You와 We로 묘사했다.

"우리는 빗속에서 그들의 대화를 들었다."(224)
"We stood there in the rain and listened to this."

이것의 효과는 독자들과 밀접한 공감(identification)과 그의 행동에 있어서 우리의 연루를 불러일으킨다는 점이다. 헤밍웨이가 시사하고 싶은 점은 우리가 프레더릭 헨리라는 점을 나타내고 싶은 것이다. (We are all Frederic Henry.)

■ 31장 주요 작품 내용

You do not know how long you are in a river when the current moves swiftly. It seems a long time and it may be very short. The water was cold and in flood and many things passed that had been floated off the banks when the river rose. I was lucky to have a heavy timber to hold on to, and I lay in the icy water with the chin on the wood, holding as easily as I could with both hands. I was afraid of cramps and I hoped we would move toward the shore. We went down the river in a long curve. It was beginning to be light enough so I could see the bushes along the shore-line. There was a bush island ahead and the current moved toward the shore. I wondered if I should take off my boots and clothes and try to swim ashore, but decided not to. I had never thought of anything, but that I would reach the shore some way, and I would be in a bad position if I landed barefoot. I had to get to Mestre some way.(226)

I watched the shore com close, then swing away, then come closer again. We were floating more slowly. The shore was very close now. I could see twigs on the willow bush. The timber swung slowly so that the bank was behind me and I knew we were in an eddy. We went slowly around. As I saw the bank again, very close now, I tried holding with one arm and kicking and swimming the timber toward the bank with the other, but I did not bring it any closer. I was afraid we would move out of the eddy and, holding with one hand, I drew up my feet so they were against the side of the timber and shoved hard toward the bank. I could see the brush, but even with my momentum and swimming as hard as I could, the current was taking me away. I thought then I would drown because of my boots, but I thrashed and fought through the water, and when I looked up the bank was coming toward me, And I kept thrashing and swimming in a heavy-footed panic until I reached it. I hung to the willow branch and did not have strength to pull myself up but I knew I would not drown now. It had never occurred to me on the timber that I might drown. I felt hollow and sick in my stomach and chest from the effort, and I held to the branches and waited. When the sick feeling was gone I pulled into the willow bushes and rested again, my arms around some brush, holding tight with my hands to the branches. Then I crawled out, pushed on through the willows and onto the bank. It was half-daylight and I saw no one. I lay flat on the bank and heard the river and the rain.(227)

After a while I got up and started along the bank. I knew there was no bridge across the river until Latisana. I thought I might be opposite San Vito. I began to think out What I should do. Ahead there was a ditch running into the river. I went toward it. So far I had seen no one and I sat down by some bushes along the bank of the ditch and took off my shoes and emptied them of water. I took off my coat, took my wallet with my papers and my money all wet in it out of the inside pocket and then wrung the coat out. I took off my trousers and wrung them too, then my shirt and under clothing. I slapped and rubbed myself and then dressed again. I had lost my cap.

Before I put on my coat I cut the cloth stars off my sleeves and put them in the inside pocket with my money. My money was wet but was all right. I counted it. There were three thousand and some lire. My clothes felt wet and clammy and slapped my arms to keep the circulation going. I had woven underwear and I did not think I would catch cold if I kept moving. They had taken my pistol at the road and I put the holster under my coat. I had no cap and it was cold in the rain. (227-228)

Up the line there was a bridge over a stream that flowed into the marsh. I could see a guard too at the bridge. Crossing the field to the north I had seen a train pass on this railroad, visible a long way across the flat plain, and I though a train might come from Portogruaro. I watched the guards and lay down on the embankment so that I could see both ways along the tracks. The guard at the bridge walked a way up the line toward where I lay, then turned and went back toward the bridge. I lay, and was hungry , and waited for the train. The one I had seen was so long that the engine moved it very slowly and I was sure I could get abroad it. After I had almost given up hoping for one I saw a train coming. The engine, coming straight on, grew larger slowly. I looked at the guard at the bridge. He was walking on the near side of the bridge but on the other side of the tracks. That would put him out of sight when the train passed. I watched the engine come nearer. It was working hard. I could see there were many cars. I knew there would be guards on the train, and I tried to see where they were, but keeping out of sight, I could not. The engine was almost to where I was lying.

When it came opposite, working and puffing even on the level, and I saw the engineer pass, I stood up and stepped up close to the passing cars. If the guards were watching I was a less suspicious object standing beside the track. Several closed freight-cars passed. Then I saw a low open car of the sort they call gondolas coming, covered with canvas. I stood until it had almost passed, then jumped and caught the rear hand-rods and pulled up. I crawled down between the gondola and the shelter of the high freight-car behind. I did not think any one had seen me. I was holding to the hand- rods and crouching low, my feet on the coupling. We were almost opposite the bridge. I remembered the guard. As we passed him he looked at me. He was a boy and his helmet was too big for him. I stared at him contemptuously and he looked away. He thought I had something to do with the train.(229)

　We were past. I saw him still looking uncomfortable, watching the other cars pass and I stooped to see how the canvas was fastened. It had grummets and was laced down at the edge with cord. I took out my knife, cut the cord and put my arm under. There were hard bulges under the canvas that tightened in the rain. I looked up and ahead. There was a guard on the freight-car ahead but he was looking forward. I let go of the hand-rails and ducked under the canvas. My forehead hit something that gave me a violent bump and I felt blood on my face but I crawled on in and lay flat. Then I turned around and I fastened down the canvas. I gave in under the canvas with guns. They smelled cleanly of oil and grease. I lay and listened to the rain on the canvas and the clicking of the car over the rails. There was a little light came through and I lay and looked at the guns. They had their canvas jackets on. I thought they must have been sent ahead from third army. The bump on my forehead was swollen and I stopped the bleeding by lying still and letting it coagulate, then picked away the dried blood except over the cut. It was nothing. I had no handkerchief, but feeling with my fingers I washed away where the dried blood had been, with rainwater that dripped from the canvas, and wiped it clean with the sleeve of my coat. I did not want to look conspicuous. I knew I would have to get out before they got to Mestre because they would be taking care of these guns. They had no guns to lose or forget about. I was terrifically hungry.(229-230)

32장(Chapter XXXII)

■ 32장 주요 내용

- 부대에서 일탈했으므로 어떤 의무도 사라졌다고 고백한다.

"너는 이제 그 일에서 떠난 거야. 이제 의무도 사라졌어."(232)
You were out of it now. You had no more obligation.(232)
"분노는 모든 의무와 함께 강물에 씻겨 나갔다."(232)
Anger was washed away in the river along with any obligation.

■ 논평

나는 생각하는 존재로 만들어지지 않았다. 먹는 존재로 만들어졌다. 정말이지 그렇다.(233)

I was not made to think. I was made to eat. My God, yes.

인간에 대한 본질적인 것을 말하는 것으로 먹는 것이 생각하는 그것보다 더 선행한다는 의미이다. 극한 상황에서 생각이 먼저가 아니고 먹는 생존이 먼저라는 의미이다. 배고 픔은 어떤 생각을 떠올리게 할 수 없고 오로지 먹는 문제에 골몰하고 사랑하는 사람, 정의, 관습 등의 것을 생각할 여유가 없다.

헨리는 기차를 감싸고 있는 천 아래에서 총기들과 함께 숨어있었다. 그리고 그곳에서 탈주와 버클리에 관해서 생각했다. 제3부는 헨리의 생각이 조이스의 의식적 흐름의 스타일을 제시하면서 조용히 끝났다. 서술에서 이인칭 시점의 사용을 주목해야 한다. 헨리는 자기 자신에게 탈주를 정당화한다. 소설의 시작부터 탈주는 어떤 면에서 합리화되었다.

"너는 이제 그 일에서 떠난 거야. 이제 의무도 사라졌어."(232)
"You were out of it now. You had no more obligation."(232)

물론 이것은 소설의 제목을 주는 사건이다. 그러나 총을 운반하는 기차에서 발생했다는 점을 고려할 때 약간 역설적이다. 헤밍웨이 주인공들은 원한을 마음에 두지 않는 것이 일반적이다. 헨리도 예외는 아니다. "분노는 모든 의무와 함께 강물에 씻겨 나갔다."(232) 'Anger was washed away in the river along with any obligation.'라고 그는 우리에게 말한다. 이야기가 진행되면서 그는 이탈리아인들에게 악의적인 의지가 있지 않았다. 만약 분함(억울함)을 느낀다면 그는 적어도 그것을 표현하는데 자제를 한다.

■ 32장 주요 작품 내용

Lying on the floor of the flat-car with the guns beside me under the canvas I was wet, cold and very hungry. Finally I rolled over and lay flat on my stomach with my head my arms. My knee was stiff, but it had been very satisfactory. Valentini had done a fine job. I had done half the retreat on foot and swum part of the Tagliamento with his knee. It was his knee all right. The other knee was mine. Doctors did things to you and then it was not your body any more. The head was mine, and the inside of the belly. It was very hungry in there. I could feel it turn over on itself. The head was mine, but not to use, not to think with, only to remember and not too much remember.(231)

I could remember Catherine but I knew I would get crazy if I thought about her when I was not sure yet I would see her, so I would not think about her, only about her a little, only about her with car going slowly and clickingly, and some light through the canvas and my lying with Catherine on the floor of the car. Hard as the floor of the car to lie not thinking only feeling, having been away too long, the clothes wet and the floor moving only a little each time and lonesome inside and alone with wet clothing and hard floor for a wife.(231-232)

You did not love the floor of a flat-car nor guns with canvas jackets and the smell of vaselined metal or a canvas that rain leaked through, although it is very fine under a canvas and pleasant with guns; but you loved some one else whom

3부(Book Three)

now you knew was not even to be pretended there; you seeing now very clearly and coldly- not so coldly as clearly and emptily. You saw emptily, lying on your stomach, having been present when one army moved back and another came forward. You had lost your cars and your men as a floorwalker loses the stock of his department in a fire. There was, however, no insurance. You were out of it now. You had no more obligation. If they shot floorwalkers after a fire in the department store because they spoke with an accent they had always had, then certainly the floorwalkers would not be expected to return when the store opened for business. They might seek other employment; if there was any other employment and the police did not get them.(232)

Anger was washed away in the river along with any obligation. Although that ceased when the carabiniere put his hands on my collar. I would like to have had the uniform off although I did not care much about the outward forms. I had taken off the stars, but that was for convenience. It was no point of honor. I was not against them. I was through. I wished them all the luck. There were the good ones, and the brave ones, and the calm ones and the sensible ones and they deserved it. But it was not my show any more and I wished this bloody train would get to Mestre and I would eat and stop thinking. I would have to stop.(232)

Piani would tell them they had shot me. They went through the pockets and took the papers of the people they shot. They would not have my papers. They might call me drowned. I wondered what they would hear in the States. Dead from wounds and other causes. Good Christ I was hungry. I wondered what had become of the priest at the mess. And RinIdi. He was probably at Pordenone. If they had not gone further back. Well, I would never see him now. I would never see any of them now. That life was over. I did not think he had syphilis. It was not a serious disease anyway if you took it in time, they said. But he would worry. I would worry too if I had it. Any one would worry.(232-233)

I was not made to think. I was made to eat. My God, yes. Eat and drink and sleep with Catherine. To-night maybe. Not that was impossible. But to-morrow night, and a good meal and sheets and never going away again except together. Probably have to go dammed quickly. She would go. I knew she would go. When would we go? That was something to think about. It was getting dark. I lay and thought where we would go. There were many places.(233)

4부(Book Four)

33장 (Chapter XXXIII)

■ 33장 주요 내용

- 민간인 신분으로 밀라노(Milan)에 도착.

On the sleeves it shows very plainly where the stars have been cut away.

- 병원에 도착해 캐서린의 소식을 묻고 스트레사로 떠난 것을 확인.
- 친구 시먼스(Simmons) 찾아감.

■ Summary

헨리는 신분을 숨기고 밀라노에 도착했다. 캐서린과 퍼거슨 간호사는 병원에 없었고 휴가차 스트레사(stresa)로 떠난 상태였다. 헨리는 음악을 공부하는 친구인 시먼스(Simmons)에게 도움을 청했다.

■ 논평

헨리가 만나는 모든 사람이 퇴각에 대해서 알고 있다는 것을 발견했을 때 짧은 서론 부문에서 극적인 긴장을 유지했다. 많은 사람이 탈영 문제에 동조하는 것처럼 보이고 중요한 것은 그것이 그들에게 큰 문제가 되지 않는다는 것입니다.

예를 들어 종업원은 헨리에게 그가 제거한 배지의 모습이 선명하게 보이는 옷을 입지 말라고 충고했다. 작품을 통해서 흐르는 두 개의 주제가 33장을 통해서 극화되었다. 즉 평범한 사람들의 품위와 우정의 가치 이 두 가지다. 비록 잘 모르는 사람이지만 바텐더(Bartendar)는 사이먼이라는 친구가 했던 것처럼 헨리에게 도움을 주었다. 병원의 짐꾼(porter)도 헨리를 도와주었을 뿐만 아니라 도움에 대해 헨리가 지급하는 돈까지도 거절했다.

헨리의 소외감에도 불구하고 이 장면과 같은 장면들은 헤밍웨이가 『무기여 잘 있거라』에서 반 이탈리아인(anti-Italian)이라는 잠재적인 혐의로부터 그를 보호하고 있지만, 그가 비판적인 것은 이탈리아 군대, 특히 헌병입니다.

작가는 구체적인 사실들을 통해서 전체 장면을 지속해서 환기한다. 커피를 마시기 위해서 그가 들어간 와인 가게에서 헨리는 우리에게 다음과 같이 말한다.

"쓸어낸 먼지, 커피잔에 담긴 스푼, 와인잔이 남긴 둥그런 물 자국에서 이른 아침의 냄새가 났다." It smelled of early morning, of swept dust, spoons in coffee-glasses and the wet circles left by wine-glasses. (237) 9장에서 오스트리아의 폭격이 있는 동안 치즈 위에 있는 벽돌 가루처럼 이 같은 세부 사항들은 우리에게 현장을 생동감 있게 해 준다.

■ 33장 주요 작품 내용

I dropped off the train in Milan as it slowed to come into station early in the morning before it was light. I crossed the track and came out between some buildings and down on the street. A wine shop was open and I went in for some coffee. It smelled of early morning, of swept dust, spoons in coffee-glasses and the wet circles left by wine-glasses. Proprietor was behind the bar. Two soldiers sat at a table. I stood at the bar and drank a glass of coffee and ate a piece of bread. The coffee was gray with milk, and I skimmed the milk scum off the top with a piece of bread.

The proprietor looked at me.

"You want a glass of grappa?"

"No thanks."

"On me," he said and poured a small glass and pushed it toward me. "What's happening at the front?"(237)

"I would not know about the front."

"I saw you come down the wall. You came off the train."

"There is a big retreat."

"I read the papers. What happens? Is it over?"

"I don't think so."

He filled the glass with grappa from a short bottle. "If you are in trouble," he said, "I can keep you."

"I am not in trouble."

"If you are in trouble stay here with me."

"Where does one stay?"

"In the building. Many stay here. Any who are in trouble stay here."

"Are many in trouble?"

"It depends on the trouble. You are a South American"

"No."

"Speak Spanish?"

"A little."

He wiped off the bar.

"It is hard now to leave the country but in no way impossible."

"I have no wish to leave."

"You can stay here as long as you want. You will see what sort of man I am."

"I have to go this morning but I will remember the address to return."

He shook his head. "You won't come back if you talk like that. I thought you were in real trouble."

"I am in no trouble. But I value the address of a friend."

I put a ten-lira note on the bar to pay for the coffee.

"Have a grappa with me," I said.

"It is not necessary."

"Have one."

He poured the two glasses.(238)

"Remember," he said. "Come here. Do not let other people take you in. Here you are all right."

"I am sure."

"You are sure?"

"Yes."

He was serious. "Then let me tell you one thing. Do not go about with that coat."

"Why?"

"On the sleeves it shows very plainly where the stars have been cut away. The cloth is a different color."

I did not say anything.

"If you have no papers I can give you papers."

"What papers?"

"Leave papers."

"I have no need for papers. I have papers."

"All right," he said. "But if you need papers I can get what you wish."

"How much are you such papers?"

"It depends on what they are. The price is reasonable."

"I don't need any now."

He shrugged his shoulders.

"I'm all right," I said.

When I went out he said, "Don't forget that I am your friend."

"No."

"I will see you again," he said.

"Good," I said.

Outside I kept away from the station, where there were military police, and picked up a cab at the edge of the little park. I gave the driver the address of the hospital. At the hospital I went to the porter's lodge. His wife embraced me. He shook my hand. "You are back. You are safe."

"Yes."(239)

"Have you had breakfast?"

"Yes."

"How are you, Tenant? How are you?" his wife asked.

"Fine."

"Won't you have breakfast with us?"

"No, thank you. Tell me is Miss Barkley here at the hospital now?"

"Miss Barkley?"

"The English lady nurse."

"His girl," the wife said. She patted my arm and smiled.

"No," the porter said. "She is away."

My heart went down. "You are sure? I mean the tall blonde English young lady."

"I am sure. She is gone to Stresa."

"When did she go?"

"She went two days ago with the other lady English."

"Good," I said. "I wish you to do something for me. Do not tell any one you have seen me. It is very important."(240)

  I got into the cab and gave the driver the address of Simmons, one of the men I knew who was studying singing. Simmon lived a long way out in the town the Porta Magenta. He was still in bed and sleepy when I went to see him. "You get up awfully early, Henry," he said.

"I came in on the early train."

"What's all this retreat? Were you are at the front? Will you have a cigarette? They're in that box on the table." It was a big room with a bed beside the wall, a piano over on the far side and a dresser and table. I sat own a chair by the bed. Simmons sat propped up by the pillows and smoked. "I'm in a jam, Sim," I said.

"So am I," he said. "I'm always in a jam. Won't you smoke?"

"No," I said. "What's the procedure in going to Switzerland?"

"For you? The Italians wouldn't let you out of the country."

"Yes. I know that. But the Swiss. What will they do?"

"They intern you."

"I know. But what's the mechanics of it?"

"Nothing. it's very simple. You can go anywhere. I think you just have to report or something. Why? Are you fleeting the police?"

"Nothing definite yet."

"Don't tell me if you don't want. But it would be interesting to hear. Nothing happens here. I was a great flop at Piacenza."

"I'm awfully sorry."

"Oh yes-I went very badly. I sung well too. I'm going to try it gain at the Lyrico here."

"I'd like to be here."

"you're awfully polite. You aren't in a bed mess, are you?"

"I don't know."

"Don't tell me if you don't want. How do you happen to be away from the bloody front?"

"I think I'm through with it."(240-241)

34장(Chapter XXXIV)

■ 34장 주요 내용

- 캐서린과의 재회.

모욕감을 느끼지 않았다. 예전 같으면 나도 그들에게 모욕감을 주고 싸움을 걸었을 것이다.(243)

I did not feel insulted. In the old days I would have insulted them and picked a fight.

나는 단독강화를 맺은 것이다.(243)

I had made a separate peace.(243)

■ Summary

헨리가 기차를 타고 휴양도시인 스트레스를 여행한다. 그곳에서 간호사인 퍼거슨과 캐서린이 호텔에서 식사하는 것을 알게 된다. 그리고 헨리와 캐서린은 이 호텔에서 함께 밤을 보낸다.

■ 논평

결국, 헨리와 캐서린은 다시 만나게 됐다. 그러나 분위기는 밀라노에서 마지막에 만났던 분위기와는 매우 달랐다. 비록 캐서린이 그것을 의식하지 못한다고 할지라도 위험은 곳곳에서 맴돌고 있었다. 헨리는 자신을 민간인 복장의 가장으로 학교를 무단으로 이탈한 사람으로 범죄자로 특징지었다.

탈영한 게 아니에요. 고작 이탈리아 군대일 뿐이라고요. (251) "It's not deserting from the army. It's only the Italian army." 캐서린은 소설의 시작쯤에 시작된 합리화의 패턴을 계속하면서 그와 우리를 안심시켰다. 34장의 첫머리에서 증명된 헨리의 성격 변화를 주목하자.

같은 기차 객실에 타고 있는 적대적인 공군 조종사에 대해서 헨리는 다음과 같이 말한다.

"모욕감 느끼지 않았다. 예전 같으면 나는 그들에게 모욕감을 주고 싸움을 걸었을 것이다."(243)

사랑과 전쟁의 경험 때문에 더 이상 불안하지도 않고 모욕감을 느끼지도 않았다. 헨리가 스트레사로 가는 기차를 타고 가는 동안 비가 왔다. 그리고 도착했을 때도 비가 왔다. 헨리와 캐서린이 호텔 방에서 시간을 보낼 때도 비가 왔다. 빗속에서 캐서린 자기 죽음의 환영을 기억해 봐라. 그리고 아마도 이 소설에서 가장 잘 알려지고 가장 많이 인용되는 구절임을 부정할 수 없을 만큼 불길한 특징을 지니고 있으며 곧이어 다음과 같은 내용이 뒤따른다.

너무 큰 용기를 지닌 사람들이 있을 때 세상은 그들을 꺾어 놓기 위해 죽이려 하고 실제로 그렇게 한다. 세상 모든 사람을 부러뜨리지만, 많은 사람이 그 부러진 곳에서 더 강해진다. 그러나 세상은 부러지지 않으려는 사람들을 죽인다. 착한 사람이든 상냥한 사람이든 용감한 사람이든 가리지 않고 공평하게 죽인다. 그 어디에도 속하지 않은 사람 역시 죽이겠지만 특별히 서두르지 않을 뿐이다.(249)

여기서 작가는 매우 다른 방법으로 글을 쓴다. 평상시 작가가 좋아하는 구체적인 세부 사항들과 매우 강한 대조를 이루는 고상한 관념중 하나인 다른 방식으로 글을 쓴다. 그러나 헤밍웨이는 가장 철학적인 부분에서도 단순하고 구어적인 언어를 선호한다는 것을 주목하자.

"나는 단독강화를 맺은 것이다."(243)
"I had made a separate peace."(243)

헨리는 자신에게 34장에서 말했다. 이 작품의 3부 마지막에서 다루는 질문은 다음과 같다.
혼자서 단독강화를 맺을 수 있는가? "Can one make a separate peace?"
혼자 단독강화한다고 해서 전쟁이 종식되는가? 혼자서 전쟁에서 벗어나는 일은 가능하겠지만 전쟁 종식은 가능하지 않다. 그렇다고 해서 죽음을 눈앞에 두고서 그냥 죽음을 맞이할 수는 없는 일이다. 단독강화가 전쟁의 종식을 이바지할 수는 없지만 그렇다고 해서 그냥 그곳에 있을 수는 없다. 우리 사회에서 나 혼자 어떤 일을 해서 큰 변화가 있겠는가? 라는 말은 일부 맞을 수도 있다. 그렇지만 한 명 한 명 하다 보면 사회가 변할 수 있는 경우도 발생한다. 적절한 비유가 아닐 수 있지만, 단독강화는 전쟁 종식이란 면에서 의미가 없을 수도 있지만, 개인으로서는 생존을 위해서 필요한 일이다.

■ 34장 주요 작품 내용

In civilian clothes I felt **a masquerader**. I had been in uniform a long time and I missed the feeling of being held by your clothes. The trousers felt very floopy. I had bought a ticket at Milan for Stresa. I had also bought a new hat. I could not wear Sim's hat but his clothes were fine. They smelled of tabacco and as I sat in the compartment and looked out the window the new hat felt very new and clothes very old. I myself felt as sad as the wet Lombard country that was outside through the window. There were some aviators in the compartment who did not think much of me. They avoid looking at me and were very scornful of a civilian my age. I did not feel insulted. In the old days I would have insulted them and picked a fight. They got off at Gallarate and I was glad to be alone. I had the paper but I did not read it because I did not want to read about war. I was going to forget the war. I had made a separate peace. I felt damned lonely and was glad when the train got to Stresa.(243)

The sandwiches came and I ate three and drank a couple more martins. I had never tasted anything so cool and clean. They made me feel civilized. I had had too much red wine, bread, cheese, bad coffee and grappa. I sat on the high stool before the pleasant mahogany, the brass and the mirrors and did not think at all. The barman asked me some question.

"Don't talk about the war," I said. The war was a long way away. Maybe there wasn't any war. There was no war here. Then I realized it was over for me. But I did not have the feeling that it was really over. I had the feeling of a boy who think of what is happening at a certain hour at the schoolhouse from which he has played truant.(245)

Catherine and Helen Ferguson were at supper when I came to their hotel. Standing in the hallway I saw them at table. Catherine's face was away from me and I saw the line of her hair and her cheek and her lovely neck and shoulders. Ferguson was talking. She stopped when I came in.

"My God," she said.

"Hello," I said.

"Why it's you!" Catherine said. Her face lighted up. She looked too happy to believe it. I kissed her. Catherine blushed and I sat down at the table.

"You are a fine mess," Ferguson said. "What are you doing here? Have you eaten?"

"No," The girl who was serving the meal came in and I told her to bring a plate for me. Catherine looked at me all the time, her eyes happy.

"What are you doing in mufti?" Ferguson asked.

"I'm in the cabinet."

"You're in some mess."

"Cheer up, Fergy. Cheer up just a little."

"I'm not cheered by seeing you. I know the mess you've gotten the girl into. You're no cheerful sight to me."

Catherine smiled at me and touched me with her foot under the table.

"No one got me in a mess, Fergy. I get in my own messes."

"I can't stand him," Ferguson said. "He's done nothing but ruin you with his sneaking Italian tricks. Americans are worse than Italians."

"The Scotch are such a moral people," Catherine said.

"I don't mean that. I mean his Italian sneakiness"

"Am I sneaky, Fergy?"

"You are. You're worse than sneaky. You're like a snake. A snake with an Italian uniform:with a cape around your neck."(246)

"Don't, Fergy," Catherine said and patted her hand. "Don't denounce me. You know we like each other."

"Take your hand away," Fergurson said. Her face was red. "If you had any shame it would be different. But you're God knows how many months gone with child and you think it's a joke and are all smiles because your seducer's come back. You've no shame and no feelings." She began to cry. Catherine went over and put her arm around her. As she stood comforting Ferguson, I could see no change in her figure. "I don't care," Ferguson sobbed. "I think it's dreadful."

"There, there, Fergy. Catherine comforted her. I'll be ashamed. Don't cry Fergy. Don't cry, old Fergy."

"I'm not crying," Ferguson sobbed. "I'm not crying. Except for the awful thing you've gotten into." She looked at me. "I hate you," she said. "She can't make me not hate you. You dirty sneaking American Italian." Her eyes and nose were red with crying.

Catherine smiled at me.

"Don't you smile at him with your arm around me."

"You're unreasonable, Fergy."

"I know it," Ferguson sobbed. "You mustn't mind me, either of you. I'm so upset. I'm not reasonable. I know it. I want you both to be happy."

"We're happy," Catherine said. "You're a sweet Fergy."(247)

That night at the hotel, in our room with the long empty hall outside and our shoes outside the door, a thick carpet on the floor of the room, outside the windows the rain falling and in the room light and pleasant and cheerful, then the light out and it exciting with smooth sheets and the bed comfortable, feeling that we had come home, feeling no longer alone, waking in the night to find the other one there, and not gone away; all other things were unreal. We slept when we were tired and if we woke the other one woke too so one was not alone. Often a man wishes to be alone and a girl wishes to be alone too and if they love each other they are jealous of that in each other, but I can truly say we never felt that. We would feel alone when we were together, alone against the others. It has only happened to me like that once. I have been alone while I was with many girls and that is the way that you can be most lonely. But we never lonely and never afraid when we were together. I know that the night is not the same as the day: all that things are different, that the things of the night cannot be explained in the day, because they do not then exist, and the night can be a dreadful time for lonely people once their loneliness has started. But with Catherine there was almost no difference in the night except that it was an even better time. If people bring so much courage to this world the world has to kill them to break them, so of course it kills them. The world breaks every one and afterward many are strong at the broken places. But those that will not break it kills. It kills the very good and the very gentle and the very brave impartially. If you are none of these you can be sure it will kill you too but there will be no special hurry.(249)

"Don't you want the paper?" "You always wanted the paper in the hospital."

"No," I said. "I don't want the paper now."

"Was it so bad you don't want even to read about it?"

"I don't want to read about it."

"I wish I had been with you so I would know about it too."

"I'll tell you about it if I ever get it straight in my head."

"But won't they arrest you if they catch you out of uniform?"

"They'll probably shoot me."

"Then we'll not stay here. We'll get out of the country."

"I'd thought something of that."

"We'll get out. Darling, you shouldn't take silly chances. Tell me how did you come from Mestre to Milan?"

"I came on the train. I was in the uniform then."

"Weren't you in danger then?"

"Not much. I had an old order of movement. I fixed the dates on it in Mestre."(250)

"Darling, you're liable to be arrested here any time. I won't have it. It's silly to do something like that. Where would we be if they took you off?"

"Let's not think about it. I'm tired of thinking about it."

"What would you do if they came to arrest you?"

"Shoot them."

"You see how silly you are. I won't let you go out of the hotel until we leave here."

"Where are we going to do?"

"Please don't be that way, darling. We'll go wherever you say. But please find some place to go right away."

"Switzerland is down on the lake, we can go there."

"That will be lovely."

It was clouding over outside and the lake was darkening.

"I wish we did not always have to live like criminals," I said.

"Darling, don't be that way. You haven't lived like a criminal very long. And we never live like criminals. We're going to have a fie time."

"I feel like a criminal. I've deserted from the army."

"Darling, don't be that way. You haven't lived like criminal very long. And we never lived like criminals. We're going to have a fine time."

"I feel like a criminal. I've deserted from the army."

"Darling, please be sensible. It's not deserting from the army. It's only the Italian army."

I laughed. "You're a fine girl. Let's get back into bed. I feel fine in bed."

4부(Book Four) **297**

A little while later Catherine said, "You don't feel like a criminal do you?"

"No," I said. "Not when I'm with you."

"You're such a silly boy," she said. "But I'll look after you. Isn't it splendid, darling, that I don't have any morning-sickness?"

"It's grand."

"You don't appreciate what a fine wife you have. But I don't care. I'll get you some place where they can't arrest you and then well have a lovely time."

"Let's go there right away."

"We will, darling. I'll go any time you wish."

"Let's not think about anything."

"All right."(251-252)

35장 (Chapter XXXV)

- **35장 주요 내용**

- 스위스로 피난길을 떠날 준비.
- 그레피 백작과 만남.
- 스위스로 갈 경우를 대비한 바텐더(barman)의 언급.

"보트가 필요하시면," 그가 말했다, "언제든지 열쇠를 드리겠습니다."(256)
"Any time you want it," he said, "I'll give you the key."

- 헨리에게는 캐서린이 이 세상에 전부가 된 현 상황.

"전에 인생이 온갖 것으로 가득 차 있었지," 내가 말했다. "이제는 당신이 곁에 없으면 나는 아무것도 가진 게 없는 거야."(257)
"My life used to be full of everything," I said. "Now if you aren't with me I haven't a thing in the world."

- 아직도 사복이 어색하기만 한 헨리: 넥타이를 메고 거울을 보니 사복을 입은 모습이 어색했다.

Knotting my tie and looking in the glass I looked strange to myself in the civilian clothes.(258)

- 백작과 삶에 관한 의미 있는 이야기 나눔.

"아니. 노인이 지혜로울 거로 생각하는 건 아주 큰 착각이야. 노인들은 지혜로워지지 않아. 조심성이 많아질 뿐이지."

"No, that is the great fallacy; the wisdom of old men. They do not grow wise. They grow careful."(261)

■ Summary

캐서린이 퍼거슨 간호사를 방문하는 동안 헨리는 호텔의 바텐더(barman)와 호수에서 낚시했다. 캐서린이 방에서 쉬는 동안 헨리는 친구인 아흔네 살인 그레피 백작(Count Greffi)과 당구를 쳤다.

■ 논평

이번 장은 서술에서 과도기 장이다. 헨리가 바텐더와 낚시하고 있지만, 헨리는 이탈리아에서 중립국인 스위스로 갈 수 있는 피난길(escaping rout)을 답사했다. 캐서린에 대한 그의 사랑의 강렬함이 강조되었다. 그는 캐서린에게 우리가 떨어져 있을 때 그는 가진 것이 아무것도 없었고 그녀의 강렬한 사랑으로부터 실신할 것 같았다고 말했다. 소설의 마지막에서 헨리는 그녀를 잃었을 때 헨리의 지지에 대한 독자들의 상실감은 강렬할 것이다. 즉 독자들은 헨리를 대신해서 그녀를 잃은 상실감을 느끼게 될 것이다.

사실 그는 한때 무관심했던 헨리가 진정으로 믿을 만한 무언가를 찾았다. 그는 백작에게 자신이 가장 소중하게 여기는 것은 사랑하는 사람이며 "신앙이 아주 깊어질 수도 있겠죠."(263) 라고 말하며 자신의 종교적인 감정은 밤에 온다고 자세히 설명한다.

그레피 백작과 이야기할 때 한동안 무관심했던 헨리는 믿고 있는 무언가를 발견했다. 그는 백작에게 그가 가장 소중히 여기는 것은 그가 사랑하는 사람이다. 그리고 "신앙이 아주 깊어질 수도 있겠죠."(263)라고 말하고 그의 종교적인 느낌은 밤에 오는 것이 아니라고도 말했다.

캐서린처럼 헨리도 그들만의 사랑의 종교를 만들었다. 헨리의 부대에서 탈주에 대한 헤밍웨이의 정당화는 전쟁은 어리석은 것이라는 현명한 백작의 의견이 형태로 계속 이어갔다. 헨리는 민간인 의복에 대해 계속 이상한 느낌이 들게 한다. 그리고 그는 전쟁에 관한 토론에 대해서도 썩 좋아하지 않았고 오래 지속한 죄책감도 던져 버렸다. 작가는 우리에게 헨리의 대의명분 포기의 도덕성에 대한 의문을 제기하는 것을 막았다.

■ 35장 주요 작품 내용

Catherine went along the lake to the little hotel to see Ferguson and I I sat in the bar and read the papers. There were comfortable leather chairs in the bar and I sat in one of them and read until the barman came in. The army had not stood at the Tagliamento. They were falling back to the Piave. I remembered the Piave. The railroad crossed it near San Dona going up to the front. It was deep and slow there and quite narrow. Down below there were mosquito marshes and canals. There were some lovely villas. Once, before the war, going up to the Cortina D'Ampezzo I had gone along it for several hours in the hills. Up there it looked like a trout stream, flowing swiftly with shallow stretches and pools under the shadow of the rocks. The road turned off from it at Cadore. I wondered how the army that was up there would come down. The barman come in.

"Count Greffi was asking for you," he said.

"Who?"

"Count Greffi. You remember the old man who was here when you were here before."

"Is he here?"

"Yes, he's here with his niece. I told him you were here. He wants you to play billiards."

"Where is he?"

"He's taking a walk."

"How is he?"

"He's younger than ever. He drank three champangne cocktails last night before dinner."

"How's his billiard game?"(253-254)

The barman put on a coat and we went out. We went down and got a boat and I rowed while the barman sat in stern and let out the line with a spinner and a heavy sinker on the end to troll for lake trout. We rowed along the shore, the barman holding the line in his hand and giving it occasional jerks forward. Stresa looked very deserted from the lake. There were the long rows of bare trees, the big hotels and the closed villas. I rowed across to Isola Bella and went close to the walls, where the water deepened sharply, and you saw the rock wall slanting down in the clear water, and then up and along to the fisherman's island. The sun was under a cloud and the water was dark and smooth and very cold. We did not have a strike though we saw some circles on the water from rising fish.(254-255)

"Are you tired from rowing?"

"I'll row back," he said.

"I like to row."

"Maybe if you hold the line it will change the luck."

"All right."

"Tell me how goes the war."

"Rotten."

"I don't have to go. I'm too old, like Count Greffi."

"Maybe you'll have to go yet."

"Next year they'll call my class. But I won't go."

"What will you do?"

"Get out of the country. I wouldn't go to war. I was at the war once in Abyssinia. Nix. Why do you go?"

"I don't know. I was a fool."

"Have another vermouth?"

"All right."(255-256)

I pulled in the line and wrapped it on a stick notched at each end. The barman put the boat in a little slip in the stone wall and locked it with a chain and padlock

"Any time you want it," he said, "I'll give you the key."

"Thank you."

We went up to the hotel and into the bar. I did not want another drink so early in the morning so I went up to our room. The maid had just finished doing the room and Catherine was not back yet. I lay down on the bed and tried to keep from thinking. When Catherine came back it was all right again. Ferguson was downstairs, she said. She was coming to lunch.

"I knew you wouldn't mind," Catherine said.

"No," I said.

"What's the matter, darling?"

"I don't know."

"I know. You haven't anything to do. All you have is me and I go away."

"That's true."

"I'm sorry, darling. I know it must be a dreadful feeling to have nothing at all suddenly."

"My life used to be full of everything," I said. "Now if you aren't with me I haven't a thing in the world."

"But I'll be with you. I was only gone for two hours. Isn't there anything you can do?"

"I went fishing with the barman."

"Wasn't it fun?"

"Yes."

"Don't think about me when I'm not here."

"That's the way I worked it at the front. But there was something to do then."

"Othello with his occupation gone," she teased.

"Othello was a nigger," I said. "Besides, I'm not jealous. I'm just so in love with you that there isn't anything else."

"Will you be a good boy and be nice to Furguson?"

"I'm always nice to Ferguson unless she curses me."

"Be nice to her. Think how much we have and she hasn't anything."

"I don't think she wants what we have."

"You don't know much, darling, for such a wise boy."

"I'll be nice to her."

"I know you will. You're so sweet."

"She won't stay afterward, will she?"

"No, I'll get rid of her."

"And then we'll come up here."(256-257)

At a quarter to five I kissed Catherine good-by an went into the bathroom to dress. Knotting my tie and looking in the glass I looked strange to myself in the civilian clothes. I must remember to buy some more shirts and socks.

"Will you be away a long time?" Catherine asked. She look lovely in the bed. "Would you hand me the rush?"

I watched her brushing her hair, holding her head so the weight of her hair all came on one side. It was dark outside and the light over the head of the bed stone on her hair and on her neck and shoulders. I went over and kissed her hand with the brush and her head sunk back on the pillow. I kissed her neck and shoulders. I felt faint with loving her so much.(258-259)

"Now we will drink the other bottle and you will tell me about the war." He waited for me to sit down.

"About anything else," I said.

"You don't want to talk about it? Good. What have have you been reading?"

"Nothing," I said. "I'm afraid I am very dull."

"No. But you should read."

"What is there written in war-time?"

"There is 'Le Feu' by a Frenchman, Barbusse. There is Mr. Britling Sees Through It."

"No, he doesn't,"

"What?"

"He doesn't see through it. Those books were at the hospital."

"Then you have been reading?"

"Yes, but nothing any good."

"I thought 'Mr. Britling' a very good study of the English middle-class soul."

"Poor boy. We none of us know about the soul. Are you Croyant?"

"At night."(260-261)

Count Greffi smiled and turned the glass with his fingers. "I had expected to become more devout as I grow older but somehow I haven't," he said, "It is a great pity."

"Would you like to live after death?" I asked and instantly felt a fool to mention death. But he did not mind the word.

"It would depend on the life. This life is very pleasant. I would like to live forever," he smiled. "I very nearly have."

We were sitting in a deep leather chairs, the champagne in the ice-bucket and our glasses on the table between us.

"If you ever live to be as old as I am you will find many things strange."

"You never seem old."

"It is the body that is old. Sometimes I am afraid I will break off a finger as one breaks a stick of chalk. And the spirit is no older and not much wiser."

"You are wise."

"No, that is the great fallacy; the wisdom of old men. They do not grow wise. They grow careful."(261)

"Perhaps that is wisdom"

"It is a very unattractive wisdom. What do you value most?"

"Some one I love."

"With me it is the same. That is not wisdom. Do you value life?"

"Yes."

"So do I. Because it is all I have. And to give birthday parties,"

he laughed. "You are probably wiser than I am. You do not give birthday parties."

We both drank the wine.

"What do you think of the war really?"he asked.

"I think it is stupid."

"Who will win it?"

"Italy."

"Why?"

"They are a younger nation."

"Do younger nations always win wars?"

"They are apt to for a time."

"Then what happens?"

"They become older nations."

"You said you were not wise."

"Dear boy, that is not wisdom. That is cynicism."(262)

"It sounds very wise to me."

"It's not particularly. I could quote you the examples on the other side. But it is not bad. Have we finished the champagne?"

"Almost."

"Should we drink some more? Then I must dress."

"Perhaps we'd better not now."

"You are sure you don't want more?"

"Yes." He stood up.

"I hope you will be very fortunate and very happy and very, very healthy."

"Thank you. And I hope you will live forever."

"Thank you. I have. And if you ever become devout pray for me if I am dead. I am asking several of my friends to do that. I had expected to become devout myself but it has not come." I thought he smiled sadly but I could not tell. He was so old and his face was very wrinkled, so that a smile used as many lines that all gradation were lost.

"I might become very devout," I said. "Anyway, I will pray for you."

"I had always expected to become devout. All my family died very devout. But somehow it does not come."

"It's too early."

"Maybe it is too late. Perhaps I have outlived my religious feeling."

"My own comes only at night."

"Then too you are in love. Do not forget that is a religious feeling."

"You believe so?"

"Of course." He took a step toward the table. "You were very kind to play."

"It was a great pleasure."

"We will walk up stairs together."(262-263)

36장(Chapter XXXVI)

■ 36장 주요 내용

- 탈영으로 처형될 것이라 소식에 밤에 캐서린과 함께 스위스로 탈주.

- 호텔종업원의 도움으로 스위스로 밤 11시에 탈주한다.

"그러면 스위스로 가십시오."
"어떻게요."
"제 보트로요."
"Then go to Switzerland."
"How?"
"In my boat."(265)

■ Summary

호텔종업원은 늦은 밤에 헨리의 호텔 방에 찾아왔다. 그리고 아침에 탈영병(deserter)으로 체포할 것이라는 말을 했다. 헨리와 캐서린은 스위스로 도망가기 위해서 빨리 준비했다.

■ Commentary

다시 한번 등장인물 중에서 평범한 사람(종업원)의 품위를 주목하게 된다. 호텔종업원은 헨리에게 임박한 체포 소식을 알려줄 뿐만 아니라 그에게 낚시 보트도 주었다. 아마 이런 과정에서 종업원은 자신의 안전에 위험이 될 수도 있었다. 그런데도 종업원은 헨리와 캐서린을 적극적으로 도왔다.

비의 상징과 아이를 밴 캐서린은 직접 충돌하는 과정으로 보인다. 다음과 같은 병치(Juxtaposition)에 주목해 보자. 그녀는 배가 조금씩 불러오자 그 모습을 보지 않으려고 했다. 남문 창문을 두드리는 빗소리를 들으며 옷을 입었다. She was beginning to be a little big with the child and she did not want me to see her. I dressed hearing the rain on the windows. (266) 작가는 희망을 놓지 않았다. 그러나 작가는 '호수를 가로지르는 바람은 차갑고 축축하지만, 산지에는 눈이 내리고 있는 것 같았다.'(267)며 희망을 품고 있었다. It was a cold, wet November wind and I knew it was snowing in the mountains.

여기서 주목할 점은 이 소설에서 눈은 평온함을 상징하고 산은 순수함 뿐만 아니라 안전함을 상징한다는 것을 기억해야 한다.

■ 36장 주요 작품 내용

That night there was a storm and I woke to hear the rain lashing the window-panes. It was coming in the open window. Some one had knocked on the door. I went to the door very softly, not to disturb Catherine, and opened it. The barman stood there. He wore his overcoat and carried his wet hat.

"Can I speak to you, Tenente?"

"What's the matter?"

"It's a very serious matter."

I look around. The room was dark. I saw the water on the floor from the window. "Come in," I said. I took him by the arm into the bathroom; locked the door and put on the light. I sat down on the edge of the bathtub.

"What's the matter, Emilio? Are you in trouble?"

"No. You are, Tenente."

"Yes?"

"They are going to arrest you in the morning."

"Yes?"(264)

"I came to tell you. I was out in the town and I heard them talking in a cafe."

"I see."

He stood there, his coat wet, holding his wet hat and said nothing.

"Why are they going to arrest me?"

"For something about the war."

"Do you know what?"

"No. But I know that they know you were here before as an officer and now you are here out of uniform. After his retreat they arrest everybody."

I thought a minute.

"What time do they come to arrest me?"

"In the morning. I don't know the time."

"What do you say to do?"

He put his hat in the washbowl. It was very wet and had been dripping on the floor.

"If you have nothing to fear an arrest is nothing. But it is always bad to be arrested-especially now."

"I don't want to be arrested."

Then go to Switzerland.

"How?"

"In a boat."

"There is a storm," I said.

"The storm is over. It is rough but you will be all right."

"When should we go?" "Right away. They might come to arrest you early in the morning."

"What about our bags?"

"Get them packed. Get your lady dressed. I will take care of them."

"Where will you be?"(265)

"I will wait here. I don't want one to see me outside in the hall."

I opened the door, closed it, and went into the bedroom. Catherine was awake.

"What is it, darling?"

"It's all right, Cat," I said. "Would you like to get dressed right away and go in a boat to Switzerland?"

"Would you?"

"No," I said. "I'd like to go back to bed."

"What is it about?"

"The barman says they are going to arrest me in the morning."

"Is the barman crazy?"

"No."

"The please hurry, darling, and get dressed so we can start."

She sat up on the side of the bed. She was still sleepy. "Is that the barman in the bathroom?"

"Yes."

"Then I won't wash. Please look the other way, darling, and I'll be dressed in just a minute."

I saw her white back as she took off her night-gown and then I looked away because she wanted me to. She was beginning to be a little big with the child and she did not want me to see her. I dressed hearing the rain on the windows. I did not have much to put in my bag.

"There's plenty of room in my bag, Cat, if you need any."

"I'm almost packed," she said. "Darling, I'm awfully stupid, but why is the barman in the bathroom?"

"Sh-he's waiting to take our bags down."

"He's awfully nice."

"He's an old friend," I said. "I nearly sent him some pipe-tobacco once."

I looked out the open window at the dark night. I could not see the lake, only the dark and the rain but the wind was quieter.(266)

"I'm ready, darling," Catherine said.

"All right," I went to the bathroom door. "Here are the bags, Emilio," I said. The barman took the two bags.

"You're very good to help us," Catherine said.

"That is nothing, lady," the barman said. "I'm glad to help you just so I don't get in trouble myself. Listen," he said to me. "I'll take these out the servants' stairs and to the boat. You just go out as though you were going for a walk."

"It's a lovely night for a walk," Catherine said.

"It's a bad night all right."

"I'm glad I've an umbrella," Catherine said.

We walked down the hall and down the wide thickly carpeted stairs. At the foot of the stairs by the door the porter sat behind his desk.

He looked surprised at seeing us.

"You're not going out, sir?" he said.

"Yes," I said. "W're going to see the storm along the lake."

"Haven't you got an umbrella, sir?"

"No," I said. "This coat sheds water."

He looked at it doubtfully. I'll get you an umbrella, sir, "he said. He went away and came back with a big umbrella." It is a little big, sir, "he said. I gave him a ten-lira note." Oh you are too good, sir. Thank you very much, "he said. He held the door open and we went out into the rain. He smiled at Catherine and she smiled at him." "Don't stay out in the storm," he said. "You will get wet, sir and lady." He was only the second porter, and his Engish was still literally translated.

"We'll be back," I said. We walked down the path under the giant umbrella and out through the dark wet gardens to the road and across the road to the trellised pathway along the lake. The wind was blowing offshore now. It was a cold, wet November wind and I knew it was snowing in the mountains. We came along past the chained boats in the slips along the quay to where the barman's boat should be. The water was dark against the stone. The barman stepped out from beside the row of trees.(267-268)

"The bags are in the boat," he said.

"I want to pay you for the boat," I said.

"How much money have you?"

"Not so much."

"You send me the money later. That will be all right."

"How much?"

"What you want."

"Tell me how much."

"If you get through send me five hundred francs. You won't mind that if you get through."

"All right."

"Here are sandwiches." He handed me a package. "Everything there are in the bar. It's all here. This is a bottle of brandy and a bottle of wine." I put them in my bag. "Let me pay you for those."

"All right, give me fifty lire."

I gave it to him. "The brandy is good," he said. "You don't need to be afraid to gave it to your lady. She better get in the boat." He held the boat, it raining and falling against the stone wall and I helped Catherine in. She sat in the stern and pulled her cape around her.

"You know where to go?"

"Up the lake."

"You know how far?"

"Past Luino."

"Past Luino, Cannero, Cannobio, Tranzano. You aren't in Switzerland until you come to Brissago. You have to pass Monte Tamara."

"What time is it?" Catherine asked.

"It's only eleven o'clock," I said.

"If you row all the time you ought to be there by seven o'clock in the morning."(268)

"Is it that far?"

"It's thirty-five kilometres."

"How should we go? In this rain we need a compass."

"No. Row Isola Bella. Then on the other side of Isola Madre go with the wind. The wind will take you to Pallanza. You will see the lights. Then go up the shore."

"Maybe the wind will change."

"No," he said. "This wind will blow like this for three days. It comes straight down from the Mattarone. There is a can to bail with."

"Let me pay you something for the boat now."

"No, I'd rather take a chance. If you get through you pay me all you can."

"All right."

"I don't think you'll get drowned."

"That's good."

"Go with the wind up the lake."

"All right," I stepped in the boat.

"Did you leave the money for the hotel?"

"Yes. In an envelop in the room."

"All right. Good luck, Tenente."

"Good luck. We thank you many times."

"You won't thank me if you get drowned."

"What does he say?" Catherine asked.

"He says good luck."

"Good luck," Catherine said. "Thank you very much."

"Are you ready?"

"Yes."

He bent down and shoved us off. I dug at the water with the oars, then waved one hand. The barman waved back deprecatingly. I saw the lights of the hotel and rowed out, rowing straight out until they were out of sight. There was quite a sea running but we were going with the wind.(269)

37장 (Chapter XXXVII)

■ 37장 주요 내용

- 호수에서 온갖 어려움을 극복하고 스위스에 도착.

스위스로 들어온 것이 틀림없었다. (276)
I was sure we were in Switzerland now.

"국경에 한참 들어온 게 분명해." 내가 말했다.
"We must be well inside the border," I said. (276)

"달링, 우리가 그 진저리나는 곳에서 빠져나와 여기 있다는 게 실감 나요?"
"Darling, do you realize we're here and out of that bloody place?"

캐서린이 올라왔고 우리는 함께 스위스 땅에 서 있었다.
Catherine stepped up and we were in Switzerland together.

■ Summary

폭풍우가 몰아치는 밤을 지나 헨리와 캐서린은 이탈리아에서 스위스로 연결되는 호수를 노를 저어갔다. 다음 날 그들은 체포가 되었고 잠시 구금되었다가 석방되었다.

■ 논평

  3부의 절정인 37장은 코믹한 안도(comic relief)-희극적인 기분 전환과 함께 흥분된 행동과 손에 땀을 쥐는 긴장감을 공교롭게도 결합했다. 헨리와 캐서린이 경찰에 의해서 석방되었을 때 이탈리아에서 그들의 탈출이 명백한 성공이었다.
  밤을 배경으로 한 상징적으로 중요한 비를 포함한 폭풍우 상태 몇 마일 노를 저어가야 하는 신체적으로 매우 힘든 도전 임신 상태이면서 여자인 캐서린의 취약한 상황 그리고 최고의 극적인 상황을 연출하기 위해서 세관 직원들의 순찰 때문에 체포되는 위험 등등을 주목해야 한다.
  여기서 보트 여행 그 자체는 헤밍웨이가 좋아하는 스테판 크레인(Stephen Crane's)의 「오픈 보트」(The open Boat)라는 단편소설의 영향이 있다는 것을 보여준다.
  예술학도로서의 헨리와 캐서린의 가장무도회와 스위스 경찰들과의 겨울 스포츠에 관한 논쟁을 통해서 제공되는 희극적인 기분 전환이다. 이 같은 기법(comic relief)은 독자와 관객들에게 전개되는 드라마의 감정적인 강도로부터 일시적으로 한숨을 돌리게 한다. 연속적인 강렬한 사건의 연속은 독자와 관객을 힘들게 할 수 있고 중간중간에 쉬어 갈 수 있는 장치가 필요하다. 음악 악보에서 쉼표처럼 그런 역할을 한다. 더욱이 비극이 발생할 때 희극적인 기분 전환이 일어나기 전과 대조가 되기 때문에 비극적인 사건의 발생이 매우 강렬한 영향을 준다. 성격묘사와 관련하여 캐서린의 대단한 불굴의 용기는 여기서 많은 증거가 나타낸다.

　임신했음에도 불구하고 캐서린은 11월 말 오픈된 보트로 여행할 뿐만 아니라 돛대처럼 작용하게 하려면 우산을 들고 있었다. 잠깐이지만 그녀는 배도 몰고 배 안에 있는 물도 퍼내고 심지어는 노도 저었다. 그리고 항상 유머 감각을 유지했다. 최근에 헨리가 세상은 용기 있는 사람을 꺾어 놓기 위해서 죽인다고 했는데 그 용기 있는 사람 중 한 사람이 캐서린인가라는 의문을 품는다.

■ 37장 주요 작품 내용

I rowed in the dark keeping the wind in my face. The rain had stopped and only can occasionally in gusts. It was very dark, and the wind was cold. I could see Catherine in the stern but I could not see the water where the blades of the oars dipped. The oars were long and there were no leathers to keep them from slipping out. I pulled, raised, leaned forward, found the water, dipped and pulled, rowing as easily as I could. I did not feather the oars because the wind was with us. I knew my hands would blister and I wanted to delay it as long as I could. The boat was light and rowed easily. I pulled it along in the dark water. I could not see, and hoped we would soon came opposite Pallanza.

We never saw Pallanza. The wind was blowing up the lake and we passed the point that hides Pallanza in the dark and never saw the lights. When we finally saw some lights much further up the lake and close to the shore it was Intra. But for a long time we did not see any lights, nor did we see the shore but rowed steadily in the dark riding with the waves. Sometimes I missed the water with the oars in the dark as a wave lifted the boat. It was quite rough; (270)

but I kept on rowing, until suddenly we were close ashore against a point of rock that rose beside us; the waves striking against it, rushing high up, then falling back. I pulled hard on the right oar and backed water with the other and we went out into the lack again; the point was out of sight and we were going in up the lake.

"We're across the lake," I said to Catherine.

"Weren't we going to see Pallanza?"

"We've missed it."

"How are you, darling?"

"I'm fine."

"I could take the oars awhile."

"No, I'm fine."

"Poor Ferguson," Catherine said. "In the morning she'll come to the hotel and find we're gone."

"I'm not worrying so much about that," I said," as about getting into the Swiss part of the lake before it's daylight and the custom guards see us."

"Is it a long way?"

"It's some thirty kilometers from here."

I rowed all night. Finally my hands were so sore I could hardly close them over the oars. We were nearly smashed up on the shore several times. I kept fairly close to the shore because I was afraid of getting lost on the lake and losing time. Sometimes we were so close we could see a row of trees and the road along the shore with the mountains behind. The rain stopped and the wind drove the clouds so that the moon shone through and looking back I could see the long dark point of Castagnola and the lake with white-caps and beyond, the moon on the high snow mountains. Then the clouds came over the moon again and the mountains and the lake were gone, but it was much lighter than it had been before and we could see the shore. I could see it too clearly and pulled out where they would not see the boat if there were custom guards along the Pallanza road. When the moon came out again we could see white villas on the shore on the slopes of the mountain and the white road where it showed through the trees. All the time I was rowing.(271-272)

The lake widened and across it on the shore at the foot of the mountains on the other side we saw a few lights that should be Luino. I saw a wedgelike gap between the mountains on the other shore and I thought that must be Luino. If it was we were making good time. I pulled in the oars and lay back on the seat. I was very, very tired of rowing. My arms and shoulders and back ached and my hands were sore.(272)

"I could hold the umbrella," Catherine said. "We could sail with that with the wind."

"Can we steer?"

"I think so."

"You take this oar and hold it under your arm close to the side of the boat and steer and I'll hold the umbrella." I went back to the stern and showed her how to hold the oar. I took the big umbrella the porter had given me and sat facing the bow and opened it. It opened with a clap. I held it on both sides, sitting astride the handle hooked over the seat. The wind was full in it and I felt the boat suck forward while I held as hard as I could to the two edges. It pulled hard. The boat was moving fast.

"We're going beautifully," Catherine said. All I could see was umbrella ribs. The umbrella strained and pulled and I felt us driving along with it. I braced my feet and held back on it, then suddenly, it buckled; I felt a rib snap on mu forehead, I tried to grab the top that was bending with the wind and the whole thing buckled and went inside out and I was astride the handle of an inside-out, ripped umbrella, where I had been holding a wind-filled pulling sail. I unhooked the handle from the seat, laid the umbrella in the bow and went back to Catherine for the oar. She was laughing. She took my hand and kept on laughing.(272)

"What's the matter?" I took the oar.(273)
"You looked so funny holding that thing."
"I suppose so."
"Don't be cross, darling. I was awfully funny. You looked about twenty feet broad and very affectionate holding the umbrella by the edge-" she choked.
"I'll row."
"Take a rest and a drink. It's a grand night and we've come a long way."
"I have to keep the boat out of the trough of the waves."
"I'll get you a drink. Then rest a little while, darling."
I held the oars up and we sailed with them. Catherine was opening the bag. She handed me the brandy bottle. I pulled the cork with my pocket-knife and took a long drink. It was smooth and hot and the heat went all through me and I felt warmed and cheerful. "It's lovely brandy," I said. The moon was under again but I could see the shore. There seemed to be another point going out a long way

ahead into the lake.

"Are you warm enough, Cat?"

"I'm splendid. I'm a little stiff."

"Bail out that water and you can put your feet down."

Then I rowed and listened to the oarlocks and the dip and scrape of the bailing tin under the stern seat.

"Would you give me the bailer?" I said. "I want a drink."

"It's awful dirty."

"That's all right. I'll rise it."

I heard Catherine rinsing it over the side. Then she handed it to me dipped full of water. I was thirsty after the bandy and the water was icy cold, so cold it made my teeth ache. I looked toward the shore. We were closer to the long point. There were lights in the bay ahead.

"Thanks," I said and handed back the tine pail.(273)

"You're ever do welcome," Catherine said. "There's much more if you want it."

"Don't you want to eat something?"

"No. I'll be hungry in a little while. We'll save it till then."

"All right."

What looked like a point ahead was a long high headland. I went further out in the lake to pass it. The lake was much narrower now. The moon was out again and the guardia di finanza could have seen our boat black on the water if they had been watching.

"How are you, Cat?" I asked.

"I'm all right. Where are we?"

"I don't think we have more than about eight miles more."

"That's a long way to row, you poor sweet. Aren't you dead?"

"No. I'm all right. My hands are sore is all."

We went on up the lake. There was a break in the mountains on the right bank, a flatteing-out with a low shore line that I thought must be Cannobio. I stayed a long way out because it was from now on that we ran the most danger of meeting guardia. There was a high dome-capped mountain on the other shore a way ahead. I was tired. It was no great distance to row but when you were out of condition it had been a long way. I knew I had to pass that mountain and go up the lake at least five miles further before we would be in Swiss water. The moon was almost down now but before it went down the sky coulded over again and it was very dark. I stayed well out in the lake, rowing awhile, then resting and holding the oars so that the wind struck the blades.

"Let me row awhile," Catherine said.

"I don't think you ought to."

"Nonsense. It would be god for me. It would keep me from being too stiff."

"I don't think you should, Cat."(274)

"Nonsense. Rowing in moderation is very good for the pregnant lady."

"All right, you row a little moderately. I'll go back, then you come up. Hold on to both gunwhales when you come up."

I sat in stern with my coat on and the collar turned up and watched Catherine row. She rowed very well but the oars were too long and bothered her. I opened the bag and ate a couple a sandwiches and took a drink for the brandy. It made everything much better and I took too another drink.

"Tell me when you're tired," I said. Then a little later, "Watch out the oar doesn't pop you in the tummy."

"If it did-Catherine said between strokes- life might be much simpler."

I took another drink of the brandy.

"How are you going?"

"All right."

"Tell me when you want to stop."

"All right."

I took another drink of the brandy, then took hold of the two gunwales of the boat and moved forward.

"No. I'm going beautifully."

"Go on back to the stern. I've had grand rest."

For a while, with the brandy, I rowed easily and steadily. Then I began to catch crabs and soon I was just chopping along again with a thin brown taste of bile from having rowed too hard after the brandy.

"Give me a drink of water, will you?" I said.

"That's easy," Catherine said.(275)

Before daylight it started to drizzle. The wind was down or we were protected by mountain that bounded the curve the lake had made. When I knew daylight coming I settled down and rowed hard. I did not know where we were and I wanted to get into Swiss part of the lake. When it was beginning to be daylight we were quite close to the shore. I could see rocky shore and the trees.(275-276)

"What's that?" Catherine and I rested on the oars and I listened. It was a motor boat chugging out on the lake. I pulled close up to the shore and lay quiet. The chugging came closer; then we saw the motor boat in the rain a little astern of us. There were four guardia di finanza in the stern, their alphini hats pulled down, their cape collars turned up and their carbines slung across their backs. They all looked sleepy so early in the morning. I could see the yellow on their hats and the yellow marks on their cape collars. The motor boat chugged on and out of sight in the rain.

I pulled out into the lake. If we were that close to the border I did not want to be hailed by a sentry along the road. I stayed out where I could just see the shore and rowed on for three quarters of an hour in the rain. We heard a motor boat once more but I kept quiet the noise of the engine went away across the lake.(276)

It was clear daylight now and a fine rain was falling. The wind was still blowing outside up the lake and we could see the tops of the white-caps going away from us and up the lake. I was sure we were in Switzerland now. There were many houses back in the trees from the shore and up the shore a way was a village with stone houses, some villas on the hills and a church. I had been looking at the road and skirted the shore for guards but did not see any.(276-277)

The road came quite close to the lake now and I saw a soldier coming out of a cafe on the road. He wore a gray-green uniform and a helmet like the Germans. He had a healthy-looking face and a little toothbrush mustache. He looked at us.

"Wave to him," I said to Catherine. She waved and the soldier smiled embarrassedly and gave a wave of his hand. I eased up rowing. We were passing the waterfront of the village.

"We must be well inside the border," I said.

"We want to be sure, darling. We don't want them to turn us back at the frontier."

"The frontier is a long way back. I think this is the customs town. I'm pretty sure it's Brissago."

"Won't there be Italians there? There are always both sides at a customs town."

"Not in war time. I don't think they let the Italians cross the frontier."

It was a nice-looking little town. There were many fishing boats along the quay and nets were spread on racks. There was a fine November rain falling but it looked cheerful and clean even with the rain.

"Should we land then and have breakfast?"

"All right."

I pulled hard on the left oar and came in close, then straightened out when we were close to the quay and bought the boat alongside. I pulled in the oars, took hold of an iron ring, stepped up on the wet stone and was in Switzerland. I tied the boat and held my hand down to Catherine.

"Come on up, Cat. It's a grand feeling."

"What about the bags?"

"Leave them in the boat."

Catherine stepped up and we were in Switzerland together.

"What a lovely country," she said.

"Isn't it grnad?"(277)

"Let's go and have breakfast"

"Isn't it a grand country? I love the way it feels under my shoes."

"I'm so stiff I can't feel it very well. But it feels like a splendid country. Darling, do you realize we're here and out of that bloody place?"

"I do. I really do. I've never realized anything before."

"Look at the houses. Isn't this a fine square? There's a place we can get breakfast."

"Isn't the rain fine? They never had rain like this in Italy. It's cheerful rain."

"And we're here, darling! Do you realize we're here?"(278)

"Why do you enter Switzerland this way in a boat?"

"I am a sportman," I said. "Rowing is my great sport. I always row when I get a chance."

"Why do you come here?"

"For the winter sport. We are tourists and we want to do the winter sport."

"This is no place for winter sport."

"We know it. We want to go where they have the winter sport."

"What have you been doing in Italy?"

"I have been studying architecture. My cousin has been studying art."

"Why do you leave here?"

"We want to do the winter sport. With the war going on you cannot study architecture."

"You will please stay where you are," the lieutenant said. He went back into the building with our passports.

"You're splendid, darling" Catherine said. "Keep on the same track. You want to do the winter sport."

"Do you know anything about art?"

"Rubens," said Catherine.

"Large an fat," I said.

"Titian," Catherine said.

"Titian-haired," I said. "How about Mantegna?"

"Don't ask hard ones," Catherine said. "I know him though-very bitter."

"Very bitter," I said. "Lots of nail holes."

"You see I'll make you a fine wife," Catherine said. "I'll be able to talk art with your customers."

"Here he comes," I said. The thin lieutenant came down the length of the custom house, holding our passports.

"I will have to send you into Locarno," he said. "You can get a carriage and a soldier will go in with you."

"All right," I said. "What about the boat?"

"The boat is confiscated. What have you in those bags?"

He went all through the two bags and held up the quarter-bottle of brandy. "Would you join me in a drink?" I asked.(279-280)

"No thank you." He straightened up. "How much money have you?"

"Twenty -five hundred lire."

He was favorably impressed. "How much has your cousin?"

Catherine had a little over twelve hundred lire. The lieutenant was pleased. His attitude toward us became less haughty.

"If you are going for winter sports," he said. "Wengen is the place. My father has a very fine hotel at Wengen. It is open all the time.(281)

"That's splendid," I said. "Could you give me the name?"

"I will write it on a card." He handed me the card very politely.

"The soldier will take you into Locarno. He will keep your passports. I regret this but it is necessary. I have good hopes they will give you a visa or a police permit at Locarno."

He handed the two passports to the soldier and carrying the bags we started into the village to order a carriage. "Hi," the lieutenant called to the soldier. He said something in a German dialect to him. The soldier slung his rifle on his back and picked up the bags.

"It's a great country," I said to Catherine.

"It's so practical."

"Thank you very much," I said to the lieutenant. He waved his hand.

"Service!" he said. We followed our guard into the village. We drove to Locarno in carriage with the soldier sitting on the front seat with the driver. At Locarno we did not have a bad time. They questioned us but they were polite because we had passports and money. I do not think they believed a word of the story and I thought it was silly but it was like a law-court. You did not want something reasonable, you wanted something technical and then stuck to it without explanations. But we had passports and we would spend the money. So they gave us provisional visas.(281)

Could we go wherever we wanted? Yes. Where did we want to go?

"Where do you want to go, Cat?"

"Montreux."

"It is very nice place," the official said. "I think you will like that place."

"Here at Locarno is a very nice place," another official said. "I am sure you would like it here very much at Locarno. Locarno is a very attractive place."

"We would like some place where there is winter sport."

"There is no winter sport at Montreux."

"I beg your pardon," the other official said. "I come from Montreux. There is very certainly winter sport on the Montreux Oberland Bernois railway. It would be false for you to deny that."

"I do not deny it. I simply said there is no winter sport at Montreux."

"I question that," the other official said. "I question that statement."

"I hold to that statement."

"I question that statement. I myself have luge-ed into the streets of Montreux. I have done it not once but several times. Luge-ing is certainly winter sport."

The other official turned to me.

"Is luge-ing your idea of winter sport, sir? I tell you you would be very comfortable here in Locarno. You would find the climate healthy, you would find the environs attractive. You would like it very much."

"The gentleman has expressed a wish to go to Montreux."

"What is luge-ing?" I asked.

"You see he has never even heard of luge-ing!"(282)

"How did you happen to pick out Montreux?" I asked Catherine. "Do you really want to go there?"

"It was the first place I could think of," sh said. "It's not a bad place. We can find some place up in the mountains."

"Are you sleepy?"

"I'm sleepy right now."

"We'll get a good sleep. Poor Cat, you had a long bad night."

"I had a lovely time," Catherine said. "Especially when you sailed with the umbrella."

"Can you realize we're in Switzerland?"

"No, I'm afraid I'll wake up and it won't be true."

"I am too."

"It is true, isn't it, darling? I'm not just driving down to the stazione in Milan to see you off."

"I hope not."

"Don't say that. It freightens me. Maybe that's where we're going."

"I'm so groggy I don't know," I said.

"Let me see your hands."

I put them out. They were both blistered raw.

"There's no hole in my side," I said.

"Don't be sacrilegious."

I felt very tire and vague in the head. The exhilaration was all gone. The carriage was going along the street.

"Poor hands," Catherine said.

"Don't touch them," I said. "By God I don't know where we are."

"Where are we going, driver? The driver stopped his horse."

"To the Hotel Metropole. Don't you want to go there?"

"Yes," I said. "It's all right, Cat."

"It's all right, darling. Don't be upset. We'll get a good sleep and you won't feel groggy to-morrow."

"I get pretty groggy," I said. "It's like a comic opera to-day. Maybe I'm hungry."

"You're just tired, darling. You'll be fine." The carriage pulled up before the hotel. Some one came out to take our bags.

"I feel all right," I said. We were down on the pavement going into the hotel.

"I know you'll be all right. You're just tired. You've been up a long time."

"Anyhow we're here."

"Yes, we're really here."

We followed the boy with the bags into the hotel.(284-285)

38장(Chapter XXXVIII)

■ 38장 주요 내용

- 계절의 변화: 가을

- 목가적인 살레(Chalet) 지역묘사: 한 폭의 그림을 보는 듯한 묘사.

- 주인공과 캐서린은 목가적인 살레 지역과 마찬가지로 편안하고 순수하며 목가적인 삶을 살아가는 모습을 소설이 시작한 이후에 처음으로 보여 준다.

■ Summary

헨리와 캐서린은 몽퇴뢰(Montreux)지역 산 앞에 있는 살레(Chalet)로 이사했다. 헨리는 전투가 이탈리아에 불리하다는 것을 신문을 읽고 알았다.

■ 논평

이 소설의 상징과 관련해서 주목해야 할 점은 작품에서 묘사된 겨울에 눈이 매우 늦게 왔다는 것이다. That fall the snow came very late. (289)

결과적으로 전투는 지속하였고 헨리는 전쟁은 다른 대학에서 벌어지는 축구 경기처럼 아득히 멀게 느껴졌다. The war seemed as far away as the football games of some one else's college.(291)라고 말했다.

그러나 리날디와 신부인 그의 동료들에 대해서 걱정했다. "전쟁은 생각하고 싶지도 않고 나는 전쟁에서 이미 손을 뗐어." "About Rinaldi and the priest and lots of people I know. But I don't think about them much. I don't think about the war. I'm through with it."(298)이라고 헨리가 캐서린에게 말했다. 여전히 헨리는 밤에 잠을 잘 자지 못한다. 아마도 탈영에 대한 죄책감의 결과인 듯하다. 그러나 헨리와 캐서린이 온통 눈으로 덮여 있는 산에서 자신들을 발견함으로써 두 가지 상징이 뒤얽혀 있다는 것을 알 수 있다.

적어도 그들은 순간적으로 순수함과 안전을 겸비한 삶을 이룩되었다. 이 경치는 작품 초반에 묘사된 신부의 고향인 아브루치(Abruzzi)를 상기시킨다.

헤밍웨이의 강력한 묘사의 힘 덕분에 38장은 작가가 강조하고자 하는 바를 잘 표출했다. 38장의 순수하고 안전한 생활의 묘사는 작가의 이야기 구성의 전략에 의해서 나온 산물이다. 이같이 목가적이고 편안하고 순순한 장면과 대비되는 비극적인 장면을 이후에 배치해서 극적인 효과를 전달하고자 하는 작가의 의도가 깔려 있다.

주변이 눈으로 덮여 있어서 목가적이고 순수하고 안전한 곳과 나중에 일어날 끔찍한 일을 비교하여 더욱 선명해진다. 작가는 이 같은 선명성을 강조하기 위해서 현재의 자신들이 거주하고 있는 지역을 눈으로 덮인 차분하고 조용한 곳으로 묘사했다.

헨리가 결혼하고자 제안했을 때 캐서린은 임신한 상태로 결혼하는 것을 거부했다. 나중에 아이 출산하고 날씬할 때 하자고 한다. 몽퇴뢰에 그들이 알고 있는 사람이 한 명도 없으므로 중요하지 않다. 그러나 그들의 이 같은 고립은 이전보다 그들을 더 가깝게 만들어 준다. 사실 캐서린은 둘이 비슷하게 보이기 위해서 머리를 같은 길이로 하자고 제안했다.

"아 달링. 나는 당신을 너무나 원해서 당신이 되고 싶어질 정도예요."(299)
헨리는 "이미 그래. 우리는 한 몸이야."라고 답했다.(299)
"Oh, darling, I want you so much I want to be you too."

"You are. We're the same one." 이 장에는 기술적이며 명백하게 불길한 성격을 예고하는 내용도 포함되어 있다. 캐서린의 의사는 그녀가 골반이 좁다고 말했다. 이것은 나중에 아이 출산과 관련돼서 문제가 된다.

■ 38장 주요 작품 내용

That fall the snow came very late. We lived in a brown wooden house in the pine trees on the side of the mountain and at night there was frost so that there was thin ice over the water in the two pitchers on the dresser in the morning. Mrs. Guttingen came into the room early in the morning to shut the windows and started a fire in the tall porcelain stove. The pine wood crackled and sparked and then the fire roared in the stove and the second time Mrs. Guttingen came into the room she brought big chunks of wood for the fire and a pitcher of hot water. When the room was warm she brought in breakfast. Sitting in bed eating breakfast we could see the lake and the mountains across the lake on the French side. There was snow on the tops of the mountains and the lake was a gray steel-blue.(289)

Outside, in front of the chalet a road went up the mountain. The wheel nuts and ridges were iron hard with the frost, and the road climbed steadily through the forest and up and around the mountains to where there were meadows, and barns and cabins in the meadows at the edge of the woods looking across the valley.

The valley was deep and there was a steam at the bottom that flowed down into the lake and when the wind blew across the valley you could hear the stream in the rocks.(289-290)

Sometimes we went off the road and on a path through the pine forest. The floor of the forest was soft to walk on; the frost did not harden it as it did the road. But we did not mind the hardness of the road because we had nails in the soles and heels of our boots and the heel nails bit on the frozen ruts and with nailed boots it was good walking on the road and invigorating. But it was lovely walking in the woods.

In front of the house where we lived the mountain went down steeply to the little plain along the lake and we sat on the porch of the house in the sun and saw the winding of the road down the mountain-side and the terraced vineyards on the side of the lower mountain, the vines all dead now for the winder and the fields divided by stone walls, and below the vineyards the houses of the town on the narrow plain along the lake shore. There was an island with two trees on the lake and the trees looked like the double sails of a fishing-boat. The mountains were sharp and steep on the other side of the lake and down at the end of the lake was the plain of the Rhone Valley flat between the two ranges of mountains; and up the valley where the mountains cut it off was the Dent du Midi. It was a high snowy mountain and it dominated the valley but it was so far away that it did not make a shadow.(290)

There was a box of wood in the hall outside the living room and I kept up the fire from it. But we did not stay up very late. We went to be in the dark in the big bedroom and when I was undressed I opened the windows and saw the night and the cold stars and the pine trees below the window and then got into bed as fast as I could. It was lovely in bed with the air so cold and clear and the night outside the window. We slept well and if I woke in the night I knew it was from only one cause and I would shift the feather bed over, very softly so that Catherine would not be wakened and then go back to sleep again, warm and with the new lightness of thin covers. The war seemed as far as the football game of some one else's college. But I knew from the papers that they were still fighting in the mountains because the snow would not come.(291)

Sometimes we walked down the mountain into Montreux. There was a path went down the mountain but it was steep and so usually we took the road and walked down on the wide hard road between fields and then below between the stone walls of the vineyards and so down between the houses of the villages along the way. There were three villages; Chernex, Fontanivent, and the other I forget. Then along the road we passed an old square-built stone chateau on a ledge on the side of the mountain-side with the terraced fields of vines, each vine tied to a stick to hold it up, the vines dry and brown and the earth ready for the snow and the lake down below flat and gray as steel. The road went down a long grade below the chateau and then turned to the right and went down very steeply and paved with cobbles, into Montreux.(291-292)

We did not know any one in Montreux. We walked along beside the lake and saw the swans and the many gulls and terns that flew up when you came close and screamed while they looked down at the water. Out on the lake there were flocks grebes, small and dark, and leaving trails I the water when they swam.

In the town we walked along the main street and looked in the windows of the shops. There were many big hotels that were closed but most of the shops were open and the people were very glad to see us. There was a fine coiffeur's place where Catherine went to have her hair done. The woman who ran it was very cheerful and the only person we knew in Montreux. While Catherine was there I went up to a beer place and drank dark Munich beer and read the papers. I read Corriere della Sera and the English and American papers from Paris. All the advertisements were blacked out, supposedly to prevent communication in that way with the enemy. The papers were bad reading. Everything was going very badly everywhere. I sat back in the corner with a heavy mug of dark beer and an opened glazed-paper package of pretzels and ate the pretzels for the salty flavor and the good way they made the beer taste and read about disaster. I thought Catherine would come by but she did not come, so I hung the papers back on the rack, paid for my beer and went up the street to look for her. The day was cold and dark and wintry and the stone of the houses looked cold. Catherine was still in the hair-dresser's shop. The woman was waving her hair. I sat in the little booth and watched. It was exciting to watch and Catherine smiled and talked to me and my voice was a little thick from being excited. The tongs made a pleasant clicking sound and I could see Catherine in three mirrors and it was pleasant and warm in the booth.(292)

Then the woman put up Catherine's hair, and Catherine looked in the mirror and changed it a little, taking out and putting in pins; then stood up. "I'm sorry to have taken such a long time."

"Monsieur was very interested. Were you not, monsieur?" the woman smiled.

"Yes," I said.

We went out and up the street. It was cold and wintry and the wind was blowing. "Oh, darling, I love you so," I said.

"Don't we have a fine time?" Catherine said. "Look. Let's go some place and have beer instead of tea. It's very good for young Catherine. It keeps her small."

"Young Catherine," I said. "That loafer."

"She's been very good," Catherine said. "She makes very little trouble. The doctor say beer will be good for me and keep her small."

"If you keep her small enough and she's a boy, maybe he will be a jockey."

"I suppose if we really have this child we ought to get married," Catherine said. We were in the beer place at the corner table. It was getting dark outside. It was still early but the day was dark and the dusk was coming early.

"Let's get married now," I said.

"No," Catherine said. "It's too embarrassing now. I show too plainly. I won't go before any one and be married in this state."

"I wish we'd gotten married."

"I suppose it would have been better. But when could we, darling?"

"I don't know."

"I know one thing. I'm not going to be married in this splendid matronly state."

"You're not matronly."

"Oh yes, I am, darling. The hairdresser asked me if this was our first. I lied and said no, we had two boys and two girls."

"When will we be married?"

"Any time after I'm thin again."(292-293)

"We want to have a splendid wedding with every one thinking what a handsome young couple."

"And you're not worried?"

"Darling, why should I be worried? The only time I ever felt badly was when I felt like a whore in Milan and that only lasted seven minutes and besides it was the room furnishings. Don't I make you a good wife?"

"You're a lovely wife."

"Then don't be too technical, darling. I'll marry you as soon as I'm thin again."

"All right."

"Do you think I ought to drink another beer? The doctor said I was rather narrow in the hips and it's all for the best if we keep young Catherine small."

"What else did he say ?" I was worried.

"Nothing. I have a wonderful blood-pressure, darling. He admired my blood-pressured greatly."

"What did he say about you being too narrow in the hips?"

"Nothing. Nothing at all. He said I shouldn't ski."

"Quite right."

"He said it was too late to start if I'd never done it before. He said I could ski if I wouldn't fall down."

"He's just a big-hearted joker."

"Really he was very nice. We'll have him when the baby comes."

"Did you ask him if you ought to get married?"

"No. I told him we'd been married four years. You see, darling, if I marry you I'll be an American and any time we're married under American law the child is legitimate."

"Where did you find that out?"

"In the **New York World** Almanac in the library."

"You're a grand girl."(293-294)

Snow did not come until three days before Christmas. We woke one morning and it was snowing. We stayed in bed with the fire roaring in the stove and watched

the snow fall. Mrs Guttingen took away the breakfast trays and put more wood in the store. It was a big snow storm. She said it had started about midnight. I went to the window and looked out but could not see across the road. It was blowing and snowing wildly. I went back to bed and we lay and talked.

"I wish I could ski," Catherine said. "It's rotten not to be able to ski."

"We'll get a bobsled and come down the road. That's no worse for you than riding in a car."

"Won't it be rough?"

"We can see."

"I hope it won't be too rough."

"After a while we'll take a walk in the snow."

"Before lunch," Catherine said, "so we'll have a good appetite."

"I'm always hungry."

"So am I."

We went out in the snow but it was drifted so that we could not walk far. I went ahead and made a trail down to the station but when we reached there we had gone far enough. The snow was blowing so we could hardly see and we went into the little inn by the station and swept each other off with a broom and sat on a bench and had vermouths.

"It is a big storm," the barmaid said.

"Yes."(296)

"No. Sometimes I wonder about the front and about people I know but don't worry. I don't think about anything much."

"Who do you wonder about?"

"About Rinaldi and priest and lots of people I know. But I don't think about them much. I don't want to think a about the war. I'm through with it."

"What are you thinking about now?"

"Nothing."

"Yes you were. Tell me."

"I was wondering whether Rinaldi had the syphilis."

"Was that all?"(298)

"Yes."

"Has he the syphilis?"

"I don't know."

"I'm glad you haven't. Did you ever have anything like that?"

"I had gonorrhea."

"I don't want to hear about it. Was it very painful, darling?"

"Very."

"I wish I'd had it."

"No you don't."

"I do. I wish I'd had it to be like you. I wish I'd stayed with all your girls so I could make fun of them to you."

"That's a pretty picture."

"It's not a pretty picture you having gonorrhea."

"I know it. Look at it snow now."

"I'd rather look at you. Darling, why don't you let your hair grow?"

"How grow?"

"Just grow a little longer."

"It's long enough now."

"No, let it grow a little longer and I could cut mine and we'd be just alike only one of us blonde and one of us dark." "I wouldn't let you cut yours."

"It would be fun. I'm tired of it. It's an awful nuisance in the bed at night."

"I like it."

"Wouldn't you like it short?"

"I might. I like it the way it is."(299)

"It might be nice short. Then we'd both be alike. Oh, darling, I want you so much I want to be you too."

"You are. We're the same one."

"I know it. At night we are."

"The nights are grand."(299)

"I want us to be all mixed up. I don't want to go away. I just said that. You go if you want to. But hurry right back . Why, darling, I don't live at all when I'm not with you." "I won't ever go away." I said. "I'm no good when you're not there. I haven't any life at all any more."

"I want you to have a life. I want you to have a fine life. But we'll have it together, won't we?"

"And now do you want me to stop growing my beard or let it go on?"

"Go on. Grow it. It will be exciting. Maybe it will be done for New Year's."

"Now do you want to play chess?"

"I'd rather play with you."

"No. Let's play chess."

"And afterward we'll play?"

"Yes."

"All right."

I got out the chess-board and arranged the pieces. It was still snowing hard outside.(300)

One time in the night I woke up and knew that Catherine was awake too. The moon was shining in the window and made shadows on the bed from the bars on the window-panes.

"Are you awake, sweetheart?"

"Yes. Can't you sleep?"

"I just woke up thinking about how I was nearly crazy when I first meet you. Do you remember?"

"You were just a little crazy."

"I'm never that way any more. I'm grand now. You say grand so sweetly. Say grand."

"Grand."

"Oh, you're sweet. And I'm not crazy now. I'm just very, very, very happy."

"Go on to sleep," I said.

"All right. Let's go to sleep at exactly the same moment."

"All right."

But we did not. I was awake for quite a long time thinking about things and watching Catherine sleeping, moonlight on her face. Then I went to sleep, too. (300-301)

39장 (Chapter XXXIX)

■ 39장 주요 내용

- 헨리와 캐서린은 가족에 관해 이야기한다.

"가족 생각은 조금도 안 해요?"
"하지. 그런데 너무 자주 다투다 보니 애정이 식었어."
"Don't you care anything about them?"
"I did, but we quareled so much it wore itself out."

■ Summary

다가올 운명에 끊임없는 전조가 지속하듯이 헨리와 캐서린은 가족에 관해 이야기한다.

■ 논평

목가적인 생활은 지속한다.

"뭘 원하는 거지? 사랑으로 파멸되는 거?"
"응, 파멸시킬 거예요."(305)

What do you want to do?

Ruin me?

"Yes, I want to ruin you."

38장과 39장은 매우 목가적이고 평온한 생활을 보여 주고 있다. 소설이 마지막으로 결론과 너무나도 대조적인 배치를 한다. 소설의 마지막 장인 41장과 너무도 대조적인 면을 소설의 마지막 앞에 배치함으로써 극적인 효과를 최대한 끌어올리는 헤밍웨이만의 구성 방식을 볼 수 있다. 캐서린과 아이가 죽는 장면 앞에 너무도 행복한 부부가 스위스의 포근하고 따스한 겨울을 보내는 면은 마지막에서의 비극적인 면을 상상할 수 없고 그런 일을 접할 때 독자들은 너무도 충격으로 다가올 수 있는 효과를 준다. 마지막에 캐서린과 아이가 죽고 헨리는 외로이 호텔을 떠나는 장면을 극적인 효과를 주기 위해서 사랑하는 사람과 함께 평온하게 생활하는 모습을 대조적으로 배치했다.

■ 39장 주요 작품 내용

By the middle of January I had a beard and the winter had settled into bright cold days and hard cold nights. We could walk on the roads again. The snow was packed hard and smooth by the haysleds and wood-sledges and the log that were hauled down the mountain. The snow lay over all the country, down almost to Montreux. The mountains on the other side of the lake were all white and the plain of the Rhone Valley was covered. We took long walks on the other side of the mountain to the Bains de l'ALLiaz. Catherine wore hobnailed boots and a cape and carried a stick with a sharp steel point. She did not look big with the cape and we would not walk too fast but stopped and sat on logs by the roadside to rest when she was tired.(302)

We sat close together on the logs. Ahead the road went down through the forest.

"She won't come between us, will she? The little brat."

"No. We won't let her."

"How are we for money?"

"We have plenty. They honored the last sight draft."

"Won't your family try and get hold of you now they know you're in Switzerland?"

"Probably. I'll write them something."

"Haven't you written them?"

"No. Only the sight draft."

"Thank God I'm not your family."

"I'll send them a cable."

"Don't you care anything about them?"

"I did, but we quarrelled so much it wore itself out."

"I think I'd like them. I'd probably like them very much."

"Let's not talk about them or I'll start to worry about them."

After a while I said, "Let's go on if you're rested."

"I'm rested."

We went on down the road. It was dark now and the snow squeaked under our boots. The night was dry and cold and very clear.

"I love our beard," Catherine said. "It's a great success. It looks so stiff and fierce and it's very soft and a great pleasure."

"Do you like it better than without"

"I think so. You know, darling, I'm not going to cut my hair now until after young Catherine's born. I look too big and matronly now. But after she's born and I'm thin again I'm going to cut it and then I'll be a fine new and different girl for you. We'll go together and get it cut, or I'll go alone and come and surprise you."

I did not say anything.

"You won't say I can't, will you?"

"No. I think it would be exciting."

"Oh, you're so seet. And maybe I'd look lovely, darling, and be so thin and exciting to you and you'll fall in love with me all over again."

"Hell," I said. "I love you enough now. What do you want to do? Ruin me?"

"Yes. I want ruin you."

"Good," I said, "that's what I want too."(304-305)

40장(Chapter XL)

■ 40장 주요 내용

- 아이를 출산하기 위해 로잔으로 출발.

On the morning of the third day of rain we decided to go down into town.(307)
"We have to be near the hospital anyway on account of Madame," I said.(307)

■ Summary

겨울이 끝날 무렵 헨리와 캐서린은 로잔(Lausanne)에 있는 호텔에 가기 위해서 산을 떠난다.

■ 논평

상징은 헨리와 캐서린의 두 번째 목가적인 생활이 결론에 다가가고 있다는 것을 우리에게 알려준다. 자연의 휴전인(nature's cease-fire) 겨울은 이미 끝났다.
그래서 헨리는 밤에 비가 내리기 시작했다. 산 위쪽에도 비가 내렸다.(306) In the night it started raining. …. It was raining high up the mountain.(306)라고 우리에게 보고하며 말했다. 로잔에 기차로 도착해서 그는,

"차창으로 우리가 살던 쪽을 바라보았지만, 산은 구름에 가려 보이지 않았다."(308)라고 보고했다. Looking out the window toward where we had lived you could not see the mountains for the clouds. (308) 따라서 그 부부가 죽음으로부터 피할 수 있는 은신처가 없다. 여기서 문제는 애정행각에 의한 죽음인가? 아니면 태아에 의한 죽음인가? 이것은 아직 명확하지 않다. 그러나 40장의 예감은 거의 참을 수 없을 정도로 극단적이다.

■ 40장 주요 작품 내용

We had a fine life. We lived through the months of January and February and the winter was very fine and we were very happy. There had been short thaws when the wind blew warm and the snow softened and the air felt like spring, but always the clear hard cold and come again and the winter had returned. In March came the first break in the winter. In the night it started raining. It rained on all morning and turned the snow to slush and made the mountain-side dismal. There were clouds over the lake and over the valley. It was raining high up the mountain. Catherine wore heavy overshoes and I wrote Mr.Guttingen's rubber boots and we walked to the station under an umbrella, through the slush and the running water that was washing the ice of the roads bare, to stop at the pub before lunch for a vermouth. Outside we could hear the rain.

"Do you think we ought to move into town?"

"What do you think?" Catherine asked.

"If the winter is over and the rain keeps up it won't be fun up here. How long is it before young Catherine?"(306)

"About a month. Perhaps a little more."

"We might go down and stay in Montreux."

"Why don't we go to Lausanne? That's where the hospital is."

"All right. But I thought maybe that was too big a town."

"We can be as much alone in a bigger town and Lausanne might be nice."

"When should we go?"

"I don't care. Whenever you want, darling. I don't want to leave here if you don't want."

"Let's see how the weather turns out."

It rained for three days. The snow was all gone now on the mountain-side below the station. The road was torrent of muddy snow-water. It was too wet and slushy to go out. On the morning of the third day of rain we decided to go down town.

"That is all right, Mr Henry," Catherine said. "You do not have to give me any notice. I did not think you would want to stay now the bad weather is come."

"We have to be near the hospital anyway on account of Madame," I said.

"I understand," he said. "Will you come back some time and stay, with the little one?"

"Yes, if you would have room."

In the spring when it is nice you could come and enjoy it. We could put the little one and the nurse in the big room that is closed now and you and Madame could have your same room looking out over the lake.

"I'll write about coming," I said. We packed and left on the train that went down after lunch. Mr and Mrs. Guttingen came down to the station with us and he hauled our baggage down on a sled through the slush. They stood beside the station in the rain waving good-by.

"They were very sweet," Catherine said.

"They were fine to us."(307)

We took the train to Lausanne from Montreux. Looking out the window toward where we had lived you could not see the mountains for the clouds. The train stopped in Very. then went on, passing the lake on one side and on the other the wet brown fields and the bare woods and the wet houses. We came into Lausanne and went into a medium-size hotel to stay. It was still raining as we drove through the streets and into the carriage entrance of the hotel. The concierge with the brass keys on his lapels, the elevator, the carpet on the floors, and the white washbowls with shining fixtures, the brass bed and the big comfortable bedroom all seemed very good luxury after the Guttingens. The windows of the room looked out on a wet garden with a wall topped by an iron fence. Across the street, which sloped steeply, was another hotel with a similar wall and garden. I looked out at the rain falling in the fountain of the garden.

Catherine turned on all the lights and commenced unpacking. I ordered a whiskey and soda and lay on the bed and read the papers I had bought at the station. It was March , 1918, and the German offensive had started in France. I drank the whiskey and soda and read while Catherine unpacked and moved around the room.(308)

Sometimes Catherine and I went for rides out in the country in a carriage. It was nice to ride when the days were pleasant and we found two good places where we could ride out to eat. Catherine could not walk very far now and I loved to ride out along the country roads with her. When there was a good day we had a splendid time and we never had a bad time. We knew the baby was very close now and it gave us both a feeling as though something were hurrying us and we could not lose any time together.(311)

41장 (Chapter XLI)

- **41장 주요 내용**

- 소설의 마지막 장.

- 아들의 죽음 The baby was dead. (327)

- 헨리와 캐서린과의 이별.

그녀는 내내 의식이 없었고, 오래지 않아 숨을 거뒀다.
She was unconscious all the time, and it did not take her very long to die. (331)

- 전쟁으로 인한 비극적인 결말.

Poor, poor dear Cat. And this was the price you paid for sleeping together. This was the end of the trap. This was what people got for loving each other. (320)

- **Summary**

이 소설의 마지막 장이다. 헨리는 캐서린을 병원에 입원시키고 그곳에서 캐서린은 아이 출산 과정에서 오랜 시간 고통스러운 과정을 경험한다.

그 결과 탯줄에 호흡이 제대로 제공되지 못해서 먼저 아이가 죽는다. 그리고 캐서린은 과다 출혈로 사망했다.

■ 논평

마지막 장인 41장은 이 소설의 앞부분(1장에서 40장까지)에서 공들여 준비한 것에 의해서 비극적이면서도 강력한 효과를 이루어 낸다. 예를 들면 캐서린이 병원에 도착했을 때 간호사는 그녀에게 잠옷(night-gown) 바꿔 입으라고 지시한 것은 헨리 캐서린 부부가 지난밤 밀리노 호텔에 머물기 위해서 구매한 잠옷을 연상시킨다.

이마도 이것은 임신한 캐서린이 아이를 낳아야 할 때가 밤이 아닌지를 암시해 준다.

"Here is a night-gown for you to wear."
"I have a nightgown," Catherine said.
"It is better for you to wear this night-gown," the woman said.(313)

마찬가지로 불행한 분만을 하는 동안 헨리가 밥을 먹으려고 간 카페에서 고객들의 카드 게임(Card game)은 체스나 브릿지(Chess and Bridge)처럼 그들의 연애 시작에서 지나친 오해를 우리에게 연상시킨다.

주목해야 할 것은 캐서린이 간호사에게 자신이 종교를 갖고 있지 않다는 것을 인정한다.

She said she had no religion.(313)

제왕절개에 관해서 헨리는 "종교재판을 그린 그림을 보는 것 같았다." (325)

It looked like a drawing of the Inquisition. 라고 우리에게 말했다. 헨리 자신조차도 매우 고통스럽다고 인정하고 아이가 세례를 받지 않은 것에 대해서 유감스러워했고 자신의 마음을 바꾸었다. They supposed he would come around and start breathing probably. I had no religion but I knew he ought to have been baptized.(327)

이제는 캐서린이 죽을지도 모른다. 그게 인간이 하는 일이다. 인간은 죽는다. 죽음이 뭔지도 모르는 채 죽는다. 그것을 깨우칠 시간도 없다. 인간을 구장에 내던지고 규칙을 말해준 뒤 베이스에서 발을 떼는 것이 보이자마자 죽이는 것이다. 또는 아이모처럼 아무 이유도 없이 죽인다. 또는 리날디처럼 매독에 걸리게 한다. 하지만 결국은 모두 죽인다. 그건 분명한 사실이다. 잠시 머물게 하지만 결국은 죽인다.(327)

Now Catherine would die. That was what you did. You did not know what it was about. You never had time to learn. They threw you in and told you the rules and the first time they caught you off base they killed you. Or they killed you gratuitously like Aymo. Or gave you the syphilis like Rinaldi. But they killed you in the end. You could count on that. Stay around and they would kill you.(327)

헨리는 불타고 있는 이 세상을 모닥불의 장작으로 묘사했다. 자신이 구세주(to be a messiah)가 될 수 있다는 충동에도 불구하고 무리를 지어 장작으로 들어가는 개미들을 그는 구하지 못했다. 죽어가고 있는 캐서린을 두고 볼 수밖에 없는 상황을 묘사했다.

모든 사람이 그런 것처럼 캐서린의 임박한 죽음 앞에서 필사적으로 신과 협상하려고 시도했다. 반면에 그녀는 자신의 신념에 대한 용기를 끝까지 간직하고 있었다. 그리고 헨리가 "신부님이나 누구 데려올까요?"(330) 라고 했을 때 그녀는 "당신이면 돼요."(330) 라고 헨리에 대해 반응했다.

"Do you want me to get a priest or any one to come and see you?"
"Just you," she said.(330)

그 어떤 것보다도 죽어가는 그 순간까지도 캐서린에게 있어서 종교는 사랑이었다. 절체절명의 순간에 캐서린에게 가장 신중한 것은 신, 신부, 성직자가 아니고 자신이 사랑하는 사람 그 사람의 사랑이다. 헨리가 그 용감함이 죽을 운명이라고 자신의 관점을 우리와 공유했기 때문에 작품 전체를 통해서 캐서린의 용감한 개념과 용감이라는 단어가 소름 끼치는 인상을 준다.

"달링 온몸이 조각난 것 같아."(322)
darling I'm going all to peaces.

이 소설에서 가장 잘 알려진 구문을 캐서린이 헨리에게 말하므로 인해서 우리에게 상기시켜 준다. 잠시 뒤 헨리는 그녀에게 용감하다. 라고 말했다. 그러자 그녀는 "나는 더 이상 용기를 낼 수가 없어요. 달링 나는 완전히 부서져 버렸어. 이 사람들이 나를 부서뜨렸어요."(323)라고 반응했다.

You be brave, because I can't do that all the time. It might kill you. "I'm not brave any more, darling. I'm all broken. they've broken me."(323)

"그녀는 고통이 심해지는 것이 더 좋은 거로 생각했다."(314)
When the pains were bad, she called them good ones.(314)

불편한 아이 출산에 대해서 처음으로 캐서린은 유쾌하게 반응했다. 이 같은 반응은 이탈리아에서 위험하게 탈출할 때나 작품 전체를 통해서 그녀의 성격묘사와 항상 일치한다. 웃지 않고 나중에 웃을 때는 그녀의 고통이 매우 극심하다는 의미이다.

그녀는 힘들지만 참고 난 후에 자신이 인내한 고통에 대해서 웃음으로 넘긴다. 옆에 있는 사랑하는 사람에게 자신이 겪은 고통을 토로하지 않고 그냥 웃는다. 아니면 농담조로 말한다.

마찬가지로 헨리는 전쟁 중에 많은 고통을 경험했지만, 제왕절개 수술을 볼 수 없었다. 너무 소름이 끼치는 수술이다. 고뇌와 죽음은 서로 사랑하는 사람들이 치르는 대가이다. (320) This was what people got for loving each other.

헨리는 우리에게 작가의 사랑, 섹스, 죽음(love-sex-death) 연속성을 계속 반복하면서 말한다. 주목해야 할 점은 헨리가 카페에서 신문을 읽으면서 알게 되는 것처럼 분명히 전쟁은 계속 진행되고 있다는 것이다.

상징적으로 중요한 날씨에 관해서는 헨리가 점심을 먹기 위해서 병원을 떠날 때 "날을 흐렸지만 해가 구름 사이로 나오려고 하고 있었다. (318) The day was cloudy but the sun was trying to come through.

수술하는 동안 그는 창문 밖을 보고 비가 오는 것을 지켜봤다. 간호사가 아이가 죽었다고 그에게 말한 직후에 헨리는 또 밖을 다시 봤다.

보이는 거라곤 창밖으로 새어 나오는 빛에 비치는 비와 어둠뿐이었다.(327)
I could see nothing but the dark and the rain falling across the light from the window.

이 장에서 또 다른 상징은 "커피 찌꺼기와 먼지와 시든 꽃들뿐이었다." (315)

there was nothing on top but coffee-grounds, dust and some dead flowers.

커피와 먼지 그리고 시든 꽃들만이 있는 쓰레기통을 포함한 것이 이 장에서 또 다른 상징이다. 더 이상 인생의 암울한 광경을 상상할 수 없다. 날씨를 통해서 현재 캐서린의 상태를 잘 설명하고 있다. 해가 구름 사이에 나오려 하고 있다는 표현 그리고 비와 어둠뿐이라는 표현은 헨리와 캐서린의 상황을 생생하게 독자들에게 보여 준다.

자신을 많이 지도해 준 거트루드 스타인(Gertrude Stein) 여사의 문체적인 예를 잘 따르면서 헤밍웨이는 후렴(refrain)과 같은 두 개의 구문을 계속 반복해서 사용했다.

고통을 감소시켜 주는 이산화질소에 관해서 캐서린은 "대주세요."(Give it to me) (318)를 반복했다. 그러자 헨리는 "안 죽을 거야"(320) She won't die 이 같은 반복을 통해서 극적인 결과를 연출한다. 즉 참혹한 느낌에 긴장감을 직접 인용함으로써 작가는 제임스 조이스의 의식적 흐름의 기법을 많이 활용했다.

병원에 되돌아왔을 때 무슨 일이 전개될지에 대해서 궁금하게 생각하기 때문에 캐서린이 시련을 감당하는 동안 헨리가 카페를 자주 방문하는 것은 긴장을 더욱 고조시킨다. 또한, 비극적이지만 이와 같은 것은 캐서린이 죽음을 맞이한 후에 헨리가 자신의 인생을 위해서 일종의 무의식적인 연습을 하게 해주는 역할을 한다. 결과적으로 우리는 그녀가 떠난 이후에 그가 얼마나 외로운지를 잘 안다. 사실 헨리의 외로움은 캐서린이 죽자마자 시작되었다. 의사가 도움과 동료애를 제공하지만, 헨리는 둘 다 거부한다. 이것은 마지막에 도움에 대해 캐서린은 끝까지 도움을 거부한 것과 일치한다. 헨리의 질문에 대한 그녀의 답은 다음과 같다.

"신부님이나 누구 데려올까요?"(330)

그녀는 "당신이면 돼요."(330) 라고, 답한다.

"Do you want me to get a priest or any one to come and see you."

"Just you," she said. (330)

캐서린이 이렇게 된 것이 자신과의 사랑으로 인한 것인가? 아니면 전쟁으로 인한 비극인가?

아니면 전쟁 중에서 전쟁에 열심히 하지 않고 사랑놀이를 한 결과 벌을 받는 것인가? 우리는 전쟁에 참전하면 24시간 전쟁만 해야 한다고 생각하지만 전쟁 중에 잠도 자고 이야기도 하고 밥도 먹는 일상의 생활을 하게 된다. 소설의 앞부분에서 언급한 것처럼 파시니는 파스타를 먹는 중에 적의 공격을 받아서 죽고 영웅도 다친다. 영웅이 이렇게 말하는 것은 전쟁을 일으킨 사람이 따로 있고 전쟁에 참전하는 사람이 따로 있고 전쟁으로 돈을 버는 사람 따로 있다고 말한 것처럼 캐서린과 영웅의 사랑을 전쟁으로 인한 희생자이다.

Poor, poor dear Cat. And this was the price you paid for sleeping together. This was the end of the trap. This was what people got for loving each other. (320)

And this was the price you paid for sleeping together. (320)

역설적으로 헨리와 캐서린의 단독강화는 성공적이었다. 적어도 단독(분리)(separation) 속에서 그들은 극단적인 도움이 필요할 때 도움을 제공해 주는 공동체가 없다는 것을 스스로 알게 된다. 이 작품을 통해서 작가는 그들이 존재할 때조차도 공동체가 우리 자신들의 죽음으로부터 구해 줄 수 없다는 것을 강조한다. 우리 자신들의 암울한 상황의 죽음으로부터 공동체들 즉 국가가 우리들의 죽음으로부터 구해 줄 수 없다는 것이다.

부대에서 탈출은 자신이 살기 위한 몸부림이다. 국가와 지도자들이 만들어 놓은 정쟁이란 덫에서 젊은이들은 조국을 위해서 죽고 조국을 위해서 싸우다 어른들과 국가가 만들어 놓은 부조리한 현장에서 살아남기 위한 필사적인 몸부림이다. 탈영병이라고 손가락질하는 것은 국가가 만들어 놓은 불합리한 덫에 있는 젊은이들에게 손가락질하는 것이다. 전쟁이란 국가들이 자신들의 욕심과 야욕을 채우기 위해서 일으킨 것이다. 그러나 자신들은 그 전쟁터에 가지 않고 아무것도 모르는 젊은이들을 전쟁터에 보내는 아주 불합리한 일들이 세계 각지에서 발생했다. 순수한 젊은 청년들은 조국을 위해서 싸우다 죽어갔다. 아니면 헨리 중위처럼 상처를 입기도 한다. 운이 좋게 헨리처럼 살 수 있으면 다행이다. 어떤 젊은이는 평생 장애인으로 살아가는 사람들을 흔히 볼 수 있다. 조국은 우리를 위해서 무엇을 해주었는가? 백번 양보해서 조국을 지키다 죽을 수 있다. 그렇지만 전쟁이 왜 발생했는지 꼭 발생해야만 하는 전쟁이었는지 국가지도자들의 욕심과 야욕에 의한 전쟁은 아니었는지 따져봐야 할 일이다. 헨리 중위가 탈영하기 직전의 심정은 어떠했을까? 살기 위한 단독강화였다. 같은 부대의 군인들에 의해서 죽음의 총부리를 맞이한 헨리는 죽기 살기로 도주할 수밖에 없었다. 그를 도와주는 사람은 누구도 없었다.

애초에 전쟁이 없었다면 헨리와 캐서린은 전쟁터에 만나지 않았고 서로 사랑을 하지 않았다. 전쟁터에서 만난 두 남녀의 사랑은 시작부터 불안했고 결말도 좋지 못했다. 서로 사랑하게 돼서 아이를 갖게 되고 그 아이들 출산하다가 캐서린과 아이는 죽음을 맞이한다. 사랑하는 남편도 캐서린의 어떻게 도와줄 수 없다. 결국, 전쟁이 낳은 죽음이고 고통이다. 이 고통과 죽음에서 도와줄 수 있는 사람은 아무도 없다. 그냥 죽음을 맞이할 뿐이다. 이렇게 된 처지에 대한 원망이 부질없는 일이다. 그래서 전쟁터에서 귀향한 젊은이들이 방황하고 기존의 가치관 질서를 부정하고 자신들이 경험만을 의지하는 세대가 되었다.

■ 41장 주요 작품 내용

One morning I woke about three o'clock hearing Catherine stirring in the bed.

"Are you all right, Cat?"

"I've been having some pains, darling."

"Regularly?"

"No, not very."

"If you have them at all regularly we'll go to hospital."

I was very sleepy and went back to sleep. A little while later I woke again.

"Maybe you'd better call up the doctor," Catherine said. "I think maybe this is it."

I went to the phone and called the doctor. "How often the pains coming?" he asked. "How often are they coming, Cat?"

"I should think every quarter of an hour."

"You should go to the hospital," the doctor said. "I will dress and go there right away myself."

I hung up and called the garage near the station to send up a taxi. No one answered the phone for a long time. Then I finally got a man who promised to send up a taxi at once.(312)

Catherine was dressing. Her bag was all packed with the things she would need at the hospital and the baby things. Outside in the hall I rang for the elevator. There was no answer. I went downstairs. There was no one downstairs except the night-watchman. I brought the elevator up myself, put Catherine's bags in it,

She stepped in and we went down. The night-watchman opened the door for us and we sat outside on the stone slabs beside the stairs down to the driveway and waited for the taxi. The night was clear and the stars were out. Catherine was very excited.

"I'm so glad it's started," she said. "Now in a little while it will be all over."(313)

At the hospital we went in and I carried the bag. There was a woman at the desk who wrote down Catherine's name, age, address, relatives and religion, in a book. She said she has no religion and the woman drew a line in the space after that word. She gave her name as Catherine Henry.

"I will take you up to your room," she said. We went up in an elevator. The woman stopped it and we stepped out and followed her down a hall. Catherine held tight to my arm.

"This is the room," the woman said. "Will you please undress and get into bed? Here is a night-gown for you to wear."

"I have a night-gown," Catherine said.

"It is better for you to wear this night-gown," the woman said.

I went outside and sat on a chair in the hallway.(313)

"You can come in now," the woman said from the doorway. Catherine was lying in the narrow bed wearing a plain, square-cut night-gown that looked as though it were made of rough sheeting. She smiled at me.

"I'm having fine pains now," she said. The woman was holding her wrist and timing the pains with a watch.

"That was a big one," Catherine said. I saw it on her face.

"Where's the doctor?" I asked the woman.

"He's lying down sleeping. He will be here when he is needed."

"I must do something for Madame, now," the nurse said.

"Would you please step out again?"

I went out into the hall. It was a bare hall with two windows and closed doors all down the corridor. It smelled of hospital. I sat on the chair and looked at the floor and prayed for Catherine.(314)

"That was a real one. Do you want to put your hand on my back again, nurse?"

"If it helps you," the nurse said.

"You go away, darling," Catherine said. "Go out and get something to eat. I may do this for a long time the nurse says."

"That first labor is usually protracted," the nurse said.

"Please go out and get something to eat," Catherine said. "I'm fine, really."

"I'll stay awhile," I said.

The pains came quite regularly, then slackened off. Catherine was very excited. When the pains were bad she called them good ones. When they started to fall off she was disappointed and ashamed.(314)

"You go out, darling," she said. "I think you are just making me self-conscious." Her face tied up. "There. That was better. I so want to be a good wife and have this child without any foolishness. Please go and get some breakfast, darling, and then come back. I won't miss you. Nurse is splendid to me."

"You have plenty of time for breakfast," the nurse said.

"I'll go then. Good-by, sweet."

"Good-by," Catherine said, and "have a fine breakfast for me too."

"Where can I get breakfast?" I asked the nurse.

"There's a cafe down the street at the square," she said. "It should be open now."

Outside it was getting light. I walked down the empty street to the cafe. There was a light in the window. I went in and stood at the zinc bar and an old man served me a glass of white wine and a brioche. the brioche was yesterday's. I dipped it in the wine and then drank a glass of coffee.

"What do you do at this hour?" the old man asked.

"My wife is in labor at the hospital."

"So. I wish you good luck."

"Give me another glass of wine."

He poured it from the bottle slopping it over a little so some ran down on the zinc. I drank this glass, paid and went out. Outside along the street were the refuse cans from the houses waiting for the collector. A dog was nosing at one of the cans.

"What do you want?" I asked and looked in the can to see if there was anything I could pull out for him; there was nothing on top but coffee-grounds, dust and some dead flowers.

"There isn't anything, dog," I said. The dog crossed the street. I went up the stairs in the hospital to the floor Catherine was on and down the hall to her room. I knocked on the floor. There was no answer.(315)

I opened the door; the room was empty, except for Catherine's bag on a chair and her dressing-gown hanging on a hook on the wall.(315-316) I went out and down the hall, looking for somebody. I found a nurse.

"Where is Madame Henry?"

"A lady has just gone to the delivery room."

"Where is it?"

"I will show you."

She took me down on the end of the hall. The door of the room was partly open. I could see Catherine lying on a table, covered by a sheet. The nurse was on one side and the doctor stood on the other side of the table beside some cyclinders. The doctor held a rubber mask attached to a tube in one hand.

"I will give you a gown and you can go in," the nurse said. "Come in here, please."

She put a white gown on me and pinned it at the neck in back with a safety pin.

"Now you can go in," she said. I went into the room.

"Hello, darling," Catherine said in a strained voice. "I'm not doing much."

"You are Mr.Henry?" the doctor asked.

"Yes. How is everything going, doctor?"

"Things are going very well," the doctor said. "We came I here where it is easy to give gas for the pains."

"I want it now," Catherine said. The doctor placed the rubber mask over her face and turned a dial and I watched Catherine breathing deeply and rapidly. Then she pushed the mask away. The doctor shut off the petcock.

"That's wasn't a very big one. I had a very big one a while ago. The doctor made me go clear out, didn't you, doctor?" Her voice was strange. It rose on the word doctor.

The doctor smiled. "I want it again," Catherine said. She held the rubber tight to her face and breathed fast.(315-317)

I heard her moaning a little. Then she pulled the mask away and smiled.

"That was a big one," she said. "That was a very big one. Don't you worry, darling. You go away. Go have another breakfast."

"I'll stay," I said.

We had gone to the hospital about three o'clock in the morning. At noon Catherine was still in the delivery room. The pains had slackened again. She looked very tired and worn now but she was still cheerful.

"I'm not any good, darling," she said. "I'm so sorry. I thought I would do it very easily. Now-there's one-" she reached out her hand for the mask ans held it over her face. The doctor moved the dial and watched her. In a little while it was over.

"It wasn't much," Catherine said. She smiled. "I'm a fool about the gas. It's wonderful."

"We'll get some for the home," I said.

"**There one comes**," Catherine said quickly. The doctor turned the dial and looked at her watch.

"What is the interval now?" I asked.

"About a minute."

"Don't you want lunch"

"I will have something pretty soon," he said.

"You must have something to eat, doctor," Catherine said. "I'm so sorry I go on so long. Couldn't my husband give me the gas?"

"If you wish," the doctor said. "You turned it to the numeral two."

"I see," I said. There was a marker on a dial that turned with a handle.

"*I want it now*," Catherine said. She held the mask tight to her face. I turned the dial to number two and when Catherine put down the mask I turned it off. It was very good of the doctor to let me do something.(317)

"Did you do it, darling?" Catherine asked. She stroke my wrist.

"Sure."

"You're so lovely." She was a little drunk from the gas.

"I will eat from a tray in the next room," the doctor said. "You can call me any moment." "While the time passed I watched him eats, then, after a while, I saw that he was lying down ans smoking a cigarette. Catherine was getting very tired.

"Do you think I'll ever have this baby?" she asked.

"Yes, of course you will."

"I try as hard as I can. I push down but it goes away. **There it comes**. Give it to me."

At two o'clock I went out and had lunch. There were a few men in the cafe sitting with coffee and glasses of kirsch or marc on the tables. I sat down at a table. "Can I eat?" I asked the waiter.

"It is past time for lunch."

"Isn't there anything for all hours?"

"You can have *choucroute*."

"Give me *choucroute* and beer."

"A demi or a bock?"

"A light demi."

The waiter brought a dish of sauerkraut with a slice of ham over the top and a sausage buried in the hot wine-soaked cabbage. I ate it and drank the beer. I was very hungry. I watched the people at the table in the cafe. At one table they were playing cards. Two men at the table next me were talking and smoking. The cafe was full of smoke. The zinc bar, where I had breakfasted, had three people behind it now; the old man, a plump woman in a black dress who sat behind a counter and kept track of everything served to the tables, and a boy in an apron. I wondered how many children the woman had and what it had been like.

When I was through with *choucroute* I went back to the hospital. The street was all clean now. There were no refuse cans out. The day was cloudy but the sun was trying to come through.(318)

I rode upstairs in the elevator, stepped out and went down the hall to Catherine's room, where I had left my white gown. I put it on and pinned it in back at the neck. I looked in the glass and saw myself looking like a fake doctor with a beard. I went down the hall to the delivery room. The door was closed and I knocked. No one answered so I turned the handle and went in. The doctor sat by Catherine. The nurse was doing something at the other end of the room.

"Here is my husband," the doctor said.

"Oh, darling, I have the most wonderful doctor," Catherine said in a very strange voice. "He's been telling me the most wonderful story and when the pain came too badly he put me all the way out. He's wonderful. You're wonderful, doctor."

"You're drunk," I said.

"I know it," Catherine said. "But you shouldn't say it." Then "*Give it to me. Give it to me.*" She clutched hold of the mask and breathed short and deep, pantingly, making the respirator click. Then she gave a long sigh and the doctor reached with his left hand and lifted away the mask.

"That was a very big one," Catherine said. Her voice was very strange. "**I'm not going to die now**, darling. I'm pasty where **I was going to die**. Aren't you glad?"

"Don't you get in that place again."

"I won't. I'm not afraid of it though. **I won't die**, darling."

"You will not do any such foolishness," the doctor said. "You would not die and leave your husband."

"Oh, no. **I won't die**. I wouldn't die. It's silly to die. There it comes. *Give it to me*."

After a while the doctor said, "You will go out, Mr. Henry, for a few moments and I will make an examination."

"He wants to see how I am doing," Catherine said. "You can come back afterward, darling, can't he, doctor?"(319)

"Yes," said the doctor. "I will send word when he can come back."

I went out the door and down the hall to the room where Catherine was to be after then baby came. I sat in a chair there and looked at the room. I had the paper in my coat that I had bought when I went out for lunch and I read it. It was beginning to be dark outside and I turned the light on to read. After a while I stopped reading and turned off the light and watched it get dark outside. I wondered why the doctor did not send for me. Maybe it was better I was away. He probably wanted me away for a while. I looked at my watch. If he did not send for me ten minutes I would go down anyway.

Poor, poor dear Cat. And this was the price you paid for sleeping together. This was the end of the trap. This was what people got for loving each other. Thanks God for gas, anyway. What must it have been like before they were anesthetics? Once it started, they were in the mill-race. Catherine had a good time in the time of pregnancy. It wasn't bad. She was hardly ever sick. She was not awfully uncomfortably until toward the last. So now they got her in the end. You never got away with anything. Get away hell! It would have been the same if we had been married fifty times. And **what if she should die?** She won't die. **People don't die** in childbirth nowadays. That was what all husbands thought. Yes, but **what if she should die? She won't die.** She's just having a bad time. The initial labor is usually protracted. She's only having a bad time. Afterward we'd say what a bad time and Catherine would say it wasn't really so bad. But **what if she should die? She can't die.** Yes, but **what if she should die?** She can't, I tell you. Don't be a fool. It's just a bad time. It's just nature giving her hell. It's only the first labor, which is almost always protracted. Yes, but **what if she should die? She can't die. Why would she die? What reason is there for her to die?** There's just a child that has to be born, the by-product of good nights in Milan.(320)

It makes trouble and is born and then you look after it and get fond of it maybe. But what if she should die? **She won't die.** But **what if she should die?** She won't. She's all right. But **what if she should die? She can't die.** But **what if she should die?** Hey, What about that? **What if she should die?**

The doctor came into the room.

"How does it go, doctor?"

"It doesn't go," he said.

"What do you mean?"

"Just that. I made an examination-" He detailed the result of the examination. "Since then I've waited to see. But it doesn't go."

"What do you advise?"

"There are two things. Either a high forceps delivery which can tear and be quite dangerous besides being possibly bad for the child, and a Caesarean?"

"What if she should die!"

"It should be no greater than the danger of an ordinary delivery."

"Would you do it yourself"

"Yes. I would need possibly an hour to get things ready and to get the people I would need. Perhaps a little less."

"What do you think?"

"I would advise a Caesarean operation. If it were my wife I would do a caesarrean."

"What are the after effects?"

"There are none. There is only the scar."

"What about infection?"

"The danger is not so great as in a high forceps delivery."

"What if you just went on and did nothing?"

"You would have to do something eventually. Mrs. Henry is already losing much of her strength. The sooner we operate now the safer."

"Operate as soon as you can," I said.(321)

"I will go and give the instruction."

I went into the delivery room. The nurse was with Catherine who lay on the table, big under the sheet, looking very pale and tired.

"Did you tell him he could do it?" she asked.

"Yes."

"Isn't that grand. Now it will be all over in an hour. I'm almost done, darling. I'm going all to pieces. Please give me that. **It doesn't work**. Oh, *it doesn't work!*"

"Breathe deeply."

"I am. Oh, **it doesn't work** any more. **It doesn't work**!"

"Get another cylinder," I said to the nurse.

"That is a new cyclinder."

"I'm just a foo, darling," Catherine said. "But **it doesn't work** any more." She began to cry. "Oh, I wanted so to have this baby and not make trouble, and now I'm all done and all gone to pieces and it doesn't work. Oh, darling, **it doesn't work** at all. I don't care if I die if it will only stop. Oh, please make it stop. There it comes. *Oh Oh Oh!*" She breathed sobbingly in the mask. "**It doesn't work**. it doesn't work. Don't mind me, darling. Please don't cry. Don't mind me. I'm just gone all to pieces. You poor sweet. I love you so and I'll be good again. I'll be good this time. Can't they give me something? If they could only give me something." I will make it work. I'll turn it all the way.

"Give it to me now."

I turned the dial all the way and as she breathed hard and deep her hand relaxed on the mask. I shut off the gas and lifted the mask. She came back from a long way away.

"That was lovely, darling. Oh, you're so good to me."

"You be brave, because I can't do that all the time. It might kill you."(322)

"I'm not brave any more, darling. I'm all broken. They've broken me. I know it now."

"Everything is that way."

"But it's awful. They just keep it up till they break you."

"In an hour it will be over."

"Isn't that lovely? Darling, I won't die, will I?"

"No. I promise you won't."

"Because I don't want to die and leave you, but I get so tired of it and I feel I'm going to die."

"Nonsense. Everybody feels that."

"Sometimes I know I'm going to die."

"You won't. You can't."

"But what if I should?"

"I won't let you."

"Give it to me quick. **Give it to me!**"

Then afterward, "I won't die. I won't let myself die."

"Of course you won't."

"You'll stay with me?"

"Not to watch it."

"No, just to be there."

"Sure. I'll be there all the time."

"You're so good to me. There, give it to me. Give me some more. **It's not working!**"

I turned he dial to three and then four. I wish the doctor would come back. I was afraid of the numbers above two.

Finally a new doctor came in with two nurses and they lifted Catherine onto a wheeled stretcher and we started down the hall. The stretcher went rapidly down the hall and into the elevator where every one had to crowd against the wall to make room; then up, then an open door and out of the elevator and down the hall on rubber wheels to the operating room.(323)

I did not recognize the doctor with his cap and mask on. There was another doctor and more nurses.

"**They've got to give me something**," Catherine said. "**They've got to give me something**, Oh please, doctor, give me enough to do some good!"

One of the doctors put a mask over her face and I looked through the door and saw the bright small amphitheatre of the operating room.

"You can go in the other door and sit up there," a nurse said to me. There were benches behind a rail that looked down on the white table and the lights. I looked at Catherine. The mask was over her face and she was quiet now. They wheeled the stretcher forward. I turned away and walked down the hall. Two nurses were hurrying toward the entrance to the gallery.

"It's Caesarean," one said. "They're going to do a Caesarean."

The other one laughed. "We're just in time. Aren't we Lucky?"

They went in the door that led to the gallery.

Another nurse came along. She was hurrying too.

"You go right in there. Go right in," she said.

"I'm staying outside."

She hurried in. I walked up and down the hall. I was afraid to go in. I looked out the window. It was dark but in the light from the window I could see it was raining.

I went into a room at the far end of the hall and looked at the labels on bottles in a glass case. Then I came out and stood in the empty hall and watched the door of the operating room.

A doctor came out followed by a nurse. He held something in his two hands that looked like a freshly skinned rabbit and hurried across the corridor with it and in through another door. I went down to the door he had gone into and found them in the room doing things to a new born child. The doctor held him up for me to see. He held him by the heels and slapped him.

"Is he all right?"(323-324)

"He's magnificent. He'll weight five kilos."

I had no feeling for him. He did not seem to have anything to do with me. I felt no feeling of fatherhood.

"Aren't you proud of your son?" the nurse asked. They were washing him and wrapping him in something. I saw the little dark face and dark hand, but I did not see him move or hear him cry. The doctor was doing something to him again. He looked upset.

"No," I said. "He nearly killed his mother."

"It isn't the little darling's fault. Didn't you want a boy?"

"No," I said. The doctor was busy with him. He held him up by the feet and slapped him. I did not wait to see it. I went out in the hall. I could go in now and see. I went in the door and a little way down the gallery. The nurses who were sitting at the rail motioned for me to come down where they were. I shook my head. I could see enough where I was

    I thought Catherine was dead. She looked dead. Her face was gray, the part of it that I could see. Down below, under the light, the doctor was sewing up the great long, forcep-spread, thick-edged, wound. Another doctor in a mask gave the anesthetic. Two nurses in masks handed things. It looked like a drawing of the Inquisition. I knew as I watched I could have watched it all, but I was glad I hadn't. I do not think I could have watched them cut, but I watched the wound closed into a high welted ridge with quick skilful-looking stitches like a cobbler's and was glad. When the wound was closed I went out into the hall and walked up and down again. After a while the doctor came out.

"How is she?"

"She is all right. Did you watch?"

He looked tired.

"I saw you sew up. The incision looked very long."

"You thought so?"

"Yes. Will that scar flatten out?"

"Oh, yes."(325)

    After a while they brought out the wheeled stretcher and took it very rapidly down the hallway to the elevator. I went along beside it. Catherine was moaning. Downstairs they put her in the bed in her room. I sat in a chair at the foot of the bed. There was a nurse in the room. I got up and stood by the bed. It was dark in the room. Catherine put out her hand. "Hellow, darling," she said. Her voice was very weak and tired.

"Hellow, you sweet."

"What sort of baby was it?"

"Sh-don't talk," the nurse said.

"A boy. He's long and wide and dark."

"Yes," I said. "He's fine."

I saw the nurse look at me strangely.

"I'm awfully tired," Catherine said. "And I hurt like hell. Are you all right, darling?"

"I'm fine. Don't talk."

"You were lovely to me. Oh, darling, I hurt dreadfully. What does he look like?"

"He looks like a skinned rabbit with a puckered-up old-man's face."

"You must go out," the nurse said. "Madame Henry must not talk."

"I'll be outside."

"Go and get something to eat."

"No. I'll be outside." I kissed Catherine. She was very gray and weak and tired.

"May I speak to you?" I said to the nurse. She came out in the hall with me. I walked a little way down the hall.

"What's the matter with the baby?" I asked "Didn't you know?"

"No."(326)

"He wasn't alive."

"He was dead?"

"They couldn't start him breathing. The cord was caught around his neck or something."

"So he's dead."

"Yes. It's such a shame. He was such a fine big boy. I thought you knew."

"No," I said. "You better go back in with Madame."

I sat down on the chair in front of a table where there were nurses' report hung on clips at the side and looked out of the window. I could see nothing but the dark and the rain falling across the light from the window. So that was it. The baby was dead. That was why the doctor looked so tired. But why had they acted the way they did in the room with him? They supposed he would come around and start breathing probably. I had no religion but I knew he ought to have been baptized. But what if he never breathed at all. He hadn't. He had never been alive. Except in Catherine. I'd felt him kick there often enough. But I hadn't for a week. Maybe he was choked all the time. Poor little kid. I wished the hell I'd been choked like that. No I didn't. Still there would not be all this dying to go through. Now Catherine would die. That was what you did. You died. You did not know what it was about. You never had time to learn. They threw you in and told you the rules and the first time they caught you off base they killed you. Or they killed you gratuitously like Aymo. Or gave you the syphilis like Rinaldi. But they killed you in the end. You could count on that. Stay around and they would kill you.

Once in camp I put a log on the top of the fire and it was full of ants. As it commenced to burn, the ants swarmed out and went first toward the centre where the fire was; then turned back and ran toward the end. When there were enough on the end they fell off into the fire. Some got out, their bodies burnt and flattened, and went off not knowing where they were going.(327)

But most of them went toward the fire and then back toward the end and swarmed on the cool end and finally fell off into the fire. I remember thinking at the time that it was the end of the world and a splendid chance to be a messiah and lifted the log off the fire and throw it out where the ants could get off onto the ground. But I did not do anything but throw a tin cup of water on the log, so that I would have the cup empty to put whiskey in before I added water to it. I think the cup of water on the burning log only steamed the ants.(327-328)

So now I sat out in the hall and waited to hear how Catherine was. The nurse did not come out, so after a while I went to the door and opened it very softly and looked in. I could not see at first because there was a bright light in the hall and it was dark in the room. Then I saw the nurse sitting by the bed and Catherine's head on a pillow, and she was all flat under the sheet. The nurse put her finger to her lips, then stood up and came to the door.
"How is she ?" I asked.
"She's all right?" the nurse said. "You should go and have your supper and then come back if you wish"
I went down the hall and then down the stairs and out the door of the hospital and down the dark street in the rain to the cafe. It was brightly lighted inside and

there were many people at the tables. I did not see a place to sit, and a waiter came up to me and took my wet coat and hat and showed me a place at a table across from an elderly man who was drinking beer and reading the evening paper. I sat down and asked the waiter what the plat du jour was.

"Veal stew-but it is finished."

"What can I have to eat?"

"Ham and eggs, eggs with cheese, or **choucroute**."

"I had **choucroute** this noon," I said.

"That's true," he said.

"That's true. You ate choucroute this noon." He was a middle-aged man with a bald top to his head and his hair slicked over it. He had a kind face.(328)

"What do you want? Ham and eggs or eggs with cheese?"

"Ham and eggs," I said, "and beer."

"A demi-blonde?"

"Yes," I said.

"I remembered," he said. "You took a demi-blonde this noon."

I ate the hams and eggs and drank the beer. The ham and eggs were in a round dish- the ham underneath and eggs on top. It was very hot and at first mouthful I had to take a drink of beer to cool my mouth. I was hungry and I asked the waiter for another order. I drank several glasses of beer. I was not thinking at all but read the paper of the man opposite me. It was about the break through on the British front. When he realized I was reading the back of his paper, he fold it over. I thought of asking the waiter for a paper, but I could not concentrate. It was hot in the cafe and the air was bad. Many of the people at the table knew one another. There was several card games going on. The waiters were busy bringing drinks from the bar to the tables. Two men came in and could find no place to sit. They stood opposite the table where I was. I ordered another beer. I was not ready to leave yet. It was too soon to go back to the hospital. I tried not to think and to be perfectly calm. The men stood around but no one was leaving, so they went out. I drank another beer. There was quite a pile of saucers now on the table in front of me. The man opposite me had taken off his spectacles, put them away in a case, folded his paper and put it in his pocket and now sat holding his liqueur glass and looking out at the room. Suddenly I knew I had to get back. I called the waiter, paid the reckoning, got into my coat, put on my hat and started out the door. I walked through the rain up to the hospital.

Upstairs I met the nurses coming down the hall.

"I just called you at the hotel," she said. Something dropped inside me.

"What is wrong?"(329)

"Mrs. Henry has had a hermorrhage."

"Can I go in?"

"No, not yet. The doctor is with her."

"Is it dangerous?"

"It is very dangerous." The nurse went into the room and shut the door. I sat outside in the hall. Everything was gone inside of me. I did not think. I could not think. **I knew she was going to die** and I prayed that she would not. **Don't let her die. Oh, God, please don't let her die.** I will do anything for you **if you won't let her die.** Please, please, please, dear God, **don't let her die. Dear God, don't let her die. Please, please, please don't let her die. God please make her not die.** I'll do anything you say **if you don't let her die. You took the baby but don't let her die.** That was all right but **don't let her die.** Please, please, dear God, **don't let her die.**

The nurse opened the door and motioned with her finger for me to come. I followed her into the room. Catherine did not look up when I came in. I went over to the side of the bed. The doctor was standing by the bed on the opposite side. Catherine looked at me with and smiled. I bent down over the bed and started to cry.

"Poor darling," Catherine said very softly. She looked gray.

"You're all right, Cat," I said. "You're going to be all right."

"I'm going to die," she said; then waited and said, "I hate it." I took her hand. "Don't touch me," she said. I let go of her hand. She smiled. "Poor darling."

"You touch me all you want."

"You'll be all right, Cat. I know you'll be all right."

"I meant to write you a letter to have if anything, happened, but I didn't do it."

"Do you want me to get a priest or any one to come and see you?"

"Just you," she said. Then a little later, "I'm not afraid, I just hate it."

"You must not talk so much," the doctor said.(330)

"All right," Catherine said.

"Do you want me to do anything, Cat? Can I get you anything?"

Catherine smiled, "No," Then a little later, "You won't do our things with another girl, or say the same things, will you?"

"Never."

"I want you to have girls, though."

"I don't want them."

"You are talking too much," the doctor said. "Mr. Henry must go out. He can come back again later. You are not going to die. You must not be silly."

"All right," Catherine said. "I'll come and stay with you nights," she said. It was very hard for her to talk.

"Please go out of the room," the doctor said. "You cannot talk."

Catherine winked at me, her face gray. "I'll be right outside," I said.

"Don't worry, darling," Catherine said. "I'm not a bit afraid. It's just a dirty trick."

"You dear, brave sweet."

I waited outside in the hall. I waited a long time. The nurse came to the door and came over to me. "I'm afraid Mrs. Henry is very ill," she said. "I'm afraid for her."

"Is she dead?"

"No, but she is unconscious."

It seems she had one hemorrhage after another. They couldn't stop. I went into the room and stayed with Catherine until she died. She was unconscious all the time, and it did not take her very long to die.

Outside the room, in the hall, I spoke to the doctor, "Is there anything I can do to-night?"

"No, There is nothing to do. Can I take you to your hotel?"

"No, thank you. I am going to stay here a while."

"I know there is nothing to say. I cannot tell you"(331)

"No," I said. There's nothing to say.

"Good-night," he said. "I cannot take you to your hotel?"

"No, thank you."

"It was the only thing to do," he said. "The operation proved"

"I do not want to talk about it," I said.

"I would like to take you to your hotel."

"No, thank you."

He went down the hall. I went the door of the room.

"You can't come in now," one of the nurses said.

"Yes, I can," I said.

"You can't come in yet."

"You get out," I said. "The other one too."

But after I had got them out and shut the door and turned off the light it wasn't any good. It was like saying good-by to a statue. After a while I went out and left the hospital and walked back to the hotel in the rain.(332)

THE END

전쟁, 사랑, 죽음

　인간이 인간을 돕고 행복하게도 하지만 인간이 인간을 참으로 괴롭히고 못살게 군다. 인간이 행한 가장 나쁜 행위, 가장 폭력적인 행위 중의 하나가 전쟁이다. 전쟁은 가장 비인간적인 행위이다. 그렇지만 인간들은 그 잔혹한 행위를 한 번도 아니고 여러 번이나 반복했으며 지금도 세계 각 지역에서는 총성이 그치지 않고 있다. 시민 어린아이 임산부 등 연약한 민간인들이 죽어가고 있다. 우리는 인간의 만행을 지금도 뉴스를 통해서 지켜볼 수 있다. 인간이 본성적으로 잔인한 존재인지 인간의 욕심을 채우기 위해 상대의 목숨도 앗아가는 존재인지 알 수 없다.

　『무기여 잘 있거라』는 전쟁을 배경으로 한 작품이다. 전쟁이란 한 가지 주제만을 다루는 작품은 아니라 전쟁의 현장에서 전우들과 그 밖의 사람들과의 관계 속에서 일어나는 모든 일을 다루는 작품이라 할 수 있다. 즉 이 글의 주제는 한마디로 말할 수 없으며 보는 사람의 관점에 따라 다양한 주제를 논할 수 있다. 이 작품의 주제를 전쟁, 사랑, 죽음, 상실 등 하나의 주제로만 보기는 어려우며 이 같은 주제들이 서로 얽혀 있다고 보는 것이 타당할 수 있다. 이 작품의 전반적인 내용과 작품을 통해서 작가가 말하고자 하는 바가 무엇인지를 생각해 보자.

　작품의 내용은 간단히 말하면 다음과 같다. 미국인 프레더릭 헨리는 자진해서 이탈리아 엠블런스 부대에 자원입대해서 미국인 장교로 전쟁에 참전한다. 그곳 전선에서 부상을 입은 군인들을 운송하는 일을 하면서 가족처럼 전우들과 같이 잘 지내는 평범한 젊은 군인이다. 그곳에서 영국 출신인 간호사 캐서린 버클리는 만나서 사랑을 하게 되고 그중에 헨리는 부상을 입고 병원에 입원하게 되고 그 병원에 캐서린이 배정되어서 헨리를 간호하면서 서로의 사랑을 키워간다. 헨리의 부상이 완쾌되자 부대로 복귀하라는 통지서를 받고 헨리는 부대로 복귀하려 하는데 그때 캐서린은 임신 3개월이라는 사실을 헨리에게 말을 한다.

그렇지만 헨리는 캐서린을 남겨두고 부대로 복귀한다. 부대로 복귀한 후 전시 상황이 좋지 못해서 퇴각하게 된다. 퇴각하는 중 차량행렬과 짐마차 등의 합류와 비로 인해 길이 진흙탕이 되어서 차를 놓고 퇴각을 하는 중 부대를 이탈했다는 이유로 헌병들에 의해서 이탈리아 장교들이 사살되는 것을 목격했고 독일 정보원(spy)으로 몰릴지 걱정한다. 그래서 그는 결국 이탈리아 부대를 버리고 강으로 뛰어 들어갔다. 강한 조류에도 불구하고 해안가에 도착했다. 그는 걸어서 베니스의 평원지역을 넘어갔다. 그리고 달리는 기차에 가까스로 올라탔다. 헨리는 신분을 숨기고 밀라노에 도착했고 캐서린과 퍼거슨은 휴가차 스트레사(Stresa)에 떠난 것을 알게 된다. 헨리는 기차를 타고 스트레사로 가서 호텔에서 캐서린과 재회를 한다.

그 이후로 헨리는 캐서린과 헤어지지 않고 같이 생활했고 호텔에 근무하는 직원(barman)으로부터 자신을 체포하려고 내일 아침에 온다는 소식을 듣고 밤 11시에 직원이 준비한 보트를 타고 임신한 캐서린과 함께 스위스로 출발한다.

　밤에 스위스로 가는 동안 비와 바람 때문에 힘들었지만, 우여곡절 끝에 스위스 땅에 도착하여 체포되고 잠시 구금되었다가 석방된다. 헨리와 캐서린은 몽퇴뢰(Montreux) 지역의 산 앞에 있는 샬레(Chalet)라는 곳에서 즐겁게 지낸다. 얼마 후 아이를 낳기 위해서 로잔으로 출발하고 병원에 입원한 후 아이를 출산하기까지 오랜 시간 고통스러운 과정을 겪는다. 그 결과 탯줄에 산소가 제대로 제공되지 못해 아이가 먼저 죽는다. 그리고 캐서린 역시 과다 출혈로 사망하게 되고 비가 오는 밤에 헨리는 병원을 떠나 호텔로 가면서 소설은 끝이 난다.

　주인공인 프레더릭 헨리는 전쟁의 참혹함, 그 속에서 피어나는 사랑, 전쟁의 부조리한 점들을 직면하면서 비극적인 사랑을 겪는다.
　이 소설의 주요 주제 중 하나는 전쟁의 비극성이다. 헨리는 전사로서 전쟁의 비인간적이고 반복적인 고통을 마주하며, 전쟁이 인간 존재에 얼마나 많은 고뇌를 가져다주는지를 체감하게 된다. 그는 평범한 일상이 전쟁으로 인해 얼마나 쉽게 파괴될 수 있는지를 깨닫게 되며, 이러한 경험을 통해 사랑의 소중함을 느낀다. 특히, 그의 사랑인 캐서린 바클리와의 관계는 전쟁 속에서도 피어나는 순수한 사랑을 상징하지만, 그 또한 전쟁의 어두운 그림자 아래에서 상실로 이어지는 슬픈 운명을 겪게 된다. 젊은 남녀가 사랑하는 것은 식사 시간이 되어서 밥을 먹는 것처럼 당연한 일이지만 평범한 일상의 사랑보다 전쟁터에서 이루어진 사랑이 얼마나 힘들고 어려운 일인지를 보여 준다. 일상생활 속에서 아이를 낳다 아이와 산모가 죽는 충격의 여파가 크다. 작가는 이런 전쟁으로 인한 부조리한 일들과 비극을 말하고자 한다.

> 전쟁보다 더 나쁜 것은 없다. There is nothing worse than war.(50)
> "모든 사람이 이 전쟁을 증오합니다." Everybody hates this war.(51)

작가는 전쟁의 문제를 다루기도 하지만 전쟁이 일으킨 원인이나 일으킨 사람들에 대한 원망과 미움을 더 잘 드러낸다. 전쟁을 일으킨 사람과 전쟁에 참전한 사람이 다르고 또한 전쟁으로 인해 돈 버는 사람이 따로 있다는 말속에서 많은 부조리한 점을 지적한다. 또한, 이 나라를 지배하는 사람들은 지배할 능력도 없다고 말한다. 자신의 소신에 의해서 전쟁에 참전했지만, 막상 참전한 전쟁터가 자기 생각과 다르다는 것을 느끼며 너무 심각한 상황에서 외로움과 괴로움을 느낀다. 전쟁에 참전하는 것이 국가를 위한 신성, 영광, 희생이라고 주장하는 지도자들을 향해 주인공은 강 이름이나 날짜 같은 구체적인 단어들 앞에서 외설스럽기까지 하다고 주장한다. 젊은이들을 전쟁터에 참전시키기 위한 수단에 불과하다는 메시지가 오히려 우리에게 더 많은 울림을 준다.

이 나라를 지배하는 세력들은 어리석고 아무것도 깨닫지 못하고 깨달을 수도 없는 계급이 지배하고 있어서 이 같은 전쟁을 우리가 겪어야 한다고 맹비난한다. 게다가 전쟁으로 돈까지 벌어들이는 사람이라고 비난한다.

> "There is a class that controls a country that is stupid and does not realize anything never can. That is why we have this war." "Also they make money out of

it."(50-51)

패배는 전쟁 그 자체보다 더 안 좋은 것이다. defeat is worse.(50)

나는 신성이니 영광이니 희생이니 하는 말과 헛되다는 표현을 들을 때마다 곤혹스러워진다. 그런 말들은 때로는 고함을 질러야 겨우 들릴 정도로 소리도 잘 들리지 않는 빗속에서 들었고, 포고문 위에 겹겹이 덧붙여 놓은 포고문들에서도 아주 오랫동안 읽어 왔지만, 나는 신성한 것은 아무것도 보지 못했고, 영광스럽다고 하는 것들에는 영광이 없으며, 희생은 고깃덩어리를 땅속에 파묻는 것 말고는 할 일이 없는 시카고 도축장에서 벌어지는 살육이나 다름없었다. 참고 듣기 힘든 말이 너무 많았기 때문에 나중에는 지명만이 위엄을 갖게 되었다. 숫자와 날짜 같은 것들만이 지명과 더불어 우리가 말할 수 있고 의미를 부여할 수 있는 유일한 것이 되었다. 영광이니 명예니, 용기니, 신성이니 하는 추상적인 말들은 마을 이름이나 도로 번호, 강 이름, 연대번호, 날짜 같은 구체적인 말 앞에서 외설스럽게 느껴졌다.(185)

I was always embarrassed by the words sacred, glorious, and sacrifice and the expression in vain. We had heard them, sometime standing in the rain almost out of earshot, so that only the shouted words came through, and had read them, on proclammation that were slapped up by billposters over other proclamations, now for a long time, and had seen nothing sacred, and the things that were glorious had no glory and the sacrifices were like the stockyards at Chicago if nothing was done with the meat except to bury it. There were many words that you could not stand to hear and finally only the names of places had dignity. Certain numbers were the same way and certain dates and these with the names of the places were all you could say and have them mean anything. Abstract words such as glory, honor, courage, or hallow were obscene beside the concrete names of villages, the numbers of roads, the names of rivers, the numbers of regiments and dates.(185)

부조리한 전쟁터를 보여 주는 장면은 많다. 부상이 아니면 수송차에 탈 수 없다는 규정은 전쟁터에 있는 군인들을 힘들게 하는 면이다. 일부러 아픈 척한다는 그들의 주장에 힘들어하는 것은 병사들뿐이다. 병사의 고통은 전쟁과 전쟁을 만든 사람들에 대한 원망과 증오로 변해만 간다.

이윽고 말이 끄는 구급차 한 대가 길가에 서 있는 것이 보였다. 두 사람이 탈장된 병사를 들어 올려 차에 태우고 있었다. 그들이 병사를 데리러 돌아온 것이었다. 병사는 나를 향해 고개를 저었다. 철모는 벗겨지고 이마에서는 아래로 피가 흐르고 있었다. 콧등이 까지고 피가 흐르는 부분과 머리카락은 먼지투성이였다.(36)

Then we saw a horse ambulance stopped by the road. Two men were lifting the hernia man to put him in. They had come back for him. He shook his head at me. His helmet was off and his forehead was bleeding below the hair line. His nose was skinned and there was dust on the bloody patch and dust in his hair.(36)

이런 참혹한 전쟁을 지도자들은 왜 그만두지 못할까? 모두가 두려워하고 일어나서는 안 되는 일을 왜 그만두지 못하고 계속해야 하는가? 지도자들은 젊은이들의 절규와 매일 전투에서 죽어가는 젊은 병사들의 참혹함을 보고 받지 못했는가? 전쟁을 통해서 국가의 지도자들이 얻고자 하는 것은 무엇인가?

전쟁보다 더 나쁜 것은 없다. 그게 얼마나 나쁜 건지 구급차를 운전하는 우리야 아무것도 모르겠죠. 그걸 깨닫는다고 하더라도 모두가 이미 미쳐버려 멈추게 할 수도 없을 거고요. 절대 깨닫지 못하는 사람들도 있습니다. 그냥 장교들을 두려워하는 사람들도 있고요. 그런 사람들 때문에 전쟁이 계속되는 겁니다.

"There is nothing worse than war. We in the auto-ambulance cannot even realize at all how had it is. When people realize how bad it is they cannot do anything to stop it because they go crazy. There are some people who never realize. There are people who are afraid of their officers. It is with them the war is made."(50)

"모든 사람이 이 전쟁을 증오합니다." Everybody hates this war.(51)라고 파시니가 말했다.

"한쪽이 그만두어야 합니다. 왜 우리는 그만두지 못하는 겁니까? 만약 적들이 이탈리아로 쳐들어온다 해도 결국은 지쳐 물러갈 겁니다."(50)

"One side must stop fighting. Why don't we stop fighting? If they come down into Italy they will get tired and go away."

파시니는 어느 한쪽이 전쟁을 그만두어야만 전쟁이 종식될 수 있다고 주장한다. 과연 한쪽이 전쟁을 그만두면 전쟁은 종식되는가? 그렇지 않을 것이다. 끝까지 찾아가서 그들이 가진 모든 것을 빼앗고 힘없는 여자들을 괴롭히고 폭력을 행할 것이 분명하다. 파시니가 말한 전쟁 종식이란 쉽지 않고 어느 한쪽이 죽거나 항복을 선언한다고 할지라도 보복과 더 많은 것들을 얻어내려고 할 것이다. 전쟁은 한번 발생하면 종식하는 일은 매우 어렵다. 결국, 가장 좋은 것은 전쟁은 일어나지 않는 것이다.

이 소설의 주요한 또 다른 주제는 헨리와 캐서린과의 사랑이라 할 수 있다. 캐서린은 한 번도 아니고 두 번씩이나 전쟁으로 인해 사랑하는 사람과 헤어지는 고통을 경험한다. 약혼자인 남자친구가 전쟁터에서 죽고 친구를 잊지 못해서 전쟁터를 서성이다가 헨리를 만나 다시 사랑하게 되지만, 그와의 사랑도 상실로 이어진다. 캐서린의 용기 있는 행동 중 하나가 분만의 결정이다. 그렇지만 분만을 하는 동안 주목해야 할 것은 캐서린이 간호사에게 자신이 종교를 갖고 있지 않다는 것을 인정한다.

She said she had no religion.(313)
제왕절개에 관해서 헨리는
"종교재판을 그린 그림을 보는 것 같았다."(325)

'It looked like a drawing of the Inquisition.'라고 우리에게 말했다. 헨리 자신조차도 매우 고통스럽다고 인정하고 아이가 세례를 받지 않은 것에 대해서 유감스러워했고 자신의 마음을 바꾸었다. They supposed he would come around and start breathing probably. I had no religion but I knew he ought to have been baptized.(327)

이제는 캐서린이 죽을지도 모른다. 그게 인간이 하는 일이다. 인간은 죽는다. 죽음이 뭔지도 모르는 채 죽는다. 그것을 깨우칠 시간도 없다. 인간을 구장에 내던지고 규칙을 말해준 뒤 베이스에서 발을 떼는 것이 보이자마자 죽이는 것이다. 또는 아이모처럼 아무 이유도 없이 죽인다. 또는 리날디처럼 매독에 걸리게 한다. 하지만 결국은 모두 죽인다. 그건 분명한 사실이다. 잠시 머물게 하지만 결국은 죽인다.(327)

Now Catherine would die. That was what you did. You did not know what it was about. You never had time to learn. They threw you in and told you the rules and the first time they caught you off base they killed you. Or they killed you gratuitously like Aymo. Or gave you the syphilis like Rinaldi. But they killed you in the end. You could count on that. Stay around and they would kill you.(327)

헨리는 불타고 있는 이 세상을 모닥불의 장작으로 묘사했다. 자신이 구세주(to be a messiah)가 될 수 있다는 충동에도 불구하고 무리를 지어 장작으로 들어가는 개미들을 그는 구하지 못했다. 죽어가고 있는 캐서린을 두고 볼 수밖에 없는 상황을 묘사 한 것이다.

언젠가 캠프에 있을 때 모닥불 위에 장작 하나를 얹었는데 장작이 개미투성이였다. 장작이 타기 시작하자 개미들이 떼 지어 처음에는 불이 붙은 중심부로 몰렸다가 곧 돌아서 장작 끝으로 달아났다. 끝에 다다른 개미들은 불 속으로 떨어졌다. 어떤 놈들은 불에 타서 몸이 납작해진 채 빠져나와 어디로 가는지도 모르는 채 무작정 기어갔다. 하지만 대부분은 불 쪽으로 갔다가 다시 방향을 돌려 뜨겁지 않은 끝 쪽으로 몰려갔다가 결국 불 속으로 떨어졌다. 그때 나는 그것이 세상의 종말이며 내가 장작불을 불에서 꺼내 개미들이 땅 위로 도망칠 수 있는 곳으로 던져줄 구세주가 될 멋진 기회라고 생각했다. 하지만 그저 양철 컵의 물을 장작 위에 끼얹기만 했는데, 컵의 물을 버린 뒤 위스키를 따르고 다시 물을 타기 위해서였다. 불타는 장작에 물을 끼얹었으니, 개미들은 쪄 죽었을 것이다.

Once in camp I put a log on the top of the fire and it was full of ants. As it commenced to burn, the ants swarmed out and went first toward the end. When there were enough on the end they fell off into the fire. Some got out, their bodies burnt and flattened, and went off not knowing where they were going. But most of them went toward the fire and then back toward the end and swarmed on the cool end and finally fell off into the fire. I remember thinking at the time that it was the end of the world and a splendid chance to be a messiah and lifted the log off the fire and throw it out where the ants could get off onto the ground. But I did not do anything but throw a tin cup of water on the log, so that I would have the cup empty to put whiskey in before. I added water to it. I think the cup of water on the burning log only steamed the ants.(327-328)

모든 사람이 그런 것처럼 캐서린의 임박한 죽음 앞에서 필사적으로 신과 협상하려고 시도했다. 반면에 그녀는 자신의 신념에 대한 용기를 끝까지 간직하고 있었다. 그리고 헨리가 "신부님이나 누구 데려올까요?"(330)라고 했을 때 그녀는

"당신이면 돼요."(330)라고 헨리에 대해 반응했다.

"Do you want me to get a priest or any one to come and see you?"
"Just you," she said.(330)

그 어떤 것보다도 죽어 가는 그 순간까지도 캐서린에게 있어서 종교는 사랑이었다. 절체절명의 순간에 캐서린에게 가장 소중한 것은 신, 신부, 성직자가 아니고 자신이 사랑하는 사람 그 사람의 사랑이었다.

"달링 온몸이 조각난 것 같아."(322) darling I'm going all to peaces.
그것이 우리가 함께 잠을 자서 당신이 치르는 대가야. 그 함정의 끝. 고뇌와 죽음은 서로 사랑하는 사람들이 치르는 대가이다.(320)
And this was the price you paid for sleeping together. This was the end of the trap. This was what people got for loving each other.(320)

캐서린이 이렇게 된 것이 자신과의 사랑으로 인한 것인가? 아니면 전쟁으로 인한 비극인 것인가? 그것도 아니면 전쟁 중에 전쟁에 참여하지 않고 사랑놀이를 한 결과의 벌을 받는 것인가? 우리는 전쟁에 참전하면 24시간 전쟁만 해야 한다고 생각하지만 전쟁 중에 일상이 이어진다. 소설의 앞부분에서 언급한 것처럼 파시니는 파스타를 먹는 중에 적의 공격을 받아서 죽고 헨리는 다친다. 헨리가 이렇게 말하는 것은 전쟁을 일으킨 사람이 따로 있고, 전쟁에 참전하는 사람이 따로 있고, 전쟁으로 돈을 버는 사람 따로 있다고 말한 것처럼, 캐서린과 헨리의 사랑은 결국 전쟁으로 인한 희생되었기 때문이다.

Poor, poor dear Cat. And this was the price you paid for sleeping together. This was the end of the trap. This was what people got for loving each other.(320)

And this was the price you paid for sleeping together.(320)

　전쟁터에서 만난 두 남녀의 사랑은 시작부터 불안했고 결말도 좋지 못했다. 서로 사랑하게 돼서 아이를 갖게 되고 그 아이를 출산하다가 캐서린과 아이는 죽음을 맞이했다. 사랑하는 남편도 캐서린을 어떻게 도와줄 수 없었다. 이것은 전쟁이 낳은 죽음이고 고통이다. 이 고통과 죽음에서 도와줄 수 있는 사람은 아무도 없었다. 그냥 죽음을 맞이할 뿐이다. 이렇게 된 처지에 대한 원망은 부질없는 일이다. 그래서 전쟁터에서 귀향한 젊은이들이 방황하고 기존의 질서를 부정하며 자신들의 경험만을 의지하는 세대가 되어 기성세대에 대한 불만과 불신을 갖게 되는 것은 그 당시 젊은이들의 생각을 대변해 준다. 그래서 헤밍웨이는 잃어버린 세대(Lost Generation)의 대변자로 불렸다.

　이 소설의 또 다른 주제는 전쟁터에서 탈출(탈영)하는 문제이다. 설령 전쟁이 발생해서 적과 아군으로 나누어서 싸우는 현장에서 적어도 자기의 동료인 아군에게는 위협하는 행위를 하지 않는 것이 전쟁터에서 규칙이 아닌가? 자발적으로 전쟁에 참전한 헨리는 자진해서 전쟁터에서 탈출한다. 자신의 신념과 생각을 행동으로 옮긴 헨리는 스스로 생각한 전쟁과 전쟁터의 상황이 너무도 달라서 그곳을 떠나지 않을 수 없는 상황에 직면하게 된다. 그래서 살기 위해서 그곳을 탈출한다. 헨리와 캐서린 단독강화에 성공한다. 탈출에 성공은 했지만, 헨리는 마음 한구석에는 부대의 탈출과 자기 동료들의 생각이 마음에서 떠나지 않는다. 심지어는 자신에게 몰려온 불행한 일들이 탈영한 것으로 인한 것이 아닌지 하는 생각을 하기도 한다. 아들과 캐서린의 죽음을 맞이한 헨리는 비를 맞으면서 병원을 떠나 호텔로 가는 길에 헨리의 마음속에는 많은 생각이 있겠지만 왜 나에게 이런 혹독한 시련이 오는가? 라는 생각 속에서 부대를 탈영했기 때문이라는 생각도 있지 않았을까 생각해 본다.

역설적으로 탈영(단독강화)(separation) 상태에서 그들은 절대적 도움이 필요할 때 도움을 제공해 주는 공동체가 없다는 것을 깨닫게 된다. 이 작품을 통해서 작가는 공동체가 우리 자신들의 죽음으로부터 구해 줄 수 없다는 것을 강조한다. 우리 죽음을 공동체들 즉 국가가 구해 줄 수 없다는 것이다. 부대에서 탈출은 자신이 살기 위한 몸부림이다. 국가와 지도자들이 만들어 놓은 정쟁이란 덫에서 젊은이들은 조국을 위해서 죽고 조국을 위해서 싸운다. 어른들과 국가가 만들어 놓은 부조리한 현장에서 살아남기 위한 필사적인 몸부림을 친다. 탈영병이라고 손가락질하는 것은 국가가 만들어 놓은 불합리한 덫에 걸린 젊은이들에게 손가락질하는 것과 같다. 전쟁이란 국가들이 자신들의 욕심과 야욕을 채우기 위해서 일으킨 것이다. 그러나 정작 자신들은 그 전쟁터에 나가지 않고 아무것도 모르는 젊은이들을 전쟁터에 보내는 아주 불합리한 일들이 세계 각지에서 발생하고 있다. 순수한 젊은 청년들은 조국을 위해서 싸우다 죽어갔다. 아니면 헨리 중위처럼 상처를 입기도 한다. 운이 좋게 헨리처럼 살 수 있으면 다행이다. 어떤 젊은이는 평생 장애인으로 살아가기도 한다. 조국은 우리를 위해서 무엇을 해주었는가? 백번 양보해서 조국을 지키다 죽을 수 있다. 그렇지만 전쟁이 왜 발생했는지 꼭 발생해야만 하는 전쟁이었는지 국가지도자들의 욕심과 야욕에 의한 전쟁은 아니었는지 따져봐야 할 일이다. 헨리 중위가 탈영하기 직전의 심정은 어떠했을까? 살기 위한 단독강화였다. 같은 부대의 군인들에 의해서 죽음의 총부리를 맞이한 헨리는 죽기 살기로 도주할 수밖에 없었다. 그를 도와주는 사람은 아무도 없었다.

헨리만을 남겨 놓고 캐서린은 아이를 낳는 중에 아이와 함께 죽는다. 참전, 사랑, 탈영, 재회, 분만, 죽음으로 이어지는 소설의 내용은 헨리와 캐서린에게 명백히 가혹한 상황이고 비극적인 상황이다. 참전과 사랑 그리고 죽음으로서 모든 것을 상실한 헨리와 캐서린은 국가가 만들어낸 비극의 희생양이다. 이런 복합적인 내용을 한 편의 영화처럼 작가는 잘 짜인 구조로 독자들에게 전달한다. 결국, 소설은 행복한 결말이 아닌, 캐서린의 죽음으로 이어지며 독자는 사랑이 얼마나 안타깝게 소멸하는지를 깨닫는다. 이러한 비극적인 결말은 전쟁의 잔혹함과 그 전쟁 속에서 이루어진 진실한 사랑조차도 덧없음을 강조한다. 이는 헤밍웨이가 자주 다루었던 실존적 고뇌와 의미 없는 세계에서 인간 존재 의의를 탐구하는 방식의 하나로 볼 수 있습니다. 이러한 요소들 덕분에 『무기여 잘 있거라』는 전쟁 문학 속에서 중요한 위치를 차지하며, 전쟁, 사랑, 죽음, 상실에 대한 깊은 통찰을 제공한다. 소설을 읽는 독자들은 헨리의 경험을 통해 전쟁 속에서 사랑과 상실의 아픔을 공유하며, 전쟁이 인간에게 미치는 영향을 다시 한번 생각하게 된다.

중심인물들(Characterization and Central Characters)

　아리스토텔레스는 인격보다 행동을 우선시하지만, 위대한 작가들은 그들의 줄거리보다 인간상에 대한 강력한 창조물로 더 잘 알려져 있다. 우리가 셰익스피어의 위대한 비극을 생각할 때 우리는 항상 헴릿, 오셀로, 맥베스, 리어왕 같은 그의 위대한 작품들을 생각한다. 의심할 여지 없이 구성(plot)은 19세기 중반까지 소설에서 가장 중요한 역할을 했고 캐릭터는 행동에 종속되어 있었다. 그러나 19세기 후반과 그 후 더 빠르게 세기가 바뀌는 동안 균형은 캐릭터 쪽으로 기울었다. 즉 행동은 캐릭터에 종속되었다.

　헨리 제임스는 캐릭터와 행동의 분리를 반대하지만, 그것들을 서로 생각하면서 "사건의 결정을 제외하고 캐릭터란 무엇인가?"(What is character but the determination of incident) 인물 묘사에 사건이란 무엇인가?(What is incident but the illustration of character?) 서사의 두 측면은 비평적인 편의를 위해서라도 계속 별개로 다루어져야 한다. 헤밍웨이 시대에 인물은 이전의 어느 때보다 작가와 비평가에 더 큰 관심을 두게 되었다.
　헨리 버그슨(Henry Bergson), 윌리엄 제임스(William James), 지그문트 프로이드(Sigmund Freud)의 심리학 연구 이전에는 행동이 사람의 성격을 드러내는 주요 장치로 여겨졌다.
　그러나 현재 심리학의 등장으로 작가들은 독백과 의식의 흐름, 꿈과

직관 등의 매우 정교한 도구를 갖게 되었고 이러한 도구를 인간의 정신을 묘사하는 데 충분히 활용하게 되었다. 헤밍웨이는 작가의 관심이 사람의 마음속으로 좁혀지는 것을 인정하지 않는 근세 작가 중 한 명이었다.

스토리텔링 기술에 있어서 모더니스트들보다 현실주의자들에게 더 가까이 있으면서 그는 서사는 객관적이고 극적으로 만드는 장치를 모더니스트들로부터 흡수했다.

이와 관련하여 그의 친분은 조셉콘래드(Joseph Conrad)제임스 조이스(James Joyce)포드 마독스(Ford Madox), D.H 로렌스(D.H Lawrence)등이 잘 알려져 있다. 서사 소설에서 인물의 기술에서 더 널리 받아들여지는 구분은 말하기(telling)와 보여주기(showing)의 기술 사이에 있다.

말하기(telling)에서 저자는 인물들의 신체, 몸짓, 습성, 생각, 묘기, 행동 등을 묘사하고 평가하기까지 하고 "보여 주기(showing)"에서 저자는 인물들이 자기 행동과 표현을 통해 조각을 드러내도록 제시할 뿐 인물들을 평가하는 것은 독자에게 맡긴다. 당연히 말하기는 인물화의 교훈적 방법으로 불리는데 보여 주기는 허구적 서사에서 인물을 그리는 극적인 방법으로 간주한다.

헤밍웨이와 같은 젊은 작가들에게 이 기법의 미덕을 보여 준 세기의 전환기를 전후하여 보여 주기 방식의 이론가이자 실천가는 구스타프 플로베르(Gustav Flaubert)와 헨리 제임스(Henry James)였다. 이후 말하기 방식은 대부분의 현대 작가에게 예술성에 대한 침해로 간주했다. 인물을 이야기하거나 그리는 이러한 현대적인 방식을 미화하면서 일반적으로 작가가 자신의 예술을 완전히 객관적으로 만들기 위해서는 그의 글에서 사라져야 한다고 권고한다. 헤밍웨이는 조이스처럼 그의 서사에서 완전히 사라지지 않으며 적어도 그의 인물을 소개하거나 발표하기 위해 그의 서사 페르소나(narrative persona)를 사용했다. 그러나 그의 서술자들은 제1인은 물론 제3인은 (third person) 자기 인물들의 생각과 감정과 행동에 대해 가능한 한 직접적인 언급을 하지 않도록 주의를 기울인다.

헤밍웨이는 거의 전적으로 그가 좋아하는 대화 장치에 의존하는 극적인 인물 묘사(characterization) 방법으로 항상 찬사를 받아왔다. 영어권 소설가들 사이에서 그는 아마도 대화를 가장 효과적인 특성화 장치로 사용하는 데 있어서 선도적인 작가일 것이다. 바깥에서 인물을 판단하는 것에 관해 말하자면 헤밍웨이는 그 인물의 모든 측면이 드러나도록 동시에 그가 밖에서 보이도록 그의 중심인물을 다른 인물들과 직접적으로 만나게 하는데 그 이유는 자신의 표현들은 자기 인물에 대한 표현이기 때문이다. 헤밍웨이는 또한 사건을 특성화의 장치로 효과적으로 활용한다. 소설가는 인물을 다른 상황에 놓음으로써 다른 사건을 만나게 함으로써 자기 인물들이 그들의 성격이 다른 측면들을 드러내도록 할 수 있다.

게다가 헤밍웨이는 때때로 서로에 대한 정보를 제공하거나 서로의 행동과 생각을 평가함으로써 서로를 묘사하기 위해 그의 캐릭터를 사용한다.

따라서 헤밍웨이는 대체로 그의 이야기에서 벗어나 그의 소설의 성격을 깊이 있게 묘사하기 위해 다양한 극적인 장치를 사용한다.

『무기여 잘 있거라』는 헤밍웨이 특성화 기술의 가장 좋은 예중 하나로 우리는 기억에 남는 많은 인물 즉 프레더릭 헨리(Frederic Henry), 캐서린 버클리(Catherine Barkley), 사제(the Priest), 리날디(Rinaldi), 파시니(Passini), 마네라(Manera), 보넬로(Bonello), 에토레(Ettore), 닥터 발렌타인(Doctor Valintine), 그레피 백작(Count Greffi), 헬렌(Helen), 반 캠펜(Van Campen), 미스 게이지(Miss Gage), 포터와 그의 아내(the porter and his wife)들을 만나게 되는데 이들은 소설 줄거리에서 중요한 역할을 하고 우리의 기억에 남을 정도로 설득력이 있게 그려진다.

이제『무기여 잘 있거라』의 많은 등장인물 중에는 소설의 '전면'을 구성한다고 말할 수 있는 주요 등장인물들이 있지만 다른 인물들은 비록 기억에 남지만 소설의 '배경'의 일부를 구성하는 사소한 인물들이다.

주요 등장인물들은 프레더릭 헨리와 캐서린 버클리, 리날디와 사제지만 다른 등장인물들은 사소한 등장인물(minor characters)들입니다. 또한 주요 인물 중 주인공은 헨리와 캐서린뿐인 데 반해 사제와 리날디는 병치를 통해 영웅의 강인함을 드러내기 위해 서로 다른 관점을 제시하여 돋보이게 한다는 점에 있어서 조 연진들 이지만 그 역할은 주요 인물들 못지않게 큰 역할을 한다. 마찬가지로 소설 속 헬렌(Helen)과 다른 간호사들도 캐서린으로 대표되는 간호사에게 상반된 의견을 제시함으로써 여주인공의 더 복잡한 성격을 드러낼 수 있도록 돕기 위한 것이다. 다른 마이너 캐릭터(minor characters)들의 경우, 그들의 기능은 주로 제한된 목적을 위해 각각 지엽적이며 (제한적이며) 따라서 소설의 구조에 다양한 차원을 추가한다. 이제 소설 속 주인공마다 어떻게 그려지는지, 각자의 역할은 무엇인지, 어떻게 등장인물로 떠올리는지, 소설의 전체 그림에 대한 개인의 기여는 무엇인지를 알아보자.

중심인물들(Characterization and Central Characters)

프레더릭 헨리(Frederic Henry)

헨리는 소설의 감정과 시각의 중심이고 소설의 주인공이다. 『무기여 잘 있거라』의 주인공은 분명 프레더릭 헨리이다. 덴마크 왕자인 햄릿이 주인공인 것처럼, 헤밍웨이 소설도 프레더릭 헨리의 이야기라 할 수 있는데 헨리의 운세 변화가 소설의 행동 방향을 결정하기 때문이다. 다른 모든 등장인물은 각자의 위치에서 중요하지만 다른 상황이나 다른 문제에서 영웅의 위치와 평행하거나 대조되는 자세를 취할 뿐이다. 헨리는 소설 행동의 시작부터 끝까지 우리의 눈에 남아 있는 유일한 인물이고 소설의 진행을 지배하고 우리의 감탄을 얻고, 우리의 운명에 관여하며, 작가의 인생관에 가깝게 보이는 인물이다. 다른 등장인물들은 제한된 상황에서 등장하며, 그 상황에서 지엽적인 기능을 전반적으로 수행해야 한다.

물론 헨리는 『무기여 잘 있거라』의 주인공으로 작가 자신이 삶의 경험에 자신을 노출할 준비가 되어 있고 그 경험을 흡수할 수 있는 능력을 갖추고 있다는 점에서 시작 자이며 현대적인 의식을 가지고 있고, 합리적인 삶의 관점에 헌신하고 있으며, 종교와 신화, 의식과 관점에 대한 맹목적인 믿음에 의해 알려지는 단순하거나 원시적인 삶의 관점으로의 회귀로부터 자신을 구할 수가 있을 뿐만 아니라, 어떤 지속적인 삶의 가치에 헌신할 수 없음과 표류하고 자기 파괴적인 단어로 퇴보하는 경향으로 알려진 "잃어버린 세대"의 냉소와 허무주의의 늪에 빠지는 것으로부터 자신을 구할 수 있다.

영웅은 사랑이든 전쟁이든 항상 그 상황에서 존경할 만한 위치를 차지함으로서 다른 사람들을 능가합니다. 즉 이기적이기보다는 사심 없이 비인간적이기보다는 용감하게 비인간적이기보다는 인간적으로 극단적이기보다는 온건하게 행동함으로써 프레더릭 헨리는 사회의 더 큰 대의에 대한 그의 헌신에 대한 확실한 이상주의를 가진 젊은 미국인이다. 그가 이탈리아에서 부상병을 치료하기 위해 미국에서 멀리까지 자원봉사자로 왔다는 사실은 그가 사회적 대의에 헌신하고 싶은 충동이 있음을 보여준다. 그는 자화자찬(Self-praise)을 부끄러워할 사람 중 한 명이다. 사실 그는 자신에 대해 말하는 것이 창피할 사람 중 한 명이다. 예를 들어 그는 왜 유럽에서 전쟁에 참여하기로 했는지 설명해 달라는 요청을 받을 때마다 답변을 피하려고 하지만, 단지 민주주의, 개인의 자유, 인간의 존엄성이라는 더 큰 대의를 위해 싸우는 그의 숭고한 사명에 대해 말하는 당혹감을 피하기 위해서이다.

소설 초기에 영국 병원의 수간호사가 이탈리아인들과 함께 일하기로 한 이유에 관해서 묻자, 그의 대답은 그가 우연히 이탈리아에 있었기 때문이고, 이탈리아어를 할 수 있었기 때문이다. 또 한번은 스트레사(Stresa) 술집 주인이 왜 전쟁에 참여했느냐고 물었을 때 그는 다시 "모르겠어. 난 바보였어."("I don't know, I was a fool.")라고 얼버무린다.

나는 신성이니 영광이니 희생이니 하는 말과 헛되다는 표현을 들을 때마다 곤혹스러워진다. 그런 말들은 때로는 고함을 질러야 겨우 들릴 정도로 소리도 잘 들리지 않는 빗속에서 들었고, 포고문 위에 겹겹이 덧붙여 놓은 포고문들에서도 아주 오랫동안 읽어 왔지만, 나는 신성한 것은 아무것도 보지 못했고, 영광스럽다고 하는 것들에는 영광이 없으며, 희생은 고깃덩어리를 땅속에 파묻는 것 말고는 할 일이 없는 시카고 도축장에서 벌어지는 살육이나 다름없었다. 참고 듣기 힘든 말이 너무 많았기 때문에 나중에는 지명만이 위엄을 갖게 되었다. 숫자와 날짜 같은 것들만이 지명과 더불어 우리가 말할 수 있고 의미를 부여할 수 있는 유일한 것이 되었다. 영광이니 명예니, 용기니, 신성이니 하는 추상적인 말들은 마을 이름이나 도로 번호, 강 이름, 연대번호, 날짜 같은 구체적인 말 앞에서 외설스럽게 느껴졌다.

I was always embarrassed by the words sacred, glorious, and sacrifice and the expression in vain. We had heard them, sometime standing in the rain almost out of earshot, so that only the shouted words came through, and had read them, on proclammation that were slapped up by billposters over other proclamations, now for a long time, and had seen nothing sacred, and the things that were glorious had no glory and the sacrifices were like the stockyards at Chicago if nothing was done with the meat except to bury it. There were many words that you could not stand to hear and finally only the names of places had dignity. Certain numbers were the same way and certain dates and these with the names of the places were all you could say and have them mean anything. Abstract words such as glory, honor, courage, or hallow were obscene beside the concrete names of villages, the numbers of roads, the names of rivers, the numbers of regiments and dates.(185)

젊은이들을 속여 이곳에서 전쟁을 벌이고 있는 상황에서 정치인이 사용하는 공허한 수사에 대한 메스꺼움은 교활한 정치인이 수사에 대한 영웅의 진지함을 간접적으로 보여주는 증거이다.

영웅은 전쟁에서 어떤 신선함이나 희생도 보지 못했을 것이고 모든 사람의 자유에 신성함을 부여하고 자유라는 이상을 지키기 위해 목숨을 바칠 준비가 되어 있는 사람 중 한 명이다.

이러한 영웅의 희생 가치에 대한 애착은 개미의 비유에 대한 그의 일화에서도 유추할 수 있다.

언젠가 캠프에 있을 때 모닥불 위에 장작 하나를 얹었는데 장작이 개미투성이였다. 장작이 타기 시작하자 개미들이 떼 지어 처음에는 불이 붙은 중심부로 몰렸다가 곧 돌아서 장작 끝으로 달아났다. 끝에 다다른 개미들은 불 속으로 떨어졌다. 어떤 놈들은 불에 타서 몸이 납작해진 채 빠져나와 어디로 가는지도 모르는 채 무작정 기어갔다. 하지만 대부분은 불 쪽으로 갔다가 다시 방향을 돌려 뜨겁지 않은 끝 쪽으로 몰려갔다가 결국 불 속으로 떨어졌다. 그때 나는 그것이 세상의 종말이며 내가 장작을 불에서 꺼내 개미들이 땅 위로 도망칠 수 있는 곳으로 던져줄 구세주가 될 멋진 기회라고 생각했다. 하지만 그저 양철 컵의 물을 장작 위에 끼얹기만 했는데, 컵의 물을 버린 뒤 위스키를 따르고 다시 물을 타기 위해서였다. 불타는 장작에 물을 끼얹었으니, 개미들은 쪄 죽었을 것이다.

Once in camp I put a long on top of the fire and it was full of ants. As it commenced to burn, the ants swarmed out and went first toward the centre where the fire was; then turned back and ran toward the end. When there were enough on

프레더릭 헨리(Frederic Henry)

the end they fell off into the fire. Some got out, their bodies burned and flattened, and went off not knowing there they were going. But most of them went toward the fire and then back toward the end and swarmed on the cool end and finally fell off into fire and throw it out where the ants could get off onto the ground. But I did not do anything but throw a tin cup of water on the log, so that I would have the cup empty to put whiskey in before I added water to it. I think the cup of water on the burning log only streamed the ants.(328)

이제 중심인물에 대한 냉소적으로 보이는 이 행동은 위기의 순간에 인류를 위해 봉사하려는 이상주의를 숨기고 있습니다. 개미들의 비유는 분명 영웅 헨리가 참전하고 있는 전쟁을 상징합니다. 개미들에게 메시아 역할을 해 주겠다는 당신의 생각은 사실 세계대전의 불 속에 빠져 번진 서구 문명의 구원자가 되겠다는 영웅의 열망입니다.

이 구절을 이루고 있는 아이러니(irony)와 냉소(cynicism)는 헨리의 영웅적 이상주의를 드러내는데, 너무 이상적인 것이어서 실현할 수 있지 못한 것으로 생각되는 면이 있다. 그래서 이것은 소설의 비극적인 비전을 심화시키는 역할을 한다. 사랑과 전쟁에서 대조적인 만남의 연속을 통해 극적으로 그려지는 프레더릭 헨리의 인물은 다양한 상황에서 그를 만나게 되는 모든 사람을 무색하게, 우울하게 또는 힘들게 한다.

그 대표적인 예가 헨리이다. 과학자 리날디와 종교인 사제는 자신의 사랑과 전쟁 경험에 대한 주요 반대 견해를 제시하는데 리날디는 노출의 경험을 흡수할 능력이 없고 노출로 인해 얻은 의식의 압박으로 무너진다는 점에서 각각 성장하지 못하는 인물이지만 후자는 맹목적인 믿음의 지시에 따라 사는 것이 결코 자신을 사랑과 전쟁의 경험에 노출하지 않는다는 점이다. 영웅은 자신을 삶에 다양한 경험에 드러낼 뿐만 아니라 그러한 경험을 흡수할 수 있는 능력을 갖춘 인물이다. 그리하여 사제가 결백의 상징적인 인물이 되고 경험의 리날디가 되는 동안 헨리는 경험을 통해 유지되는 결백의 상징적인 인물이 된다.

헨리가 모든 겸손 속에서 전쟁에 참여하고 있는 개인의 자유에 대한 이상주의에 헌신하는 영웅적이고 자기희생적 성격인 것은 그가 부하들과 함께 상처를 입는 공격과정에서 행동에서도 알 수 있다. 자신이 위험한 상처를 입은 동안 그는 부하들을 찾으려 하고, 파시니가 죽어가는 것을 발견하고, 그의 옷을 붕대에 사용하여 그를 구하려고 하고, 적십자 부하들이(the Red Cross men) 그를 들어 올리려고 할 때 그는 그들에게 이렇게 말한다.

"나는 나중에 가는 게 낫겠어." 내가 말했다.
"나보다 부상이 훨씬 심한 사람들이 많아. 나는 괜찮아."(56)
나중에 야전병원에서 영국 의사들이 그에게 특권적인 치료를 하려고 할 때 그는 "나보다 훨씬 더 심한 부상자들이 있기 때문에 차라리 기다리겠다."라고 평소처럼 말한다.(58)

"I'd rather wait," I said. "There are much worse wounded than me. I'm all right."(58)

프레더릭 헨리(Frederic Henry)

야전병원의 키 큰 영국인 등 다른 인물들의 과장된 발언으로 영웅의 겸손함이 균형을 이룬다.

자, 어서요. 그가 말했다. "영웅은 버리십시오." 그러고는 이탈리아어로 말했다. "다리는 아주 조심해서 들어 다리 통증이 심하니까. 윌슨 대통령의 아드님이시다."(58)
"Come, come, he said." Don't be bloody hero. "Then in Italian: Lift him very carefully about the legs. His legs are very painful. He is the legitimate son of President Wilson."(58)

그의 타고난 겸손함 때문에 전쟁 기간 그의 영웅적인 행동이 그에 의해서 행해졌다는 사실은 전쟁으로 파괴되기 전에 오만한 리날디에 의해서 강조된다.

"안녕, 베이비? 기분은 좀 어때? 이걸 가져왔지----" 코냑 한 병이었다. 그는 당번병이 의자를 가져오자 앉았다. "좋은 소식도 가져왔어. 자네가 훈장을 받게 됐어. 실버훈장이면 좋을 텐데 브론즈일지도 몰라."
"뭘 했다고?"
"중상 입었잖아. 영웅적인 행동을 했다는 걸 증명한다면 실버를 받을 수 있어. 안 그러면 브론즈일 거고. 무슨 일이 있었는지 정확히 말해 봐. 영웅적인 행동을 했나?"
"아니," 내가 말했다. "우린 치즈를 먹다가 포탄을 맞았을 뿐이야."
"진지하게 생각해 봐. 그전이나 그 후에 분명 뭔가 영웅적인 행동을 했을 거야. 잘 떠올려 봐."
"안 했어."

"누굴 업고 옮기질 않았나? 고르디니는 자네가 여러 명을 업고 날랐다던데. 제1 구호소 군의관 소령이 그건 불가능했을 거라고 말하긴 했지만. 표창 추천서에 그 사람이 서명해야 하거든."

"나는 아무도 업어 나르지 않았어. 움직일 수도 없었다고."

"그건 상관없어." 리날디가 말했다.

그는 장갑을 벗었다.

"자네가 실버를 받도록 해 줄 수 있을 것 같은데. 남들 먼저 하라고 치료를 양보하지 않았어?"

"단호하게 한 건 아니야."

"그건 중요하지 않아. 어쩌다가 다쳤다고 생각해 봐. 늘 최전선에 가겠다고 자청한 자신의 용감한 행동을 한번 생각해 보라고. 게다가 공격 작전도 성공했어."(63)

"How are you, baby? How do you feel? I bring you this——" It was a bottle of cognac. The orderly brought a chair and he sat down. "and good news. You will be good decorated. They wanted to get you the medaglia d'argento but perhaps they can get only the bronze."

"What for?"

"Because you are gravely wounded. They say if you can prove you did any heroic act you can get the silver. Otherwise it will be the bronze. Tell me exactly what happened. Did you do any heroic act?"

"No," I said. "I was blown up while we were eating cheese."

"Be serious. You must have done something heroic either before or later. Remember carefully."

"I did not."

프레더릭 헨리(Frederic Henry)

"Didn't you carry anybody o your back? Gordini says you carried several people on your back but the medical major at the first post declares it is impossible. He had to sign the proposition for the citation."

"I didn't carry anybody. I couldn't move."

"That doesn't matter," said Rinaldi.

He took off his gloves.

"I think we can get you the silver. Didn't you refuse to be medically aided before the others?"

"Not very firmly."

"That doesn't matter. Look how you are wounded. Look at your valorous conduct in asking to go always to the first line. Besides, the operation was successful."(63)

그 대화는 코믹하고 아이러니하여 풍자적인 것을 의미합니다. 또한 헨리가 자신의 미덕을 과소평가하는 습관을 포함한 영웅적 행위에 대한 특정 사실을 밝히기 위한 것입니다. 군대에서 훈장이 조작되는 방식에 대한 헤밍웨이의 풍자는 틀림없으며 헨리가 훈장을 탈것이라는 전망에 흥분한 리날디의 전쟁 개입의 경박함을 폭로하려는 의도도 마찬가지입니다. 작가가 사용하는 코믹 양식을 통해서도 헨리의 겸손함을 강조합니다. 헤밍웨이가 프레더릭 헨리의 특징에서 보여 주는 사실주의는 영웅의 초기 이상주의와 그의 후기 냉소주의 그의 초기 영웅주의와 그의 후기 탈영의 균형을 맞추려는 데서 나타난다. 마찬가지로 저자는 캐서린에 대한 영웅의 나중 사랑과 이전의 매춘부 집을 방문했던 것의 균형을 맞춘다.

나는 그곳 대신 담배 연기 자욱한 카페들에 갔고, 밤마다 방안이 빙빙 돌아 그걸 멈추려면 벽을 쳐다봐야 했고, 그게 다인 것을 알면서도 밤이면 술에 취한 채 여자와 침대로 들어갔고, 잠에서 깼을 때는 상대가 누군지도 모르는 이상한 흥분을 느꼈으며

I had gone to no such place but to the smoke of cafes and nights when the room whirled and you needed to look at the wall to make it stop, nights in bed, drunk, when you knew that that was all there was, (13)

따라서 소설가는 "전체진실"에 대한 관심 속에서 영웅 캐릭터의 성격과 성장의 다양한 측면과 단계를 대조적인 장면을 통해 우리에게 보여준다. 일반적으로 그러하듯이 헤밍웨이 소설의 주인공은 예술가로서의 직업뿐만 아니라 감성적으로도 예술가이다. 전쟁이 발발했을 때 그는 우리에게 말해 주듯 건축을 공부하기 위해 이탈리아에 있었다. 1920년대 외국 예술가처럼 그는 많은 언어를 알고 있었다. 그는 미국 영어 이외에도 이탈리아어와 프랑스어도 알고 있었다. 그가 캐서린에게 말했듯이 그는 "이탈리아에 있었기 때문에" 그리고 "이탈리아어로 말하기" 때문에 전쟁에 참여했습니다. (23) 다시 현장 병원에서 의사들은 상처를 입은 헨리에 관해 이야기합니다.

"저 친구는 미국인이야." 다른 대위가 말했다.

"프랑스인이라고 들었던 것 같은데 프랑스어를 했잖아," 대위가 말했다. "전에 본

프레더릭 헨리(Frederic Henry)

적도 있어. 나는 전부터 이 친구가 프랑스인인 줄 알았어."(60)

"He's an America," one of the other captains said.

"I thought you said he was a Frenchman. He talks French," the captain said. "I've known him before. I always thought he was French."(60)

그의 예술적 지식과 감성은 캐서린이 병원 사무실에서 정원으로 내려올 때 늘 기다리는 과정에서 알아볼 수 있다.

모두 똑같아 보이는 대리석의 특징을 유감없이 드러내고 있었다. 조각상은 늘 따분한 느낌이 들지만, 청동상은 그나마 좀 그럴싸해 보인다. 하지만 대리석 흉상들은 모두 공동묘지처럼 보인다. 유일하게 멋진 게 있다면 피사에 있는 묘지다. 제노바에는 형편없는 대리석 흉상들이 넘친다.(28)

There were many marble busts on painted wooden pillar along the walls of the room they used for an office. The hall too, that the office opened on, was lined with them. They had the complete marble quality of all looking alike. Scalpture had always seemed a dull business- still, bronzes looked like something. But marble busts all looked like a cemetery. There was one fine cemetery though-the one at Pisa. Genoa was the place to see the bad marbles.(28)

소설의 시작 부분의 묘사는 소설의 마지막에 영웅이 죽은 캐서린과 둘이 있고 "마치 조각상에 작별 인사를 하는 것 같았다.(332) It was like saying good-by to a statue. 적절한 것이었다. 영웅의 예술적 배경은 캐서린이 "그들은 당연히 죽는다"(They died of course)라고 대답하는 용감한 사람에게 아무 일도 일어나지 않는다고 말할 때도 나온다. 캐서린은 그것이 문학 작가의 진술인 것을 즉시 알고 있지만 정확한 출처는 알지 못한다. 물론 헨리는 자신이 무지한 자세를 취하고 있지만 셰익스피어의 대사 중 정확한 표현을 인용하고 있어서 알고 있다.

"겁쟁이는 천 번 죽지만 용감한 사람은 한번 죽는다."(139)
"The coward dies a thousand deaths, the brave but one?"

나중에 연인들이 밀라노 병원에서 낭만적인 시간에 바깥세상을 잊고 살 때 캐서린의 말에

"우리는 정말 좋은 시간을 보내고." 캐서린이 말했다.
"나는 이제 다른 일에 관심 없어. 나는 당신과 결혼해서 정말 행복해요."
그때 웨이터가 들어와 그릇들을 가져갔다. 잠시 후 우리는 아무 말 없이 가만히 빗소리에만 귀를 기울였다. 저 아래 거리에서 자동차가 경적을 울렸다.(154)
"하지만 등 위에서 언제나 들리지. 날개를 단 시간의 전차가 급히 다가오는 소리가."

"We have such a fine time." Catherine said. "I don't have any interest in anything else any more. I'm very happy married to you."
The waiter came and took away the tings. After a while we were very still and we could hear the rain. Down below aon the street a motor car hooked.(154)

"But at my back I always hear

Time's winged chariot hurrying near."

* 17세기 영국시인 앤드루 마블 신인의 시「수줍어 하는 여인에게」일부

이것은 영웅의 문학적 감상을 보여 줄 뿐만 아니라 공상이나 자기기만의 사치를 용납하지 않기 때문에 그의 실재감을 증명한다. 헨리는 이성과 상식이 있는 사람이다. 민주주의 세속주의라는 자유주의적 가치에 헌신했음에도 불구하고 그는 자신이 헌신하는 가치 자체를 죽이는 것에 광신적이지 않다. 그는 항상 상대방의 관점에서 상황을 보려고 한다.

그의 성찰은 항상 그의 대화를 따라가며 그는 항상 상대방의 관점을 이해하고 감상하려고 노력하는 것을 마음속에 되새긴다. 자신에게 가장 비합리적인 전투경찰(Battle police)들과 마주치는 등 극단적인 상황에도 그는 분노를 억누르는 것이 어렵지 않다.

분노는 모든 의무와 함께 강물에 씻어 나갔다. 의무는 헌병이 내 멱살을 잡는 순간 이미 사라졌지만, 나는 외관에 별로 신경 쓰지 않는 편이지만, 군복을 벗어 버리고 싶었다. 소매에서 별을 떼어버린 것도 편의 때문이었다. 명예의 문제가 아니었다. 반감 때문도 아니었다. 그냥 완전히 손을 뗀 것이었다. 나는 모두의 행운을 빌었다. 착한 사람, 용감한 사람, 침착한 사람, 현명한 사람이 있었고, 그들은 행운을 누려 마땅하다.(232)

Anger was washed away in the river along any obligation. Although that ceased when the carabiniere put his hands on my collar. I would like to have had the uniform off although I did not care much about the outward forms. I had taken off the stars, but that was for convenience. It was no point of honor. I was not against them. I was through. I wished them all the luck. There were the good ones, and the brave ones, and the calm ones and the sensible ones, and they deserved it.(232)

따라서 헨리가 행동의 모든 과정에서 유지하는 마음의 평형과 균형은 그가 습관적으로 이성에 의존하고 있어서 가능하다.

자원한 이탈리아 군에 의해서 죽음을 당할 처지에서 가까스로 그곳을 도망치고 갖가지 우여곡절 끝에 캐서린과 재회한다. 결혼하지 않은 아내 캐서린과 새로 태어난 아들 등 그가 가진 모든 것을 잃은 채 홀로 서 있는 이 소설의 마지막 부분에서도 그를 침착하게 유지하는 것은 바로 이 이유 때문이다. 비록 그가 죽음에 대해 공포를 느끼고 일시적으로 냉소적으로 변한 것처럼 보이지만 그는 오셀로나 안토니우스처럼 그러한 순간에 그의 목숨을 앗아갈 셰익스피어 비극의 영웅처럼 행동하지 않는다. 헨리의 현실감과 이성에 대한 의지는 그를 냉정하고 침착하게 만든다.

병실 밖 복도에서 나는 의사에게 말했다. "오늘 여기서 제가 할 수 있는 일이 있습니까?"

"아니오, 아무것도 없습니다. 제가 호텔까지 모셔다드릴까요?"

"아니, 괜찮습니다. 저는 여기 잠시 있겠습니다."

"뭐라고 드릴 말씀이 없군요. 뭐라고 말씀드려야 할지----"

"아닙니다," 내가 말했다. "말씀 안 하셔도 됩니다."

"그럼 안녕히 가십시오." 그가 말했다. "정말 호텔까지 모셔다 드리면 안 될까요?"

프레더릭 헨리(Frederic Henry)

"아니, 괜찮습니다."(331)

Outside the room, in the hall, I spoke to the doctor, "Is there anything I can do to-night?"

"No. There is nothing to do. Can I take you to your hotel?"

"No, thank you. I am going to stay here a while."

"I know there is nothing to say. I cannot tell you----"

"No," I said. "There's nothing to say."

"Good-night," he said. "I cannot take you your hotel?"

"No, thank you."(332)

이는 삶을 그대로 받아들이고 이를 학습의 경험으로 만들려고 노력하는『무기여 잘 있거라』의 현실주의 영웅의 강인함을 확실히 보여 준다. 어니스트 헤밍웨이의 소설『무기여 잘 있거라』에서 "전체진실"이라는 개념은 중요한 역할을 하는데, 특히 주인공이 전쟁, 사랑, 죽음을 경험하는 방식을 통해 표현되는 방식에서 그렇다. 직접성, 단순성, 가시적인 것에 초점을 맞춘 헤밍웨이의 글쓰기 스타일은 진실을 이해하는 데 있어 더 현실적이고 때로는 가혹한 접근 방식을 시사한다. 소설에서 "전체진실"이 나타나는 몇 가지 방법은 다음과 같다.

첫째는 전쟁에 대한 환멸이다.

『무기여 잘 있거라』에서 헤밍웨이는 전쟁의 잔혹한 현실과 개인에게 미치는 영향을 묘사한다. 주인공인 헨리는 1차 세계대전 중 이탈리아 군대의 구급차 운전사이며, 헤밍웨이는 자기 경험을 통해 낭만적인 전쟁 개념과 냉혹한 전쟁의 현실 사이의 격차를 드러낸다. 프레데릭은 처음에는 의무와 명예를 믿었지만, 전쟁의 공포, 폭력, 무의미함, 무의미한 죽음을 목격하면서 환멸을 느낀다. 헤밍웨이가 제시하는 전쟁의 진실은 영광, 명애, 신성, 용기 영웅심이 아니라 고통, 혼돈, 상실이다. 헨리의 여정은 환상을 벗겨내고 갈등의 시기에 인간이 겪는 경험에 대한 냉소적이고 냉정한 진실을 드러낸다. 헤밍웨이의 간결하고 꾸밈없는 산문은 이러한 날카롭고 꾸밈없는 현실을 강조한다.

둘째는 사랑과 탈출이다.

캐서린 바클리와 헨리의 연애는 전쟁의 잔혹함으로부터 일종의 피난처를 나타내지만, 이 로맨스조차도 삶의 가혹한 현실에 물들어 있다. 그들의 관계는 처음에는 의미와 위안을 제공하는 것처럼 보이지만, 헤밍웨이는 독자가 그것이 무상함과 죽음의 세계에서 존재한다는 것을 잊지 않도록 한다. 이 맥락에서 사랑에 대한 진실은 단순히 열정이나 탈출에 대한 것이 아니라 취약성, 두려움, 궁극적으로 상실을 포함한다. 헨리와 캐서린의 관계는 진지하지만, 캐서린이 출산 중 사망하는 것과 같은 삶의 비극에서 자유롭지 않다. 그것은 인간으로서 얼쩔수 없는 사실이고 진실이다.

너무 큰 용기를 지닌 사람들이 있을 때 세상은 그들을 꺾어 놓기 위해 죽이려 하고 실제로 그렇게 한다. 세상 모든 사람을 부러뜨리지만, 많은 사람이 그 부러진 곳에서 더 강해진다. 그러나 세상은 부러지지 않으려는 사람들을 죽인다. 착한 사람이든 상냥한 사람이든 용감한 사람이든 가리지 않고 공평하게 죽인다. 그 어디에도 속하지 않은 사람 역시 죽이겠지만 특별히 서두르지 않을 뿐이다.(249)

국가와 민족을 위해서 헌신하고 봉사하는 용기 있는 자와 명예와 신념을 지키면서 상대에 대한 배려심으로 살아가는 자들을 세상은 그런 사람들을 더 봐주고 죽음을 연장시켜 주지 않고 죽이고 결국에는 죽는다고 말한다. 어찌 되었든 인간은 구별 없이 죽임을 당하고 만다는 사실을 말한다. 인류의 평화와 민주주의를 지키려는 사람들은 더 봐주고 한 번 더 용서해 주는 일은 없다. 오히려 그들은 더 빨리 가혹하고 대항할 수 없이 죽인다. 그것은 헤밍웨이가 말하는 진실이고 사실이다. 헤밍웨이는 잔혹한 세상에서 위안을 줄 수 있는 사랑조차도 사람들에게 존재하는 고통으로부터 보호할 수 없다고 말한다.

셋째는 피할 수 없는 진실로서의 죽음이다.
죽음은 『무기여 잘 있거라』에서 반복되는 주제이며, 헤밍웨이는 그것을 삶의 피할 수 없는 부분으로 취급한다. 앞에서 언급한 것처럼 전쟁이나 사랑에 대한 낭만화된 묘사와 달리, 헤밍웨이의 죽음에 대한 관점은 냉엄하고 확고하다. 죽음에는 큰 의미가 없습니다. 사람들은 무작위로, 때로는 무의미하게, 그리고 종종 별다른 의식 없이 죽습니다. 캐서린이 죽고 헨리는 홀로 남겨지는 소설의 결말은 헤밍웨이의 진실 전체에 대한 비전을 상징한다. 삶은 고통, 상실, 죽음으로 가득 차 있으며, 그것을 피하거나 완화하기 위해 할 수 있는 일은 거의 없습니다. 마지막 줄의 단순함과 간결함은 책 대부분에 스며든 실존적 무의미함을 강조한다.

넷째는 헤밍웨이의 빙산 이론으로 덮은 진실이다.
헤밍웨이의 "빙산 이론"은 이야기의 더 깊은 진실이 표면 아래에 잠겨 있고 일부만 보인다는 생각으로, "모든 진실"에 대한 그의 견해를 반영한다. 『무기여 잘 있거라』에서 등장인물의 내면에 대한 감정적 깊이와 진실 대부분은 직접적으로 언급되기보다는 암시된다. 헤밍웨이는 표면적인 세부 사항(대화, 행동, 실체적 세계)을 제시하지만, 근본적인 감정과 실존적 진실은 추론하도록 둔다. 이러한 접근 방식은 소설에서 모든 진실을 다루는 방식을 반영한다. 헨리는 전쟁, 사랑 또는 죽음에 대한 심오한 철학적 성찰을 표현하지 않을 수 있지만 이러한 경험의 무게는 그의 절제된 서술의 표면 아래에서 깊이 느껴진다.

마지막으로 실존적 현실주의이다.
『무기여 잘 있거라』는 일종의 실존적 현실주의를 구현하는데, 여기서 모든 진실은 삶의 본질적인 불확실성과 실망에 직면하는 것을 포함한다. 헤밍웨이의 등장인물들은 의미에 대한 탐구가 종종 무관심이나 비극으로 맞이하는 세상에서 살고 있다. 이 소설에는 신의 개입이나 위대한 도덕적 질서가 없다. 종교나 기타 다른 어떤 존재가 그들 앞에 놓인 고통과 시련을 절감해 줄 수 없다. 생존, 사랑, 죽음이라는 엄연한 현실만 있다. 이는 헤밍웨이가 중심인물이었던 더 큰 모더니즘 운동과 전통적 가치의 붕괴와 전후 세계에서의 의미에 대한 탐구에 대한 시대의 집착을 반영한다.

결론적으로 『무기여 잘 있거라』에서 헤밍웨이는 우리가 원하는 대로가 아닌 있는 그대로 삶의 모든 진실을 밝힌다. 어떤 것을 더하거나 빼는 일이 절대 없다. 이 소설은 쉬운 답이나 위안이 되는 환상을 제공하지 않는다. 대신, 헤밍웨이는 헨리의 경험을 통해 전쟁, 사랑, 죽음의 가혹하

프레더릭 헨리(Frederic Henry)

고 종종 고통스러운 현실을 탐구한다. 헤밍웨이의 관점에서 보면, 모든 진실은 인생이 고통, 환멸, 상실로 가득 차 있고 그것이 현실이며 그 현실을 작품을 통해서 보여 준다. 하지만 거짓된 희망이나 환상 없이 이러한 현실에 정면으로 맞서는 데에는 절제된 존엄성도 있다.

캐서린 버클리(Catherine Barkley)

『무기여 잘 있거라』의 주제와 구조적 패턴에서 중요한 프레더릭 헨리의 옆에는 전쟁 중 헨리와 사랑에 빠진 캐서린 버클 리가 있다. 그녀는 헨리보다 2년 빠른 1919년에 참전했다.

이탈리아 전쟁 전선에 있는 영국 병원의 VAD로서 "키가 크고 금발에 황갈색 피부와 회색 눈"을 가지고 있으며"장난감 라이딩크롬처럼 얇은 등나무 막대기를 들고 가죽으로 묶은 채 병원에서 헨리와 마주친다.

"작년에 전사한 남자가 가지고 있었던 거예요."
"정말 안됐군요."
"아주 좋은 사람이었죠. 저와 결혼을 약속했는데 솜강에서 죽었어요."(18)

"It belonged to a boy who was killed last year."
"I'm awfully sorry."
"He was a very nice boy. He was going to marry me and he was killed in the Somme."(18)

그녀는 소년이 전쟁에서 죽었을 때 8년 동안 그와 약혼했었다. 그녀도 전쟁에서도 로맨틱한 감상적인 소녀의 모습을 보여준다.

"약혼한 지 오래됐었습니까?"

"팔 년요. 어려서부터 같이 자랐어요."

"그런데 왜 결혼하지 않았죠?"(19)

"Had you been engaged long?"

"Eight years. We grew up together."

"And why didn't you marry?"(19)

그녀는 그가 내가 있던 병원에 올 수도 있다는 어리석은 생각을 했다.

I remember having a silly idea he might come to hospital where I was.(20)

군도에 찔려 머리에 붕대를 감고서 아니면 어깨에 총상을 입거나. 그런 그림 같은 장면을 상상했어요.(20)

With a sabre cut, I suppose and a bandage around his head or shot through the shoulder something picturesque.(20)

헤밍웨이의 가정에도 부합하듯이 실제로 일어난 일은 가짜의 사랑이었다.

"폭탄에 산산조각 나버렸죠."

They blew him all to bits.(20)

그녀는 그의 죽음을 애도하는 감상적인 몸짓을 생각했다.

"그 사람이 죽었을 때 다 잘라 버리려고 했어요."

"I was going to cut it all off when he died."(19)

약혼자가 죽은 후에 그녀는 사랑과 집을 갈망하면서 마음이 조금 불안해졌다. 심지어 리날디는 그녀의 애인 죽음으로 생긴 공간을 메울 반가운 동반자로 발견된다.

헨리가 그녀를 소개받기 전에 리날디는 그가 버클리와 결혼할지도 모른다고 소개한다.

"못 믿겠나? 그럼 오늘 오후에 당장 가 보자고. 마을에 예쁜 영국 아가씨들도 있어. 나는 미스 버클리에게 푹 빠졌어. 만나러 갈 때 데려가 주지. 어쩌면 미스 버클리와 결혼할지도 모르거든."(12)

"You don't believe me? We will go now this afternoon and see. And in the town we have beautiful English girls. I am now in love with Miss Barkley. I will take you to call. I will probably marry Miss Barkley."(12)

캐릭터가 형성되는 상황과 캐릭터의 유형을 고려할 때 소설의 행동 과정에서 그 행위를 판단할 수 있다. 『무기여 잘 있거라』 가상 세계에서 캐서린을 생각해 보면 우리는 1919년 초부터 8년 넘게 그녀가 약혼했던 연인을 잃은 채 전쟁에서 자원봉사자로 일하고 있는 젊은 여성을 보고 그녀의 이른바 '꿈같은' 모습이 매우 현실적으로 된다. 게다가 우리가 현실의 삶이 아닌 심리학적 이론에서 끌어낸 진부한 유형들을 잠시나마 잊고 헤밍웨이의 소설이 서사 속에서 캐서린을 있는 그대로 볼 수 있다면, 우리는 그녀를 독립적이고 설득력 있는 여성으로 발견할 것이고 그녀 자신만의 개성을 가지고 삶을 용감하게 마주하며 그녀의 '소녀'를 사랑하는 것은 그녀의 개성을 희생하지 않고 사랑하는 것이다.

우선 캐서린이 헨리를 처음 만났을 때 헨리가 그녀와 함께 자유롭게 있는 것을 발견하고 그녀를 위안소 여자들을 대신할 수 있는 더 편리한 사람으로 대하자.

키스하기 위해 어둠 속에서 몸을 숙인 순간 따끔하게 눈앞에서 날카로운 불꽃이 번쩍했다. 그녀가 내 얼굴을 세게 때린 것이다. 나는 코와 눈을 맞아 반사적으로 눈물이 핑 돌았다.(26)

"Please," I leaned forward in the dark to kiss her and there was a sharp stinging flash. She had slapped me face hand. Her hand had it my nose and eyes, and tears came in my eyes from the reflex.(26)

그녀는 "밤에 비번인 간호사는 이럴 거라고 생각하는 게 싫었을 뿐이에요."(26)

"I just couldn't stand the nurse's evening-off aspect of it."(26)

그녀는 그런 행위는 꿈을 꾸거나 소원을 비는 투영(projection) 때문에 이루어질 수 없다.

마찬가지로 그녀는 연애 초기에 그가 그녀를 정말 사랑하지 않았고 그녀를 사랑하는 척만 하고 있다는 것을 알고 있었으며, 그녀는 그에게 그녀가 속을 수 없으므로 더 이상 가장 하지 말라고 부탁했다.

   나는 캐서린 버클리를 사랑하지 않았고 그럴 생각도 없었다. 이건 게임이었다. 카드가 아니라 말로 하는 브리지 같은 게임. 브리지처럼 돈을 따기 위해 게임을 하거나 내기를 걸고 하는 척하면 그만이었다. 나는 아무래도 상관없다.(30)

   I knew I did not love catherine Barkley nor had an idea of loving her. This was a game, like bridge, in which you said things instead of playing cards. Like bridge you had to pretend you were playing for money or playing for some stakes.

   "우리 지금 아주 못된 게임을 하고 있는 거죠?"

"게임이요?"

"둔한 척하지 말아요."

"둔한 사람 아니에요. 일부러 그러는 거 아닙니다."

"당신은 좋은 사람이고" 그녀가 말했다. "당신이 잘 아는 방법대로 능숙하게 게임하고 있어요. 하지만 이건 못된 게임이에요." "다른 사람들 생각을 언제나 그렇게 잘 압니까?"

"늘 그렇진 않아요. 하지만 당신이라면 알아요. 나를 사랑하는 척할 필요 없어요. 오늘 밤은 그만하죠. 더 하고 싶은 말 있어요?"

"하지만 나는 당신을 사랑해요."

"제발, 쓸데없는 거짓말 말아요."(31)

"This is a rotten game we play, isn't it?"

"What game?"

"Don't be dull."

"I'm not, on purpose."

"You're a nice boy," she said. "And you play it as well as you know how. But it's rotten game."

"Do you always know what people think?"

"No always. But I do with you. You don't have to pretend you love me. That's over for the evening. Is there anything you'd like to talk about?"

"But I do love you."

"Please let's not lie when we don't have to."(31)

분명히 이 대화의 캐서린은 비평가들이 그녀에게 강요하려고 했던 틀에 맞지 않을 것이다. 그녀는 인간 본성에 대한 충분한 지식을 가진 지적이고 경험이 많은 소녀이다. 게다가 그녀는 남자 동반자를 갖고 싶어도 자기 삶에 직면할 수 있는 자립적인 소녀이다. 그녀는 전쟁에서 약혼자가 죽은 후에 그것에 직면해 왔다. 그녀가 모국에서 멀리 떨어진 곳에서 봉사하는 전문간호사라는 사실은 그녀가 자신을 매우 잘 돌볼 수 있다는 것을 증명한다.

캐서린이 자신만의 개성이 없는 그녀를 추상적인 인물로 전락시키는 것을 비판적으로 단순화한 것은 네가 원하는 것을 내가 하고 네가 원하는 것을 말하고 난 후에 나는 큰 성공을 거둘 것이다.

"당신이 원하는 걸 하고 듣고 싶어 하는 말을 한다면 나는 정말 대 성공이겠죠?"(105)

"I will do what you want and say what you want and then I'll be a great success, won't I?"(105)

이제 맥락을 벗어난 그의 진술은 소설의 상황에서 실제로 얻을 수 있는 것과는 매우 다른 의미로 해석될 수 있다.(interpreted to mean very differently from its actual import in the novel's situation.) 캐서린이 내뱉는 말은 간호사로서의 여주인공이 수술을 준비하는 시점에 밀라노 병원의 한 장면에 등장한다. 캐서린이 남녀관계에 대해 가벼운 이야기를 하는 와중에 자주 인용되는 그러나 필연적으로 잘못 해석되는 발언을 한다.

"몰라."
"물론 모르겠죠. 그 여자들도 남자에게 사랑한다고 말하나요? 말해 줘요. 그건 알고 싶어요."
"하지. 남자가 원한다면."
"남자도 그 여자에게 사랑한다고 말하나요? 제발 말해 줘요. 이건 중요해요."
"본인이 하고 싶으면 하지."(105)
"I don't know."
"Of course not. Does she say you loves him? Tell me that. I want to know that."
"Yes. If he wants her to."
"Does he say he loves her? Tell me please. It's important."
"He does if he wants to."(105)

캐서린 버클리(Catherine Barkley)

캐서린이 이렇게 진술하는 것은 그녀가 간호사로서 헨리에게 상처를 입은 다리의 수술을 준비하면서, 환자의 주의를 간호사의 상처 치료 등으로 인한 고통으로부터 멀리 떨어뜨리기 위한 대화에 관여하도록 하는 전문적인 일을 하고 있을 때의 일이다.

게다가 진술이 일어나는 것은 연인들의 놀림 놀이이고, 그런 정신으로 대화는 캐서린이 자신을 확신하고 더 교육적이고 예술적인 연인과 자신이 일치한다는 것을 증명하기 위해 날카롭고 빠른 마음을 가지고 있다는 것을 보여 준다.

그녀가 그 진술에서 실제로 의미하는 것은 그녀가 소녀 중 한 명이라는 것이 아니라 그녀가 멍청하고 유순한 소녀처럼 행동한다면 그 남자는 매우 기뻐하리라는 것이다. 비평가들이 캐서린이 자신의 개성이 없다는 것을 증명하기 위해 사용해 온 또 다른 발언은,

"당신이 원하는 게 내가 원하는 거예요. 나라는 존재는 이제 더 이상 없어 당신이 원하는 것만 있을 뿐. 따로 나를 분리하지 마세요."(106)

"I want what you want. There isn't any me any more. Just what you ant." Don't make u a separate me.(106, 115)

이제 이것은 다시 소설의 서사에서 특정한 맥락에서 나타나는데, 이를 염두에 둔다면 비평가들이 그녀에게 이런저런 유형의 신화나 심리학을 증명하기 위해 제출한 일종의 해석을 허용하지 않을 것이다. 캐서린이 말한 내용의 맥락은 연인들이 밀라노 병원에서 생활할 때 결혼에 대한

논쟁이다.

나는 정식으로 결혼하고 싶었지만, 캐서린은 그러면 자신이 여기서 쫓겨날 테고, 그저 수속만 밟아도 그들이 자신을 감시하고 우리를 갈라놓으려 할 거라고 말했다. 혼인하려면 이탈리아 법대로 해야 하는데 절차가 무척 까다로웠다. 나는 아이가 생길지도 모른다는 우려에 결혼을 하고 싶었지만, 이미 결혼한 부부처럼 지냈기 때문에 크게 걱정하지 않았고 사실 결혼하지 않고 지내는 것을 더 즐겼던 것도 같다. 어느 밤 그 문제에 관해 이야기하다가 캐서린이 말했다. "하지만 병원에서 나를 다른 데로 보낼 거예요, 달링."

"안 그럴 수도 있지."

"그럴 거예요. 나를 집으로 돌려보내면, 우리는 전쟁이 끝날 때까지 헤어져 있어야 해요."

"내가 휴가를 받아서 갈게."

"휴가 정도로는 스코트랜드까지 다녀갈 수 없어요. 게다가 나는 당신 곁을 떠나고 싶지 않아. 지금 결혼하는 게 무슨 의미가 있어요? 우리는 사실상 결혼한 거예요. 이보다 더 확실한 결혼 상태가 어디 있어요."

"당신을 위해 하려는 거야."

"나라는 존재는 없어. 내가 바로 당신이에요. 당신과 나를 떼어놓지 말아요."(115)

I want to be really married but Catherine said that if we were they would send her away and if we merely started on the formalities they would watch her and would break us up. We would have to be married under Italian law and her formalities were terrific. I wanted us to be married really because I worried about having a child if I thought about it. but we pretended to ourselves we were married and did not worry much and I suppose I enjoy not being married, really. I know one night we talked about it and Catherine said, "But, darling, they'd send me away."

"Maybe they wouldn't."

"They would. hey'd send me home and then we would be apart until after the war."

"I'd come on leave."

"You couldn't get to Scotland and back on a leave. Besides, I won't leave you. What good would it do to marry now? We're really married. I couldn't be any more married."

"I only wanted to for you."

"There isn't any me. I'm you. Don't make up a separate me."(115)

사실 그들은 공식적으로 하나가 되기를 열망한다. 하지만 복잡한 문제들이 있다. 캐서린은 헨리가 결혼을 고집하지 않도록 설득하기 위해서 말한 것이다라고 말한다.

우리는 하나이고 사랑하는 사람과 분리할 수 없다라는 생각을 말한 것은 공식적인 결혼을 피하려는 그녀의 주장이다. 이 같은 맥락에서 그녀의 주장은 그녀가 영웅과 분리된 인격체를 가지고 있지 않으며 그녀가 별 볼일 없는 존재가 아니라는 것을 보여 준다. 캐서린은 많은 사람들이 보는 앞에서 공식적인 결혼은 현실적으로 불가능하다는 판단하에 서로 사랑하고 같이 생활하는데 큰 문제가 없고 현재 당면한 문제해결에 집중하는 것이 더 좋겠다는 현실적인 캐서린의 판단이고 그에 반해 헨리는 결혼을 통해서 자신들의 사랑을 검증받고 싶어 한다는 점에서 차이가 있다.

그녀가 개성(특성)이 없다면 그녀를 사랑하는 영웅도 마찬가지라는 연인을 지칭하는 개념이다. 그녀는 이 주장을 제시하는데, 이는 캐서린 뿐만 아니라 헨리에게도 두려운 전망인 이별의 결혼에 들어가는 어려운 상황을 피할 수 있을 것이기 때문이다. 따라서 이것은 캐서린이 논쟁하는 연인을 이용하기 위해 사용하는 책략일 뿐이다. 캐서린의 "성격 없음(characterless ness)에 대한 증거발화를 사용하는 것은 단지 맥락적 의미를 왜곡하는 것이다. 캐서린이 분명 그녀만의 개성을 가지고 있는데, 헤밍웨이는 그녀가 어려운 상황과 다른 사람들과 대화를 나누는 것을 통해 그 모습을 묘사한다.

"여기도 영웅은 많아요." 그녀는 말했다. "하지만 그 사람들은 대체로 조용하죠."

"난 별로 싫지 않던데."

"그렇게 우쭐대면서 사람들을 지루하고, 지루하고, 또 지루하게 하지만 않는다면 나는 싫진 않을 거예요."

"지루하긴 하지."

"그렇게 말해 주니 고마워요. 달링. 하지만 그럴 필요 없어요. 당신은 전선에 있는 그 사람 모습을 상상할 수 있으니까, 능력이 있다는 걸 알겠지만 그 사람은 내가 아주 싫어하는 타입이에요."

"알아."

캐서린 버클리(Catherine Barkley)

"알아줘서 고마워요. 좋아하려고 노력은 해 보겠지만 그래도 정말 끔찍하고 끔찍한 남자예요."

"오늘 오후에 만났는데 대위로 진급한다더군."

"잘됐네요," 캐서린이 말했다. "아주 기분이 좋았겠네."(124)

"We have heroes too," she said. "But usually, they're much quieter."

"I don't mind him."

"I wouldn't mind him if he wasn't so conceited and didn't bore me, and bore me and bore me."

"He bores me."

"You're sweet to say so, darling. But you don't need to. You can picture him at the front and you know he's useful but he's so much the type of boy I don't care for."

"I know."

"You're awfully sweet to know, and I try and like him but he's a dreadful, dreadful boy really."

"He said this afternoon he was going to be a captain"

"I'm glad, said Catherine. That should please him."

"Wouldn't you like me to have some more exalted rank?"

"No, darling. I only want you to have enough rank so that we're admitted to the better restaurant."(124)

이것은 캐서린이 자신의 견해를 어떻게 가졌는지, 헨리가 항상 감상할 수 있는 유머 감각을 지니고 있는지, 그리고 에토레와 같은 사람들에게 어떻게 허풍을 드러낼 수 있는지를 분명히 보여준다. 캐서린은 승진하는 것에 대해서 그렇게 좋게 생각하지 않았고 좋은 레스토랑에 들어갈 수 있을 정도면 된다고 말한다.

또한 캐서린은 헨리에게 임신 소식을 전하면서, 그녀의 연인이 최선의 노력에도 불구하고 피할 수 없었던 것을 좋아하지 않았을 수도 있다는 것을 느낀다. 그녀는 그에게 "덫에 걸린"(trapped) 것 같은 느낌을 느꼈는지를 물어보자 비록 그는 그것을 받아들이지 않았지만, 그 소식에 확실히 화가 났다. 이것은 헨리가 그녀를 내버려 둔 채 곧 전선으로 돌아가야 해서 캐서린이 그들의 상황에 대해서 걱정하게 만든다. 그녀가 다소 슬픈 것을 발견한 헨리는 그녀가 용감하고 용감한 사람은 죽지 않았다고 말하면서 그녀의 사기를 북돋우려고 노력한다.
헨리의 발언에 대해 그녀의 대답은 의미심장하다.
내가 말했다.

"당신은 용감하니까 용감한 사람에게는 아무 일도 벌어지지 않아."
"그런 사람이 죽기는 하죠."(139)
I said "Because you're too brave.
Nothing ever happens to the brave."
"They die of course."

헨리가 "겁쟁이는 천 번을 죽지만 용감한 사람은 한 번 죽는다."라는

캐서린 버클리(Catherine Barkley)

셰익스피어의 말을 인용했다. 그는 겁쟁이들에 대해서는 많이 알고 있지만 용감한 사람들에 대해서는 아는 것이 없다고 말한다. 용감하고 영리한 사람이라면 아마 이천 번은 죽을 거예요. 그렇다고 말하지 않을 뿐이지라고, 말한다. 캐서린은 여기서 자신의 견해를 확신하는 독립적인 마음뿐만 아니라 자신이 직면할 수 있는 어떤 상황에서도 완전히 자립적으로 반응할 준비가 된 인물로 나타난다.

게다가 일반적인 밀라노에 있는 연인들의 목가적인 삶은 "현실"(real) 연인들의 걱정에서 벗어날 수 없다. 현실이 가져다주는 연인들의 걱정에서 벗어날 수 없고 헨리와 캐서린도 예외는 아니다. 현실과 관계없는 로맨스는 없다. (There is no romance without relation to reality)

캐서린이 전쟁 속에서 운 좋게 사랑을 나눈다면 그녀 역시 사랑을 나누는 대가에서 벗어나지 못한다. 그녀는 임신하고 정식으로 연인의 아내가 될 기회를 얻기 전에 엄마가 되는 불명에 직면했다.

인간의 성격이 두 가지 요소에 의해서 만들어진다고 생각하기 때문에 유전과 환경에 세심한 주의를 기울였던 자연주의자들과 달리 헤밍웨이는 인간의 인격은 자신의 행위와 성찰 사이의 지속적인 상호작용을 통해 만들어진다고 보고 인물들의 행위에 주목한다. 그러나 그는 자기 인물들 적어도 주요 인물들에게 국적과 부모의 배경을 더 현실적이고 설득력이 있게 보이도록 제공한다.

"우리는 헨리의 배경에 대해 아무것도 모르고 캐서린 버클리의 배경에 대해서도 아무것도 모른다."라는 말은 사실이 아닙니다.

첫째『무기여 잘 있거라』와 같은 상황에서 가족이나 사회적 배경은 그다지 관련이 없습니다. 왜냐하면 그것은 가족이나 사회문제에 대한 소설이 아니기 때문입니다. 그것은 예의에 대한 소설이 아니기 때문입니다. 둘째 헤밍웨이 소설은 상황과 관련된 배경이 무엇이든 제시된다. 소설의 맨 앞부분에서 우리는 헨리가 이탈리아에서 건축학을 공부하고 있고, 지원병으로 참전한 미국인이라고 들었다. 마찬가지로 캐서린은 한 남자와 8년 동안 약혼한 영국 소녀이며 그가 전쟁에서 사망하기 전에,

"와인 때문에 우리 아버지는 심한 통풍을 앓고 계세요."(154)
"But it's given my father gout very badly."

통풍을 앓고 있는 아버지를 두고 있다. 그리고 그녀는 1919년 초부터 영국 병원 VAD로 일하고 있다.

마지막으로 헤밍웨이는 유전이 사람의 성격을 결정한다고 생각하지 않으며 심리학자나 사회학자의 관점에서 인물을 묘사하는 것을 선택하지도 않습니다.

그의 단순화의 방법은 오로지 사건과 대화를 포함한 행동 장치에 의존한다. 또한 인물에 대한 정보는 전기나 환경에 대한 직접적인 묘가가 아닌 아이러니와 절제된 표현을 사용하여 비스듬히 드러난다. 캐서린은 단지 지적이고 민감할 뿐만 아니라 실용적인 감각도 강하다. 그녀는 언제든지 그 자리에 올라 진실하고 믿을 수 있는 동반자로서 자기 남자를 도울 수 있다. 예를 들어 전쟁터에서 탈출한 이후 밀라노에 있는 동안 헨리는 이탈리아 군경의 체포와 처벌 가능성에 직면하여 전쟁에 대한 뉴스 읽고 싶어 하지 않을 정도로 긴장감을 유지한다. 캐서린의 상황에 대

한 대응은 중요하다.

"신문 읽고 싶지 않아요? 병원에서 늘 신문을 찾았잖아."

"싫어," 내가 말했다. "이젠 읽고 싶지 않아."

"소식을 알고 싶지 않을 정도로 상황이 나빴어요?"

"전쟁 소식은 알고 싶지 않아."

"당신하고 같이 있었다면 나도 사정을 알았을 텐데."

"머릿속에 정리가 되면 말해 줄게."

"그런데 군복을 벗었다는 게 들키면 체포되지 않을까요?"

"아마 총살하겠지."

"그럼, 우리 여기 이러고 있지 말아요. 이 나라에서 떠나요."

"나도 그런 생각을 했어."

"우리 떠나요. 달링, 바보 같은 모험은 안 돼요. 메스트레에서 밀라노까지는 어떻게 왔어요?"

"기차로 왔어. 그때는 군복을 입고 있었고."

"그럼 위험한 일은 없었어요?"

"별로, 옛날에 받은 이동명령서를 가지고 있었거든. 메스트레에서 날짜를 고쳤어."

"달링, 여기 있다가는 언제 체포될지 몰라요. 그렇게 되게 두지 않을 거야. 그건 어리석어요. 당신이 잡혀가면 우린 어떻게 될까요?"

"그런 생각하지 말자. 생각만으로도 피곤해."

"당신을 체포하러 오면 어떻게 할 거예요?"

"쏴 버리지."

"어리석은 소리, 여기 떠날 때까지 절대 호텔 밖으로 나가지 말아요."(251)

"Don't you want the paper? You always wanted the paper in the hospital"

"No." I said. "I don't want the paper now."

"Was it so bad you don't want even to read about it?"

"I don't want to read about it."

"I wish I had been with you so I would know about it too."

"I'll tell you about it if I ever get it straight in my head."

"But won'they arrest you if they catch you out of uniform?"

"They'll probably shoot me."

"Then we'll not stay here. We'll get out of the country."

"I'd thought something of that."

"We'll get out. Darling, you shouldn't take silly chances. Tell me how did you come from Mestre to Milan?"

"I came on the train. I was in uniform them."

"Weren't you in danger then?"

"Not much. I had an old order of movement. I fixed the dates on it in Mestre."

"Darling, you're liable to be arrested here any time. I won't have it. It's silly to do something like that. Where would we be if they took you off?"

"Let's not think about it. I'm tired of thinking about it."

"What would you do if they came to arrest you?"

"Shoot them."

"You see how silly you are. I won't let you go out of the hotel until we leave here."(251)

여기서 캐서린은 자신이 독립적으로 생각할 뿐만 아니라 단호하게 행동한다는 것을 분명히 보여 준다. 그녀는 현재 상황의 급박함에서 발생하는 즉각적인 상황에 대해 행동하는 실용적인 감각을 지니고 있다. 게다가 그녀는 남자와 함께 그가 강제로 부대에서 이탈한 이후 직면해야 하는 걱정과 긴장뿐만 아니라 그들을 위해 목숨을 건 역경과 맞서 싸우는 두 사람이 직면해야 하는 육체적인 어려움을 공유한다. 헨리의 "팔과 어깨" 그리고 등과 손이 아프게 되면 캐서린은 노를 잡고 보트 옆에 바짝 붙어 있는 그녀의 팔 아래를 잡고 헨리가 우산을 바람에 대고 조종한다.

그렇게 하여 연인들은 호수를 건너 스위스로 탈출할 수 있다. 대부분 비평가가 그랬던 것처럼 걱정과 긴장, 위협으로 가득 찬 연인들의 삶이 목가적인 삶으로 묘사될 수 있는지 궁금하다. 게다가 캐서린처럼 두 사람이 직면해야 하는 모든 신체적인 걱정과 정신적인 걱정에 적극적으로 참여하는 여성을 어떻게 "꿈의 소녀" 혹은 "소원 투영"(wish projection)이라고 표현할 수 있는가.

그녀는 자신만의 독립적이고 복잡한 성격을 가진 진짜 여성이다. 캐서린이 마지막이자 가장 설득력 있는 용기 있는 행동은 출산의 시련이다. 그녀는 전쟁 중에 헨리가 빗속에서 강제로 떠난 이후에 여러 번 "비" 속에서 죽은 자신을 보았기 때문에 항상 "비"를 두려워했다. 이제 소설에서 그들의 여정의 마지막에 그녀는 확실한 죽음의 절망에 직면한 자신을 발견한다. 그녀는 자신이 죽을 것이라는 것을 알고 있지만, 죽음을 두려워하지 않는다.

"가여운 사람." 캐서린이 아주 부드럽게 말했다. 얼굴이 잿빛이었다.

"당신은 괜찮아, 켓." 내가 말했다. "괜찮아질 거야."

"나는 죽을 거예요." 그녀가 말했다. 그리고 잠시 후 말을 이었다.

"죽기 싫어요."(330)

"Poor darling," Catherine said very softly. She looked gray.

"You're all right, Cat," I said. "You're going to be all right."

"I'm going to die," she said; then waited and said, "I hate it."(330)

그리하여 캐서린은 냉철한 체념과 어쩔 수 없는 것에 대한 수용으로 피할 수 없는 것에 침착하게 직면하게 된다. 헨리와 달리 그녀의 사랑, 헨리 퍼거슨과의 우정, 미스 게이지와 미스 반 캠펜과의 온화한 행동까지 그리고 리날디와 같은 사람들과의 온화한 행동까지 이 모든 사실은 헨리와 다른 인물들과 함께 전쟁의 치열한 상황에서도 냉철함과 마음의 균형 미덕을 가진 성격을 드러낸다. 소설에서 그녀의 중요성은 그녀가 전쟁의 인물들에게 대항하는 사랑의 인물일 뿐만 아니라 용기와 체념의 인물이라는 점도 있다. 그녀는 분명히 복잡하거나 둥근 캐릭터이지 단순하거나 납작한(flat) 캐릭터가 아니다. 그녀의 이차원적인 인물이 아니고 다차원적인 인물이다. 그녀는 정적인(not static) 것이 아니라 역동적이다. 무엇보다도 그녀는 프레더릭 헨리보다 기억에 남을 만큼 뛰어난 캐릭터이다.

사제(Priest)

『무기여 잘 있거라』의 주제적인 패턴에서 이탈리아 신부는 중요한 인물이다. 그는 리날디와 함께 소설의 의미 패턴에서 한 쌍의 반대되는 관계를 형성한다. 리날디가 삶에 대한 이성적인 태도를 나타내는 의사라면 사제는 삶에 대한 종교적인 태도를 나타내는 신앙을 가진 사람이다. 아부르지(Abruzzi)라는 작은 마을에 속해 있는 그는 큰 도시에서 다소 불편함을 느낀다. 소설의 앞부분에서 헨리가 장교들의 엉망진창 휴가 계획을 이야기할 때, 리날디와 소령이 로마와 다른 대도시로 가라는 조언에 반대하는 것처럼 신부는 춥지만 밝고 건조한 곳, 사냥하기 좋은 곳, 농부들이 모자를 벗고 당신을 주님이라고 부르는 곳을 방문하라고 조언한다.

그리하여 사제는 소박한 수줍음, 곧음, 견고함의 대표적인 특성이 있는 목회자 적 성격이다. 그는 대도시의 산업화와 현대화에 영향을 받지 않는 농촌 생활 방식을 대표하는 유형을 이루고 있다. 그래서 헨리가 아브루치로 가자고 제안했을 때 장교 중 한 명이 이렇게 반박한다.

"아브루치라고요. 거긴 여기보다 눈이 더 많이 오는 덴데. 저 친구는 농부를 보고 싶은 게 아닙니다. 문화와 문명의 중심지로 보내야죠."(8)

Listen to him talk bout the Abruzzi. There's more snow there than here. He doesn't want to see peasants. Let him go to centres of culture and civilization.(8)

소설 내내 이름을 조심스럽게 밝히지 않은 신부님은 분명히 자신의 직업을 대변하기 위한 것입니다. 그는 로마교회에 대한 믿음이 확고한 가톨릭 기독교인이다. 장교들은 그의 신앙에 대해 계속 놀리고 교황을 조롱했다. 장교들이 어질어진 식사 시간에 그는 여전히 미끼의 주요 대상으로 남아 있다.

"교황은 이 전쟁에서 오스트리아가 이기길 바라지." 소령이 말했다. "교황은 프란츠 요제프 편이거든. 거기가 돈 나오는 데니까. 나는 무신론자야."

"『검은 돼지』라는 책을 읽어 보셨습니까?" 중위가 물었다. "제가 한 권 구해드리죠. 제 믿음을 뒤흔든 책입니다."

"더럽고 사악한 책입니다," 신부가 말했다. "당신이 그 책을 정말로 좋아할 리 없어요."

"아주 귀한 책입니다," 중위가 말했다. "사제들에 대해 뭔가 말해 주거든. 자네도 좋아할 거야." 중위가 내게 말했다. 나는 신부에게 미소를 지었고 신부도 촛불 너머로 내게 미소를 지었다. "읽지 마십시오." 신부가 말했다.

"자네도 한 권 구해 주지," 중위가 말했다.

"생각이란 걸 하는 사람들은 모두 무신론자지," 소령이 말했다. "그렇다고 프리메이슨을 믿는 건 아니야."(8)

"The Pope wants the Austrians to win the war," the major said. "He loves Franz Joseph. That's where the money comes from I am ab atheist."

"Did you ever read the 'Black Pig?" asked the lieutenant. "I will get you a copy. It was that which shook my faith."

"It is a filthy and vile book," said the priest. "You do not really like it."

"It is very valuable," said the lieutenant. "It tells you about those priest and he smiles back across the candle-light." "Don't you read it," he said.

"I will get it for you," said the lieutenant.

"All thinking men are atheists," the major said. "I do not believe in the Free Masons however."(8)

진정한 신앙인 것처럼 냉정하고 침착한 성직자는 자신의 신앙뿐만 아니라 자기 사람에 대한 장교들의 공격에도 흔들리지 않는다. 아이러니나 빈정거림을 사용하는 것에 주어진 것은 아니지만 그는 아이러니하고 빈정거리는 발언이 만들어지는 그 상황을 정신으로 신앙으로 받아들인다. 장교들이 하는 대부분의 비판은 그가 농담으로 받아들인다:

우리가 이야기를 멈추자, 대위가 소리쳤다. "신부님 행복하지 않아. 신부님 아가씨들이 없이 행복하지 않아."

"저는 행복합니다." 신부가 말했다.

"신부님 행복하지 않아. 신부는 오스트리아가 이 전쟁에서 이기기를 바라." 대위가 말했다. 다른 사람들은 듣고 있었다. 신부는 고개를 저었다.

"아닙니다." 그가 말했다.

"신부님은 우리가 공격하는 것을 원하지 않아. 우리가 절대 공격하지 않길 바라죠?"

"아닙니다. 전쟁하는 이상 우리도 공격해야죠."

"공격해야지. 공격하자!"

신부는 고개를 끄덕였다.(14)

We too stopped talking and the captain shouted, "Priest not happy. Priest not happy without girls."

"I am happy," said the priest.

"Priest not happy. priest wants Austrians to win the war," the captain said. The others listened. The priest shook his head.

"No." he said. "Priest wants us never to attack. Don't you want us never to attack?"

"No. if there is a war I suppose we must attack."

"Must attack. Shall I attack!"

The priest nodded.(14)

신부님이 화를 내고 동요하는 일 없이 온갖 더러운 농담을 냉정하고 차분하게 받아들일 수 있다는 것은 믿음의 힘을 보여준다. 종교에 대한 그의 믿음과 아브루치의 관습은 그를 이성의 맹공격으로부터 보호하고 전쟁의 붕괴 효과로부터 그를 보호한다. 리날디와 같은 사람들은 모진 전쟁으로 인해 우울해질 뿐만 아니라 마음의 균형을 잃지만, 사제는 비교적 침착하다. 사제는 전쟁에 대한 대응에서 리날디와 정반대의 입장을 구성하게 되어 있다.

리닐디는 밤낮으로 전쟁에 참여하여 노출로 인한 부식효과를 받는 반면 사제는 갈등에 있는 외부인에 더 가까우면서 그 갈등속에 들어가지 않는다. (말려들지 않는다)

육체적으로나 지적으로나 신부는 전쟁에 노출되지 않은 채 남아 있다.

"전쟁이 끝날지도 모르잖습니까."

"그렇게 되길 바라죠."

"그렇게 되면 뭘 하실 생각인가요?"

"가능하면 아브루치로 돌아갈 겁니다."

신부의 가무잡잡한 얼굴이 갑자기 환해졌다.

"아부루치를 사랑하는군요?"

"그럼요. 무척 사랑하죠."

"그럼 꼭 가야죠."

"그럼 더없이 행복할 겁니다. 거기서 살면서 하나님을 사랑하고 섬길 수 있다면."

"존경도 받으면서요." 내가 말했다.

"네, 존경받으면서요. 못 그럴 것도 없겠죠?"

"못 그럴 이유가 없죠. 신부님은 존경받아야 합니다."

"아무래도 상관없습니다. 우리 고향에서는 남자가 하나님을 사랑할 수 있다는 걸 이해합니다. 이건 상스러운 농담이 아니에요."

"압니다."

신부가 나를 보며 미소를 지었다.

"알지만 하나님을 사랑하지 않죠."

"네."(71)

"Maybe the war will be over."

"I hope so."

"what will you do then?"

"If it is possible I will return to the Abruzzi."

His brown face was suddenly very happy.

"You love the Abruzzi?"

"Yes, I love it very much."

"You ought to go there then."

"I would be too happy. If I could live there and love God and serve Him."

"and be respected. Why not?"

"no reason not. You should be respected."

"it does not matter. But there in my country it is understood that a man may love God. It is not a dirty joke."

"I understand."

He looked at me and smiled.

"You understand but you do not love God."

"No."(71)

여기서 대화 내용이 드러나듯이 영웅이 전쟁에 노출되면서 변신했고, 이전에 정착한 삶으로 돌아갈 수 없는 정도라면 사제는 실제로 경험하지 못한 전쟁 때문에 불편함 없이 곧바로 존경의 마을 삶으로 돌아가곤 했다. 그의 믿음은 장점인 동시에 약점이기도 하다. 전쟁의 허무주의적 영향으로부터 그를 보호한다는 점에 있어서 강점이며, 전쟁의 경험과 삶에 대해 무지하게 만든다는 점에서는 약점이기도 하다. 소설이 제공하는 또 다른 경험인 사랑에 대한 그의 태도는 전쟁에 대한 것만큼이나 전통적이고 관습적이다. 그는 종교의 안경을 통해 전쟁뿐만 아니라 사랑을 바라본다; 그는 단지 그의 믿음의 원칙과 관습을 따를 뿐이며, 사랑의 경험에 결코 자신을 드러내지 않는다. 분명히 그는 전쟁에 대해 무지

한 그것만큼이나 사랑에 대해서도 잘 모르고 있다:

"여자를 사랑하는 건 어떨까요? 제가 진심으로 한 여자를 사랑하게 된다면 그런 행복을 느낄까요?"

"그건 모르겠군요. 여자를 사랑해 본 적이 없어서."

"어머니는요?"

"그렇죠, 어머니는 당연히 사랑했죠."

"신부님은 늘 하나님을 사랑했습니까?"

"아주 어릴 때부터요."

"음", 내가 말했다. 무슨 말을 해야 할지 몰랐다. "착한 아이로군요," 내가 말했다.

"맞습니다," 그가 말했다. "하지만 중위님은 저를 아버지라고 부르죠."

"그게 예의니까요."

신부는 미소를 지었다.(72)

"How about loving women? If I really loved some woman would it be like that?"

"I don't know about that. I never loved any woman."

"What about your mother?"

"Yes, I must have loved my mother."

"Did you always loved God?"

"Ever since I was a little boy."

"Well," I said. I did not know what to day. "You are a fine boy," I said.

"I am a boy," he said. "But you call me father."

"That's politeness."

He smiled.(72)

이제 이것은 사제의 종교가 삶의 다양한 측면에 대한 그의 반응에 얼마나 큰 장애가 되고 있는지를 보여 준다. 그는 지적인 성장으로 볼 때 정말로 '소년'으로 남아 있다. 사랑과 전쟁에 노출되지 않은 채 그는 사랑과 전쟁에 대해서도 무지한 채로 남아 있다. 의심할 여지 없이, 그는 흔들리지 않고 바위처럼 견고하지만, 또한 그는 돌처럼 정적인 채로 남아 있다. 따라서 단순한 수줍음이 많고 곧은 사제는 과학기술로 점철된 도시 문명이 지배적인 세력인 현대와 같은 시대에 영웅 프레더릭 헨리가 삶에 대한 부적절한 반응으로 거부하는 "자연으로 희귀"의 가능성을 제시한다. 휴가에서 도시로 가지 말고 자기 고향으로 가라고 추천하는 등 자연으로의 회귀를 계속 제시한다.

의사 리날디(Doctor Rinaldi)

이 소설의 주제 계획에서 주요한 역할을 하는 신부 이외에 또 다른 이탈리아 원주민 캐릭터는 리날디 박사이다. 사제가 삶에 대한 목회적 접근과 사제적 접근을 대변하도록 의도된 것처럼, 의사도 삶에 대한 도시적 접근과 이성적 접근을 대변하도록 의도된 것이다. 소설의 시작부터 우리는 그가 도시를 마을에 대항하는 것으로 종교에 대항하는 것으로 이성을 들어 도시를 애원(찬양)하는 것을 발견한다. 만약 사제가 소설의 주제적 스펙트럼의 한쪽 극단에 서 있다면 의사는 다른 쪽 극단에 서 있다.

그는 극과 극 사이에는 두 사람이 인물의 힘을 강조하는 것처럼 두 사람의 한계를 드러내는 영웅 프레더릭 헨리가 서 있다. 리날디는 외향적이고 말이 많고 유머러스하며 열심히 일하는 사람이다. 사제와 달리 어디에 있든 존재감을 느끼게 해 준다. 그는 장교식당에서 항상 사제를 화나게 해서 활기를 불어넣는다. 게다가 그는 헨리와 방을 함께 사용하는 헨리의 활기찬 동료이다. 의사와 사제는 정반대이다: 전자는 무신론자(atheist)이고, 후자는 독실한 신봉자이며(staunch believer) 전자는 여성을 사랑하며 후자는 여성을 수줍어한다. 전자는 동료와 음식을 사랑하는 쾌락주의자이며 후자는 금식을 지키는 금식자이며, 전자는 지치지 않는 수다쟁이이며 후자는 다소 유보적이다. 리날디 박사는 비록 합리주의자이고 믿지 않는 사람이지만 처음부터 냉소적이지는 않으며, 그는 와인, 여성, 그리고 일과 같은 삶의 모든 좋은 것들을 즐긴다. 게다가 그는 즐거운 친구이다.

헨리는 그의 일에 대한 농담으로 그를 좋아한다. 헨리는 리날디와 같은 인생의 가치관을 갖는 인물은 아니지만 전쟁터에서 상처를 입은 전우들을 보살피는 군의관과 천성적으로 낙천적인 리날디를 좋아했다.

우리는 악수했고 그는 내 목을 끌어안고 키스했다.

"으윽." 내가 말했다.

"지저분해." 그가 말했다. "씻어야겠는데. 어디 가서 뭘 했어? 당장 불어."

"여기저기 다 갔지. 말라노, 피렌체, 로마, 나폴리, 빌라 산 조반니, 메시나, 타오르미나—"

"무슨 시간표라도 외우나? 그래, 멋진 모험을 했어?"

"그럼."

"어디서?"

"밀라노, 피렌체, 로마, 나폴리——"

"그건 됐어. 정말 최고였던 데나 얘기해 봐."

"밀라노."

"처음 가서 그랬겠지. 여자는 어디서 만났나? 코바였나? 어디를 갔어? 기분은 어땠어? 다 얘기해 봐. 밤새 같이 있었나?"

"그럼."

"그런 건 뭐 별것도 아니지. 이젠 여기도 예쁜 아가씨들이 와 있거든. 전선에 와본 적 없는 새로운 아가씨들."

"잘됐군."(12)

의사 리날디 (Doctor Rinaldi)

We shook hands and he put his arm around my neck and kissed me.

"Oughf," I said.

"You're dirty," he said. "You ought to wash. Where did you go and what did you do? Tell me everything at once."

"I went everywhere. Milan, Florence, Rome, Napoles, Villa San Giovanni, Messina, Taormina----"

"You talk like a time-table. Did you have any beautiful adventures?"

"Yes."

"Where?"

"Milano, Firenze, Roma, Napoli----"

"That's enough. Tell me really what was the best."

"In Milano."

"That was because it was first. Where did you meet her? In the Cova? Where did you go? How did you feel? Tell me everything at once. Did you stay all night?"

"Yes."

"That's nothing. Here now we have beautiful girls. New girls never been to the front before."

"Wonderful."(12)

이러한 삶에 대한 농담은 그를 계속 나아가게 하지만, 허무주의적인 전쟁의 맹공격에 대한 방어무기 역할도 한다. 마찬가지로, 그의 이성주의는 그에게 사랑과 전쟁의 경험에 자신을 드러내는 이점을 주지만, 동시에 그가 막다른 골목, 공허, 공허에 직면한 자신을 발견하는 탐구의 길

끝으로 데려간다. 이에 따라 의사는 우울증에 사로잡히고 의식의 압박으로 분해된다.

우리가 리날디를 두 번째 만났을 때- 헨리가 상처에서 회복된 후 전선으로 돌아왔을 때- 우리는 그가 완전히 바뀐 것을 발견하고 헨리와 사제를 상대하면서도 그는 더 이상 술과 좋은 음식을 즐기는 자발적인 자신이 아니다. 오히려 그는 우울증과 냉소주의에 사로잡힌, 분해된 성격, 금이 가고 무너지는 쓰라린 사람이다:

"될 대로 되라지." 리날디가 식탁에 앉은 우리에게 말했다. "빌어먹을 전쟁이고 뭐고 지옥으로 꺼지라고 해." 그는 도전적인 눈길로 식탁 주위를 둘러보았는데, 눈은 풀려 있고, 얼굴은 창백했다.

"맞아." 내가 말했다. "빌어먹을 전쟁 따윈 지옥으로 꺼리라지."

"아니, 아니야," 리날디가 말했다. "자네는 못 해. 자네는 못 한다고 자네는 못 한다니까. 자네는 메마르고 텅 빈 인간이고 다른 건 아무것도 없어. 다른 건 아무것도 없다고. 빌어먹을 것 하나 없어. 알아, 나는 일을 그만두면 아무것도 없어."(174)

"I don't give a damn," Rinali said to the table. "To hell with the whole business." He looked defiantly round the table, his eyes flat, his face pale.

"All right," I said. "To hell with the whole damn business."

"No, no," said Rinaldi. "You can't do it. You can't do it. I say you can't do it. You're dry and you're empty and there's nothing else. There's nothing else I tell you. Not a damned thing. I know, when I stop working."(174)

리날디는 전쟁에서 부서졌다. 그는 더 이상 자신의 의식에 대처할 수 없다. 외로움을 마주할 수 없는 것: 그리고 그 어떤 것도 그는 하루 종일 상처를 입은 군인들을 수술하는 육체적인 일로 바쁘게 지내서 육체적인 피로로 의식이 무너졌다. 리날디는 전쟁경험을 통해 허무주의적으로 성장한 만큼 사랑 경험을 통해 냉소적으로 변했다.

그 의사는 그 위안소에서 소녀들과 무차별적인 성관계를 통해 매독에 걸렸다. 그는 더 이상 어떤 여자와도 결혼하고 싶지 않다. 그는 처녀(girl)든 여자(women)든 차이가 없다고 본다. 처녀와 여자의 차이에 대해서는 처녀가 더 고통스럽다. 전쟁터에서 처녀들이 온갖 고통을 당하는 모습에서 온 경험에서 나온 생각이다. 그렇게 리날디에게 여성에 대한 사랑마저 잃은 것이다. 그에게 삶의 의미가 사라졌다. 그의 이성이 모든 것에 대한 믿음을 무너뜨렸기 때문에 그에게 발생한 일들이다. 그에게는 성직자의 신앙이 없다. 그리고 그는 헨리의 세속적 가치인 사랑, 우정, 자유와 평등에 대한 헌신하고 있지 않다. 그래서 그는 허무주의자와 냉소주의자이다. 그리하여 사제가 경험의 결실 없이 결백을 유지하는 것처럼 의사는 삶에 대한 헌신 없는 상태에서 과도한 경험의 부담으로 인해 파탄에 빠진다.

헬렌 퍼거슨(Helen Ferguson)

프레더릭 헨리가 한쪽에 리날디가 다른 한쪽에 사제와 나란히 있는 것처럼 캐서린 버클리도 한쪽에 헬렌 퍼거슨 다른 한쪽에 미스 게이지(Miss Gage)와 나란히 있다.

헨리가 중간길을 택하므로 인해서 정제된(온화한) 삶의 태도를 보이는 것과 달리 사제와 리날디는 삶에 대한 대립적인 접근을 취한다. 퍼거슨과 게이지 역시 캐서린의 중간길을 택하여 조절하는 삶에 대한 대립적인 반응을 나타낸다. 또한 소설 속에 다양한 상황에서 리날디와 사제가 영웅에게 병치를 제공함으로써 캐서린의 성격을 규정하는 데 도움을 준다.

"전 스코틀랜드인이거든요."(I'm Scotch, you see.)(21)
그러나 나는 두 오빠가 각각 25사단과 메소포타미아에 있다는 것과 그녀가 캐서린 버클리에게 무척 잘한다는 것 외에는 그녀에 대해 아는 것이 없다.(108)
I never learned anything about her except that she had a brother in the Fifty-Second Division and a brother in Mesopotamia and she was very good to Catherine Barkley.

헬렌 퍼거슨은 이탈리아의 오스트리아 전선에 있는 영국 병원의 간호사이다. 헨리와 리날디가 빌라에서 한 방을 함께 쓰듯이 퍼거슨과 캐서린은 함께 살 뿐만 아니라 항상 함께 발견된다. 두 사람은 "주노의 백조"(Juno's swan)라고 부릴 만큼 떼려야 뗄 수가 없는 한 쌍의 소녀를 만든다. 퍼거슨은 캐서린에게 깊은 애정을 품고 있어서 혼자 살기가 힘들다. 하지만 캐서린이 헨리와 사랑에 빠진 것을 발견했을 때 그녀는 그들을 내버려 두는 것을 꺼리지 않는다.

"먼저 일어날게요," 그녀가 말했다. "두 사람은 나 없이도 아주 좋을 테니까."

"가지 마, 헬렌." 미스 버클리가 말했다.

"아니, 가야 해. 편지를 써야 하거든."

"안녕히 가십시오." 내가 말했다.

"또 뵐게요. 미스터 헨리."

"검열관에게 걸릴 이야기는 쓰지 마십시오."

"걱정 말아요. 이곳이 얼마나 아름다운지, 이탈리아인이 얼마나 용감한지만 쓸 거니까."

"그러면 훈장을 타겠는데요."

"I'll leave you too," she said. "You get along very well without me."

"Don't go, Helen," Miss Barkley said.

"I'd really rather. I must write some letters."

"Good-night," I said.

"Good-night, Mr. Henry."

"Don't write anything that will bother the censor."

"Don't worry. I only write about what a beautiful place we live in and how brave Italian are."

"That way you'll be decorated."(25)

이것은 퍼거슨이 어떻게 이러한 상황에 대처하고 변화하는 삶의 상황에 건강하게 대응할 수가 있는지를 보여 준다. 애인에게 친구(캐서린)를 맡긴다는 핑계를 찾는 것부터 헨리가 제기한 검열 문제에 대한 적절한 대답을 찾는 그것까지 퍼거슨은 캐서린에 버금가는 민첩한 마음을 보여 준다.

퍼거슨은 그녀의 친구 캐서린에게 매우 헌신적이어서 그녀는 이 우정을 병원 밖에서의 삶의 직업으로 삼는다. 그녀는 캐서린을 위해 모든 이익을 희생할 것 같다. 우리는 리날디와 함께 있는 그녀를 한번 발견하지만 아마도 그녀는 리날디를 받아들이고 캐서린과 함께 헨리를 내버려 둘 것이다. 리날디 역시 그녀를 그다지 매력적으로 생각하지 않았다.

어쩌면 그녀 자신이 그다지 매력적이지 않을 수도 있고, 줄리엣(Juliet)처럼 똑같이 잘생긴 어린 헨리와 사랑에 빠지는 자신의 아름다운 친구에게 친절하게 대해주는 것에 만족감을 찾고 있을 것이다. 그러나 캐서린에 대한 그녀의 애착은 너무나 진실하고 깊어서 그녀가 곤란에 처해 있다는 생각조차 견딜 수가 없다. 그녀는 친구가 사랑을 나누는 것을 보는 것을 좋아하지만 그녀가 전쟁 전선에서 임신 문제에 휘말리는 것을 생각하면 견딜 수 없다:

"우리 결혼식에 와 줄 거죠, 퍼기?"
한번은 이렇게 내가 물었다.
"결혼은 절대 못 할걸요."
"할 겁니다."
"아니요, 못 해요."

헬렌 퍼거슨(Helen Ferguson)　　　　　　　　　　　　　　　　　　**471**

"왜 못 해요?"

"결혼하기 전에 싸울 테니까요."

"우리는 안 싸워요."

"아직은 그렇겠죠."

"우리는 안 싸운다고요."

"아니면 당신이 죽겠죠. 싸우거나 죽거나. 인간사가 다 그렇죠. 결혼은 못 할 거예요."(108)

"Will you come to our wedding, Fergy?" I said to her once.

"You'll never get married."

"We will."

"No you won't."

"Why not?"

"You'll fight before you'll marry."

"We never fight."

"You've time yet."

"We don't fight."

"You'll die then. Fight or die. That's what people do. They don't marry."(108)

여기서 헨리의 냉소는 너무 오랫동안 그곳에 있었고 너무 많은 파괴를 일으켰던 전쟁의 맥락에서 보아야 해서 그러한 냉소적인 견해를 발전시키는 것은 그동안 그곳에 있었던 모든 사람에게 매우 자연스러운 일이다.

헨렌은 전쟁이 시작된 이래로 계속 전쟁에 있었고 죽음의 참화를 너무 많이 보았기 때문에 아무도 결혼해서 행복하게 살 수 있는 행운이 있으리라고 믿을 수 없다. 게다가 전쟁에서 남자들에 대한 경험도 그녀를 냉소적으로 만들었다. 영국 병원의 간호사들에 대한 리날디의 태도로부터 우리는 병원에 있는 소녀들과 위안소에 있는 소녀들 사이에 큰 차이가 없을 것 같은 리날디와 같은 수백 명의 장교들에 대한 퍼거슨의 지식은 상상할 수 있다. 그녀는 전쟁 중에 여자들을 임신시키고 연인인 척 유혹하는 사람들에게 버림받는 소위 애정행각을 많이 보았을 것이다:

나는 손을 뻗어 그녀의 손을 잡으려고 했다. "잡지 말아요," 그녀가 말했다. "나 우는 거 아니에요. 어쩌면 당시들은 잘될 수도 있겠죠. 하지만 캐서린을 힘들게 하지 말아요. 그랬다간 내가 가만 안 놔줄 거예요."

"절대 힘들게 하지 않을게요."

"아무튼 조심해야 해요. 두 사람이 잘되길 바랄게요. 즐겁게 지내고요."

"즐겁게 지내고 있어요."

"그러니 싸우지 말고 캐서린을 힘들게 하지도 말아요."

"안 그럴게요."

"정말 조심해야 해요. 캐서린이 전쟁고아를 갖는 꼴은 보고 싶지 않으니까."(109)

I reached for her hand. "Don't take hold of me," she said. "I'm not crying. Maybe you'll be all right you two. But watch out you don't get her in trouble. You get her trouble and I'll kill you."

"I won't get her in trouble."

"We'll watch out then. I hope you'll be all right. You have a good time."

"We have a fine time."

"Don't fight then and don't get her into trouble."

"I won't."

"Mind you watch out, I don't want her any of these war babies."(109)

나중에 퍼거슨의 두려움은 현실이 된다. 그 여인들은 결혼하지 않는다. 캐서린은 공경에 빠진다. 그녀는 아이들 낳는다. 그리고 그녀는 죽습니다. 그래서 그녀의 모든 두려움이 현실이 됩니다. 헤밍웨이는 소설의 비극적인 패턴에서 퍼거슨을 장치로 사용했다. 퍼거슨이 여기서 표현하는 두려움은 우리에게 앞으로 일어날 사건들에 대한 아이디어를 주고, 동시에 우리는 긴장하게 한다. 결국 이것들은 단지 인물에 의해 표현되는 두려움일 뿐이며 신탁에 의해 예언으로 받아들일 수 없기 때문이다. 따라서 이것은 비극적인 결말에 대비할 수 있도록 준비하고 다가오는 사건에 대해 긴장감을 유지하는 이중 기능을 수행한다. 그러나 퍼거슨이 소설에서 수행해야 할 더 중요한 기능은 미스 게이지의 캐릭터뿐만 아니라 캐서린의 캐릭터에도 병치를 제공하는 것이다.

캐서린과 그녀의 대조적인 점은 그녀가 오히려 전통적인 삶의 관점에 헌신하는 반면 퍼거슨은 경험의 진실에 헌신한다는 것이다. 그녀가 미스 게이지의 성격이 제공하는 대조적인 점은 그녀가 여전히 전통 소녀로 남아 사회적 금기와 관습을 따르지만, 미스 게이지는 모든 금기를 거스르는 매우 파격적인 행동을 한다는 것이다. 전통 퍼거슨과 비전통적인 게이지 사이에 캐서린은 사회관습에 대한 경건함을 보여 줌으로써 균형을 유지하지만 동시에 자기 삶의 상황이 필요하다면 사회관습을 무시한다.

퍼거슨은 다소 융통성이 없다. 그녀는 헨리와 캐서린이 결혼 전에 아이를 낳음으로써 전통적인 행동에 대한 일종의 대담한 반항을 하지 않을 것이다. 헨리가 상처를 입은 후 전쟁에서 물러난 후 밀라노 병원에서 헨리를 보았을 때 그녀는 그가 캐서린을 곤경에 빠뜨리고 그가 사회적 관습에 관심이 없었기 때문에 그 남자를 보는 것을 참을 수조차 없었다:

"나는 이 사람 못 봐주겠는데." 퍼거슨이 말했다. "비열한 이탈리아식 수작으로 너를 망가지기만 했잖아. 미국인이 이탈리아인보다 더해."

"스코틀랜드인들은 너무 도덕적이지." 캐서린이 말했다.

"그런 말이 아니야. 이 사람의 이탈리아식 비열함을 말하는 거야."

"내가 비열합니까, 퍼기?"

"그럼요, 비열한 것보다 더 나빠요. 당신은 뱀 같아요. 이탈리아 군 군복을 입은 뱀이요. 목에 망토를 두른 뱀."

"지금은 이탈리아 군 군복을 입고 있지 않은데요."

"그게 바로 당신의 비열함을 보여주는 또 한 증거예요. 지난여름 내 내 연애를 해서 아이를 갖게 해놓고 이제 슬그머니 도망치려는 수작이겠죠."

나는 캐서린에게 미소를 지었고 캐서린도 내게 미소를 지었다.

"우린 함께 도망칠 거야." 그녀가 말했다.

"둘이 똑같네," 퍼거슨이 말했다. "나는 네가 부끄러워, 캐서린 버클리. 너는 수치도 명예도 모르는구나. 너는 이 사람만큼이나 비열해."

"그러지 마, 퍼기." 캐서린은 말하며 퍼기의 손을 토닥였다. "나를 비난하지 마. 우리가 서로 사랑한다는 거 너도 알잖아."

"손 치워." 퍼거슨이 말했다. 그녀의 얼굴이 붉어져 있었다. "네가 수치심이 있었

헬렌 퍼거슨(Helen Ferguson)

다면 이렇게 되지 않았겠지. 하지만 너는 몇 개월인지는 모르지만, 임신한 몸으로 마치 아무 일도 아니라는 듯 너를 농락한 사람이 돌아왔다는 이유만으로 얼굴에 웃음이 가득하잖아. 너는 수치심도 감정도 없어." 그녀는 울기 시작했다.(247)

"I can't stand him," Ferguson said. "I get in my own messes."

"He's done nothing but ruin you with his sneaking Italian tricks. Americans are worse than Italian."

"The Scotch are such a moral people," Catherine said.

"I don't mean that. I mean his Italian sneakiness."

"am I sneaky, Fergy?"

"You are. You're worse than sneaky. You're like a snake with an Italian uniform: with a cape around your neck"

"I haven't got a Italian uniform now."

"That's just another example of your sneakiness. You had a love affair all summer and got this girl with child and now I suppose you'll sneak off."

I smiled at Catherine and she smiled at me.

"We'll both sneak off," she said.

"You're two of the same thing," Ferguson said. "I'm ashamed of you, Catherin Barkley. You have no shame and no honor and you're as sneaky as he is."

"Don't, Fergy," Catherine said and patted her hand. "Don't denounce me. You know we like each other."

"Take your hand away," Ferguson said. Her face was red. "If you had any shame it would be different. But you're God knows how many months gone with child and you think it's a joke and are all smiles because your seducer's come back. You've no shame and no feelings." She began to cry. (247)

여기서 퍼거슨은 캐서린이 이브가 되고 헨리가 그녀의 유혹자인 수풀 속의 뱀이 되는 성경적 형상을 사용한 것은 그녀의 사고의 관습을 보여준다. 캐서린이 자신의 파격적인 행동에 수치심을 느낀다는 시늉을 할 수 있다면 그녀는 결혼 전의 아기조차도 개의치 않을 것이다. 하지만 캐서린은 자신이 한 일에 부끄럽지도 않고 자랑스럽지도 않다. 그녀는 헨리가 진정한 여인이라는 것을 경험을 통해서만 알게 되었고 그녀는 그 남자와의 사랑에서 자기 삶에 성취를 발견했다.

게다가 그녀는 전쟁과 결혼 전에 어떤 아이도 원치 않았다. 그녀는 그것을 피하려고 최선을 다했다. 하지만 그것은 피할 수 없었을 때 그녀는 그것을 직면할 준비가 되어 있다. 퍼거슨에 관해 말하자면, 그녀는 사제와 마찬가지로 관습을 뛰어넘어 실제 상황의 현실을 스스로 볼 수 없다. 그녀의 헌신은 경험에 기반한 것이 아니라 다른 방향을 지향한다. 그러나 신부와 마찬가지로 정통성과 관습성의 한계에도 불구하고 그녀는 소박함과 성실함이라는 덕목 그 때문에 호감이 가는 인물이다.

그녀는 사람들 특히 친구들에 대한 자연스러운 애정을 품고 있는 긍정적인 캐릭터이다.

만약 그녀가 여인들에게 쓰려고 비합리적으로 굴고 있다면, 그것은 단지 그녀가 곤경에 처한 것을 차마 볼 수 없는 캐서린에 대한 그녀의 사랑 강도를 드러낼 뿐이다.

미스 게이지(Miss Gage)

정통적이고 관습적인 퍼거슨과 대립하는 것은 어떠한 금기나 관습에도 금지되지 않고 어떠한 규칙이나 규정에도 구속되지 않는 미스 게이지의 성격이다. 모든 규칙과 관계없이 그녀는 상처를 입은 영웅인 프레더릭 헨리가 좋아하는 음료는 무엇이든 쾌활하게 대접한다.

미스 게이지가 물 주전자와 컵을 가져왔다. 나는 석 잔을 마셨고 간호사들이 나가자, 창밖을 좀 더 바라보다가 다시 잠들었다.(86)

She brought a pitcher of water and a glass. I drank three glasses and then they left me and I looked out of window a while and went back to sleep.(86)

그리고 조금 후에 그녀는 실제로 헨리와 술을 마신다.

그녀가 옷장 문을 열고 베르무트병을 꺼냈다. 거의 비어 있었다. "침대 밑에 있던 다른 술도 여기 넣어뒀어요." 그녀가 말했다. "왜 잔을 달라고 하지 않았어요?"
"못 마시게 할 거로 생각했거든요."
"함께 마실 수도 있었는데."
"좋은 분이군요."
"혼자 마시는 건 좋지 않아요," 그녀가 말했다. "절대 그러지 마세요."(90)
She opened the armoire door and held up the vermouth bottle. It was nearly empty. "I put the other bottle from under the bed in there too," she said. "Why

didn't you ask me for a glass?"

"I thought maybe you wouldn't let me have it."

"I'd have had some with you."

"You're a fine girl."

"It isn't good for you to drink alone," she said. "You mustn't do it."(90)

조금 후 그녀는 헨리와 술을 마신다. 금기에 대해 연연하지 않는다. (no hangover of any taboo) 그녀는 제 1차 세계대전 무렵의 사회협약에 저항하기 위해 남성과의 평등권을 주장하기 시작한 소녀 중 한 명이다. 영국 병원의 전통 여성들, 특히 미스 반 캠펜(Miss Van Campen)이나 정통 퍼거슨과 같은 엄격한 훈육자들과 비교할 때 미스 게이지의 모습은 오히려 신선하다.

그녀는 현장에 등장할 때마다 오랜 전쟁 속에서 보기 드문 사건과 기쁨을 가져다준다. 예를 들어 다음과 같은 상황을 주목해 보자.

나는 벨을 눌렀고 잠시 후 미스 게이지가 들어왔다.

"무슨 일이에요?"

"할 말이 있어서요. 미스 바클리가 당분간 야간근무를 그만해야 할 것 같지 않아요? 너무 피곤해 보여요. 왜 미스 버클리만 계속 야간근무를 하는 겁니까?"

미스 게이지는 나를 물끄러미 보았다.

"전 당신들 친구예요." 그녀가 말했다. "저한테 그런 식으로 말할 필요 없어요."

"무슨 말이죠?"

"바보 같은 소리 말아요. 그게 다예요?"

미스 게이지(Miss Gage)

"베르무트 한잔할래요?"

"좋아요. 그런데 곧 가 봐야 해요." 그녀는 옷장에서 병을 꺼내고 잔을 가져왔다.

"잔으로 마셔요." 내가 말했다. "저는 병째 마실게요."

"당신의 건강을 위해." 미스 게이지가 말했다.(110)

… I rang the bell and in a little while Miss Gage came in.

"What's the matter?"

"I just wanted to talk to you. Don't you think Miss Barkley ought to go off night duty for a while? She looks awfully tired."

"Why does she stay on so long?"

Miss Gage looked at me.

"I'm a friend of yours," she said. "You don't have to talk to me like that."

"What do you mean?"

"Don't be silly. Was that all you wanted?"

"Do you want a vermouth?"

"All right. Then I have to go." She got out the bottle from the armoire and brought a glass.

"You take the glass," I said. "I'll drink out of the bottle."

"Here's to you," said Miss Gage.(110)

게이지 양의 이해심이 풍부한 말투 그녀의 거침없는 행동 그리고 그녀의 요구 없는 우정이 그녀를 리날디의 여성 상대로 만든다. 오직 그녀만이 전쟁으로 깨지지 않고 소설의 후반부 전쟁 장면에서 리날디처럼 쓸쓸하고 냉소적이 되지 않는다.

그녀는 전쟁의 긴장도 사회적 억압도 보여주지 않는다. 그녀는 게이지와 정반대인 퍼거슨과 대조를 이룬다. 게다가 그녀는 병치를 통해 캐서린 버클리의 성격을 드러낼 수 있도록 돕습니다. 캐서린 역시 게이지처럼 사회적 관습에 대해 독단적이지 않다. 하지만 캐서린은 여전히 관습을 거스르지만, 게이지 양은 항상 관습을 거스르는데 조금의 망설임도 없이 관습을 거스를 준비가 되어 있다. 헨리와 함께 술을 마시는 그녀의 경우와 무의식은 그녀가 사회적 금기를 얼마나 가볍게 여기는지를 보여준다.

"벤 캠펀에게 뭐라고 하셨어요? 머리끝까지 화가 났던데요."

"감각을 비교해 보고 있었죠. 아이를 낳아본 적 있겠느냐고 말하려던 참이었는데—"

"바보 같군요," 게이지가 말했다. "당신 머리 가죽 벗기려 들 거예요."

"벌써 벗겨서 가졌죠." 내가 말했다. "요양 휴가를 취소시켰고 아마 군법회의에 넘길지도 몰라요. 정말 못됐어요."

"처음부터 당신을 좋아하지 않았잖아요." 게이지가 말했다. "그런데 무슨 일로 그런 거예요?"

"전선에 돌아가지 않으려고 일부러 술을 마셔서 황달에 걸렸다고 생각해요."

"세상에." 게이지가 말했다. "당신이 한 방울도 마시지 않았다고 증언해 드리죠. 모두가 그렇게 해 줄 거예요."(145)

"What did you say to Van Campen? She was furious."

"We were camping sensation. I was going to suggest that she had never experienced childbirth—"

"You're a fool," Gage said. "She's after you scalp."

"She had my scalp," I said. "She's lost me my leave and she might try and get me court-martialled. She's mean enough."

"She never liked you," Gage said. "What's it about?"

"She says I've drunk myself into jaundice so as to go back to the front."

"Pooh," said Gage. "I'll swear you've never taken a drink. Everybody will swear you've never taken a drink."(145)

그리고 그녀는 그를 도우려고 노력한다. 그녀는 모든 병을 배낭에 싸서 짐꾼에게 건네기 위해 문을 열기 시작하지만, 밴 캠펜(Van Campen)이 도착하여 자신이 소유한 병들을 가져간다. 따라서 미스 게이지는 거짓말을 하지 않거나, 술을 마시지 않거나 남자 낯선 사람들과 자유롭게 지내는 전통적인 도덕성에 대해 완전히 무관심했다. 그녀는 사회적 금기와 도덕에 전혀 구애받지 않는다. 그녀는 헨리와 미스 반 캠펜 사이에 일종의 코믹한 안도감을 제공할 뿐만 아니라 숨이 막히는 전쟁 분위기 속에서 신선한 공기를 제공한다. 그녀는 『무기여 잘 있거라』에서 기억에 남는 인물 중 한 명이다.

* Bhim S. Dayiya 『Hemingway's A Farewell to Arms A Critical Study』 Academic Foundation. 중심인물들의 내용은 이 책의 내용 중 일부를 번역하고 연구한 내용을 정리한 것임을 밝힘.

그 밖의 인물들(Minor Characters)

헨리, 캐서린, 신부, 리날디, 미스 게이지와 같은 주요한 인물들 이외에도 헤밍웨이 소설에는 소설의 주제 패턴과 구조설계에서 기능하는 몇 명의 그 밖의 인물들이 등장한다.

또한 그들은 소설의 액션에 잠깐 등장했음에도 불구하고 그들만의 고유한 모습으로 등장해서 기억에 남는다. 사제를 괴롭히는 대위(Captain) 그의 세상에 대한 비관주의와 개인적으로 쾌활함이 결합한 소령(Major) 헨리의 무릎을 고친 의사 발렌티니(Valintini) 당구를 하고 헨리가 참전한 전쟁, 정치를 논하는 고령의 그래피 백작(Count Greffi) 그리고 일반적인 삶의 만남: 밀나노 병원에서 헨리는 면도하는 반대편에서 온 장교로 의심하는 이발사(barber); 마네라(Manera) 파시니(Passini), 지노(Gino), 에토레(Ettore), 아이모(Aymo), 보넬로(Bonello)는 모두 이탈리아 쪽에서 전쟁에 참여하고 있으며, 영웅은 그들과 함께 여러 단계에서 함께 일을 해야 한다. 중사(sergeants)는 매우 중요한 순간에 카포라토(Caporatto)로 영웅의 부하들과 퇴각하는 순간에 합류한다. 경마(horse races)에서 헨리와 캐서린과 합류하는 메이어스 커플(Meyer's couple); 떠나는 영웅에게 피난처를 주고 나중에 연인이 스위스로 탈출하는 것을 돕는 스트레사의 바맨(barman at Stresa); 그리고 소설의 캔버스(Canvas)를 넓히고 서사를 앞으로 나가도록 돕는 그 밖의 인물들; 그 밖의 인물들의 서술이 매우 능숙하게 이루어졌고 짧은 공간에서 서로서로 인물들과 전체 구성에 유기적으로 잘 연결되도록 묘사되었다.

작품에 등장하는 인물들은 1929년의 헤밍웨이가 인물을 묘사하는 능력이 전혀 부족하지 않았음을 보여 주기에 충분했다. 헤밍웨이가 영웅 피난처의 배경을 더 깊게 파고들어 갔다. 그는 자기의 서사의 목적을 위해 필요한 만큼 깊이 파고들어 갔다. 이러한 기법들에서 반듯이 들어가는 것은 불필요한 것들을 제거하는 것은 항상 그의 특별한 중독 중 하나였다. 배경과 인물 및 대화를 통해서 인물의 생각과 감정 등을 전달하는 과정에서 헤밍웨이는 넘치는 것보다 약간 부족한 것을 선택하고 그 부족함의 내면에는 풍성함과 독자들의 상상력을 일깨워 주는 힘이 있다. 그 밖의 인물들은 단순히 기억에 남을 뿐만 아니라, 장면이나 상황에서 지역적으로, 그리고 일반적으로 줄거리에서 매우 기능적이며 주제 패턴의 복잡한 그물망과 마찬가지로 복잡한 『무기여 잘 있거라』 구조적으로 이바지한다. 마네라 와 파시니가 헨리와 전쟁을 주제로 나눈 대화는 전쟁 상황에 대한 영웅의 인식을 강조하는 것이었고, 발렌티니 의사는 상처 수술 부위를 다루는 데 6개월이 걸릴 3명의 의사로 구성된 의사 전문가 집단의 조언에 반하여 하루 만에 영웅의 무릎을 고친다. 이것은 경험과 지식이 가져온 결과이다. 지식만으로도 안되고 경험만으로도 안 되고 지식과 경험의 결과이다; 젊은(youth) 경륜(age)의 대조를 통해 성장의 역동을 보여 주는 그레피 백작의 영웅과의 만남; 헨리와의 만남에서 이발사가 제공하는 코믹한 에피소드(interlude), 심지어 개인적인 인간관계를 유리하게 하는 의심과 불신의 분위기를 강조하는 것 등은 헤밍웨이가 빠르게 움직이는 소설의 액션의 여러 단계에서 이 인물들이 얼마나 조심스럽게 소개되고 소설의 액션 깊이(depth)와 크기(magnitude)를 보여 준다.

배경과 인물들(Background and Characters)

　소설과 같은 예술작품에서 우리는 항상 인물의 세 가지 범주를 가지고 있다. 첫째, 소설의 행동 선두(forefront)에 남아 있고 그 행동의 주요 윤곽을 구성하는 전경(foreground) 또는 주요 인물. 둘째, 소설의 행동에 제한적으로 등장하는 줄거리-구조의 보조적인 선을 구성하는 사소한 인물. 셋째, 소설의 구성 또는 구조적인 설계에 아무런 이바지하지 않지만 그 행동의 배경을 구성하는 인물이다. 이와 같은 인물들은(셋째) 엄밀한 의미에서 실제로 인물이 아니다. 그들은 단지 마을 거리에 사람들처럼 등장할 뿐이며, 그들의 존재는 그들 앞에서 일어나는 어떤 중요한 사건에 대한 현실적인 위치를 제공한다. 따라서 이와 같은 인물들은 액션 일부가 아니라, 오히려 그들은 액션의 배경 일부이다. 우리는 『무기여 잘 있거라』의 페이지를 통해 그러한 캐릭터들이 수십 명이 있는데, 이들은 액션이 계속 진행됨에 따라 나타났다가 사라진다. 그것들은 결코 기억에 남지 않으며 스케치로서도 어떤 세부 사항도 그려지지 않기 때문에 우리는 그것들을 쉽게 잊어버린다.

　이름조차 알려지지 않은 난장판 속에 있는 여러 장교, 장교들을 위해 위안소에 있는 여러 소녀, 전선에서 싸우거나 후퇴하는 수많은 병사, 장교들을 잠재우고 총을 쏘는 전투경찰의 부하들, 다리를 건너가 강을 건너 행진하는 독일 병사들, 야전병원에 있는 부상병들, 헨리를 비롯한 부상병들을 들어 올리는 사람들, 병원과 역에 있는 짐꾼들, 헨리와 캐서린이 마주치는 스트레사에 있는 사람들, 스위스의 경비원들, 캐서린이 죽은 아이를 출산한 후 사망하는 병원에 있는 의사들, 간호사들, 캐서린이 병원에서 목숨을 건 사투를 벌이는 동안 헨리가 방문해야 하는 카페와 술집에서 술을 마시고 먹는 이야기를 나누는 사람들, 장소와 국가의 이름, 달력과 날짜와 함께 언급되는 이들과 수백 명의 다른 사람들이 모두 소설의 역사적인 배경을 이루고 있다.

날씨의 상징(Weather Symbolism)

어니스트 헤밍웨이는『무기여 잘 있거라』에서 전쟁에 대한 영웅의 설명, 후퇴, 그리고 싸우지 않을 때 군인들이 시간을 보내는 방법 등보다는 전쟁에 대한 진실을 말하려 한다. 그러나 헤밍웨이가 그의 주제에 대해 현실적으로 접하는 것은 많은 전통적인 문학적 장치의 사용을 배제하지 않습니다. 예를 들어 오늘날까지 날씨는 전쟁 경험의 기본 요소이다. 헤밍웨이는『무기여 잘 있거라』에서 날씨를 사실적으로 묘사하지만, 상징적인 목적으로도 날씨를 사용한다. 이 소설에서 흔히 생명과 성장과 동일시되는 비는 죽음을 의미하며, 눈은 완전히 희망을 상징한다.

■ Snow

잭 런던(Jack London)의 "불을 지피기 위해"(To Built a Fire)와 같은 이야기에서 눈과 얼음은 꽤 논리적으로 위험과 죽음을 나타낸다. 결국 사람은 얼어 죽을 수도 있고, 살얼음을 뚫고 떨어져 익사할 수도 있고, 눈사태 아래서 죽을 수도 있다. 반면,『무기여 잘 있거라』2장에서 묘사된 싸움을 끝내는 것은 눈입니다. 그러므로 눈은 그 반대가 아니라 더 안전한 것을 의미합니다. 그러나 눈이 맨땅을 덮고 있고 심지어 2장에서는 이탈리아 군의 포병대까지 덮고 있지만, 여름의 전투로 인해 찢어진 참나무 그루터기들이 계속해서 튀어나오고 있다는 것은 겨울이 물론 영구적인 것이 아니라 단지 전투로부터 해방된 것, 즉 휴전(cease-fire)인 것을 상기시켜 준다. 얼마 지나지 않아 프레더릭 헨리는 사제의 고향인 아브루치 지역을 "길이 철처럼 얼고 단단하며 맑고 차갑게 건조하며 눈이 건조하고 가루가 많이 나는 것"으로 묘사했다. 이 단락의 맥락은 이러한 특성이 긍정적인 특성임에 의심의 여지를 남기지 않는다. 소설 후반부에 겨울 스포츠를 둘러싼 스위스 경찰들의 논쟁은 절실히 필요한 코믹한 안도감(comic relief)을 제공할 뿐만 아니라 헨리와 캐서린 버클리의 목가적인 생활을 보여준다. 그 직후 헨리와 캐서린은 곳곳에 눈이 쌓인 스위스 알프스에 있는 자신들을 발견한다. 그리하여 그들은 일시적으로 순수함과 안전함을 동시에 갖춘 삶을 이루어 냈습니다.

■ Rain

『무기여 잘 있거라』의 첫 번째 장에서 시작하여 비는 분명히 죽음을 상징한다.

"가을에, 나뭇잎들은 모두 밤나무에서 떨어지고 가지들은 앙상하게 드러났고 나무줄기들은 비로 검게 변했습니다."(4)

in the fall when the rains came the leaves all fell from the chestnut trees and the branches were bare and the trunks with rain.(4)

"포도밭도 앙상하고 가지만 앙상하여 온 나라가 가을에 젖어 갈색으로 말라 죽었습니다."(4)

The vineyards were thin and bare-branches too and all the country wet and brown and dead with the autumn.(4)

　비의 상징은 완전히 문학적 자만심이 아닙니다. 비는 실제로 치명적인 질병인 콜레라가 발생하여 올가을에 7천 명의 죽음을 앗아가기 때문입니다. 나중에 그들의 밀라노 목가에서 캐서린은 헨리와 독자들에게 비의 상징을 분명히 합니다.

　"비가 오는 것을 두려워합니다. 왜냐하면 저는 가끔 제가 그 안에서 죽는 것을 보기 때문입니다."라고 그녀는 그에게 말한다. 그리고 가끔 그 안에서 당신이 죽어있는 것을 봅니다. "헨리와 캐서린이 그녀와 함께 마지막 밤에 무기고에서 기차역 근처 호텔로 여행하는 동안 23장 시작부터 도시를 뒤덮은 안개는 비로 바뀝니다. The fog was turning to rain. (150) 그들이 서로 작별을 고하면서 비가 계속 내리고 있습니다. 사실, 소설의 이 부분에서 캐서린의 마지막 행동은 헨리에게 비를 피하라고 신호를 보내는 것입니다. 전투의 흐름이 바뀌고 이탈리아인들이 카포레토와 전투에 참여한 독일인들로부터 퇴각을 시작하는 장(Chapter) 동안 거의 계속해서 비가 내린다. 비는 어느 날 저녁 공세가 그칠 것이라는 희망을 품고 눈으로 변하지만, 눈은 금세 녹아 비가 다시 시작된다. 운전자들 사이에서 저녁 식사와 함께 마시는 와인에 대해 토론하는 동안 아이모라는 운전자는 "내일 우리는 빗물을 마실지 모릅니다."라고, 말한다.

　이때까지 헤밍웨이는 독자들이 진정한 예감을 느낄 정도로 비의 상징성을 발전시켰으며 실제로 다음날 헨리의 해체부대(disintegrating unit)에 죽음을 가져다줄 것인 것을 예상하게 한다. 도망자 헨리가 기차를 타고 스트레사로 가는 동안 비가 내리고, 도착하면 비가 내리고 헨리와 캐서린이 호텔 방에서 함께 밤을 보내는 동안 비가 내리고 있다.

마지오레(Maggiore)를 가로지르는 오픈 보트 여행은 돛으로 사용되는 우산과 함께 빗속에서 이루어진다. (우연히 우산이 부러진다) 그리고 XL(40장)에서 헨리와 캐서린의 아이가 태어날 도시를 위해 겨울 산으로 떠나는 이별을 고할 때 헨리는 우리에게 "밤에 비가 내리기 시작했다."고 말한다.

In the night it started raining. It rained on all morning and turned the snow to slush and made the mountain-side dismal. There were clouds over the lake and over the valley. It was raining high up the mountain.(306)

마침내 캐서린이 길고 고뇌에 찬 분만을 하는 동안 헨리가 점심을 먹기 위해 병원을 떠날 때,

날은 흐렸지만, 태양은 문자 그대로 희망의 광선을 통과하려고 했습니다. 하지만 수술하는 중 창밖을 내다보았고 창문 너머로 어둠과 비가 내리는 것밖에 보이지 않았습니다.

could see nothing but the dark and he rain falling across the light from the window.(327)

소설의 마지막에 헨리는 병원을 떠나 비를 맞으며 호텔로 돌아옵니다. 사실 『무기여 잘 있거라』의 마지막 단어는 전반적으로 이야기에서 날씨의 중요한 위치를 보여주는 증거인 "비"입니다.

헤밍웨이는 우리들이 비와 눈이 주는 상징의 패턴을 감지하고 그것의 의미를 이해하는 것들에 대해 우리에게만 맡겨 놓지 않고 캐서린이 헨리에게 그들이 비를 맞고 죽은 것을 본다고 말함으로써 그의 책에서 비와 눈의 중요성을 강조한다.

그래서 『무기여 잘 있거라』에서 날씨의 상징은 분명하다. 그러나 헤밍웨이가 이 문학적 장치를 사용하는 것은 그 자체로 상징성이 거의 없다. 소설에서 비가 올 때마다 숨을 죽이고 캐서린이 그 장면 동안 죽지 않기를 기도하는 우리는 비와 눈 모두 그의 구성 속으로 몰아넣고 우리들의 관심을 계속 유지하도록 한다.

우리는 헨리가 이야기의 나레이터이기 때문에 비를 맞으며 살아남을 것인 것을 알고 있습니다. 그래서 헤밍웨이는 전쟁 중에 잔인하게 현실적인 삶의 전설을 쓰면서 『무기여 잘 있거라』 이전의 전쟁 이야기를 문학적으로 쓴 소설을 썼다. 거의 틀림없이 그것은 지금까지 말한 어떤 이야기만큼 강력합니다.

* 마지오레(Maggiore): 이탈리아 북부와 스위스 남부에 걸친 호수

참고문헌

권진아. 『무기여 잘 있거라』 문학동네. 1993

Cliffs Notes *A Farewell to Arms* by Adam Sexton, M.F.A Wily Publishing, Inc.

Ernest Hemingway. *A Farewell to Arms* published by Simon & Schuster New York.

Bhim S. Dayiya Hemingway's *A Farewell to Arms* A Critical Study Academic Foundation.